Hidden Illness in the White House

Hidden Illness in the White House

Kenneth R. Crispell and Carlos F. Gomez

Duke University Press   Durham and London 1988

© 1988 Duke University Press
All rights reserved
Printed in the United States of America
on acid-free paper ∞
Library of Congress Cataloging-in-Publication Data
appear on the last printed page of this book.

Contents

Foreword   vii

Preface   ix

Acknowledgments   xiii

1   Illness and History: An Overview   1

2   Woodrow Wilson: Strokes, Versailles, and the
Pathology of Politics   13

3   Franklin D. Roosevelt: The Diagnosis of an
"Unexpected" Death   75

4   Diplomacy and Failing Health: Roosevelt and the
Final Decline   121

5   John F. Kennedy: "I'm the Healthiest Candidate"   160

6   The Twenty-fifth Amendment and the
Decisions of History   203

Notes   243

Index   263

Foreword

Since the United States Constitution established the office of the president, most American citizens have tended to look upon their president as impervious to the physical and mental frailties that regularly afflict lesser mortals. In the populace's mind, much attention is given to a president's, or would-be president's, economic and foreign policy. Little concern is exhibited in regard to whether or not the president's health will prohibit him from performing the powers and duties of the office. Dr. Ken Crispell's book, Hidden Illness in the White House, graphically illustrates that American presidents are not supermen after all. Quite the contrary—because our presidents labor in an extremely stressful, often highly emotional political environment, the risk to their health and physical well-being is significantly greater than that confronting the average American.

Dr. Crispell combines the talents of physician and political scientist in documenting that presidents do become seriously ill like the rest of us. Of greater significance, he illustrates the impact presidential illness can have on national policy and, thus, on the governmental health and well-being of us all.

The incidents described in Hidden Illness in the White House occurred before the enactment and ratification of the Twenty-fifth Amendment to the Constitution. Hopefully, Dr. Crispell's work will stimulate future presidents and those men and women closest to them to utilize the provisions of the Twenty-fifth Amendment whenever illness threatens the president's ability to perform the powers and duties of his office. All Americans can benefit from a better understanding of the importance of the direct relationship between presidential health and public policy. This is must reading for future presidents.

Birch Bayh
U.S. Senator, 1963–81
Author of the Twenty-fifth Amendment
to the Constitution
April 1988

Preface

■■■■■■ *Hidden Illness in the White House* is an interdisciplinary collaboration between a professor of law and medicine from the University of Virginia and a medicine and public-policy fellow from the University of Chicago. The work is not intended as a classical history of the presidents we discuss (namely, Franklin D. Roosevelt, Woodrow Wilson, and John F. Kennedy). We have drawn from previously published classical histories in presenting newly researched medical histories and their public policy impact. Drawing the case studies together, we conclude with a discussion of the Twenty-fifth Amendment of the Constitution as it relates to presidential succession in the case of sudden vacancy or illness.

As an army physician stationed in France in April 1945, I was neither shocked nor surprised upon learning that President Roosevelt was dead. My associates in the medical corps and I were fully aware from his appearance that the president's health was deteriorating at an alarming pace, though nothing of the sort was mentioned in the press. What was shocking was that bulletins issued by his physician, Admiral McIntire, regarding Roosevelt's health were misleading and perhaps even false.

My interest in this subject was further piqued when, as an endocrinologist in 1955, I ran across a particularly interesting article in a leading surgical journal describing the use of cortisone in patients with Addison's disease (adrenal insufficiency) who were undergoing major surgery. One of the patients described was a young United States senator facing back surgery.[1] That young senator was John F. Kennedy.

My exposure to the effects of illness on world leaders became more personal in 1958 when I was requested by the State Department to go to Haiti to examine President Duvalier who was seriously ill. After examining the patient, I was asked by him and his staff to withhold from the press all information regarding his medical condition. My visit to Haiti was not to be known by anyone except President Duvalier's staff and officials at the State Department. However, when I returned to New York City, I received a telephone call at 3 o'clock in the morning from a reporter asking me about "Papa Doc." I stated I had no knowledge of Duvalier and the reporter in essence called me a liar. This was my first encounter with the press involving the problem of the doctor-patient relationship and confidentiality when dealing with the care of well-known political figures.

In 1970 a leading medical journal published an article by one of the Navy physicians assigned to President Roosevelt.[2] Dr. Howard Bruenn described the actual facts dealing with President Roosevelt's terminal illness and his death. His article was in response to Admiral Ross McIntire's (the president's personal physician) biography, which he felt "clouded" the actual facts of Roosevelt's failing health over the last two years of Roosevelt's life.

As we researched the health of presidents, it became evident that many had suffered major illnesses while in office. Using recent publications on presidential illness,[3] in addition to using the Freedom of Information Act to obtain sources of new material, we were amazed to find the degree to which presidential illness had been covered up either by the presidents' personal physicians or the White House staff. It also became evident that, in general, classical historians have been unaware either of serious medical illnesses in our leaders or of the possible impact that these may have had upon events in history. The real concern is that serious medical illnesses of presidents could conceivably have been major contributing factors in their decision processes, in decisions which may have affected world history.

Interest in the maladies of past presidents has kindled our interest in possible problems of presidential illness in the future. In view of even the remote possibility of nuclear warfare, we believe the issue critical. The president is the only person in the United States who can initiate nuclear war. The protocol for control of the nuclear code is clear; the code accompanies the president at all times.

What is less clear, and to us even more problematic, is the question of *who* has the powers of the presidency when the elected head of state is ill or incapacitated. In view of the unspeakable power the president can unleash, this question is more than problematic—it is of paramount importance.

The most recent attempt to solve this problem resulted in passage of the Twenty-fifth Amendment to the United States Constitution. The amendment, which was ratified by the states in 1967, is divided into four sections:

> *Section 1* clarifies a long-standing precedent that if the president dies in office, the vice president becomes the president.
>
> *Section 2* is new in that it allows the president, with the approval of Congress, to appoint a vice president if the office of the vice president becomes vacant. This was used by President Nixon to appoint Mr. Ford as vice president. When Mr. Ford became president, he used the amendment to appoint Mr. Rockefeller.
>
> *Section 3* allows the president to declare a period of personal inability to perform his or her duties, at which time the vice president becomes acting president. The president can then reassume the office when he or she declares that they are able to assume the office of president.

Section 4 offers a mechanism that would speed the removal of a president from office who was so incapacitated that he or she could not function effectively. The vice president and a majority of the cabinet are required by the Constitution to initiate the proceedings of removal and report their recommendations to the Speaker of the House and president pro tem of the Senate.

With the death of a president the line of succession is clearly spelled out. However, with a physically or emotionally impaired president uncertainties remain. For example, what is meant by "unable to discharge the powers and duties of his office" in Section 4, and who determines disability of the president? Where does the doctor-patient confidentiality end when dealing with presidential illness?

On the occasion of President Reagan's hospitalization for cancer surgery, Section 3 of the Twenty-fifth Amendment would seem to apply. But as we discuss in the final chapter of the book, the Twenty-fifth Amendment was never invoked, including the period when the president was under anesthesia. In a letter from President Reagan to the House and Senate prior to his operation he states, "I do not believe that the drafters of the Amendment intended its application to situations such as the instant one."

It is our hope that this book will bring to the attention of historians, members of Congress, and the general public the fact that urgent problems still exist with the Twenty-fifth Amendment. It is crucial that some solutions be found in the near future.

Kenneth R. Crispell
and Carlos F. Gomez

Acknowledgments

████████ We are grateful and deeply indebted to a number of individuals and groups who counseled, corrected, and supported our work these past few years. Without their help, this project would never have come to fruition.

The W. Alton Jones Foundation was generous and steadfast in its support of the early research for this book. In later stages of writing and editing, Professor Kenneth W. Thompson, director of the White Burkett Miller Center of Public Affairs at the University of Virginia, provided a stimulating series of forums and seminars where many of our early ideas matured. Professor Thompson was also instrumental in the formation of the National Commission on the Twenty-fifth Amendment. The hearings held by the commission helped to shape and inform many of our recommendations.

Many of our friends and colleagues not only gave needed encouragement but took the time to read and critique early drafts of this work: Mr. Staige Blackford, Ms. Kathleen C. Blackmer, Dr. Bland Cannon, Mr. Mortimer Caplin, Ms. Lynn Carter, Professor James F. Childress, Dr. Merlin K. DuVal, Professor Joseph Fletcher, Professor Julian N. Hartt, Dr. Thomas Hunter, Mr. Richard Johnson, Professor Robert Kellogg, Mr. C. Brian Kelly, Dr. Norman Knorr, Mr. Kurt Luedtke, Mr. Daniel Meador, Ms. Karen O'Neill, Dr. John Owen,

Dr. Raymond Pruitt, Dr. David Solomon, Mr. Paul Stephan, and Dr. Oscar A. Thorup. We would especially like to thank Dr. Daniel Ruge and Dr. William Lukash for their invaluable advice and comments on later versions of the manuscript. We owe special thanks to Mrs. Jean Bergmark, who kindly gave us access to Dr. Jonas Robitscher's unpublished work on this subject.

We would also like to thank the staffs at the following libraries for their quick and efficient replies to our requests: Manuscripts Room, Alderman Library, University of Virginia; the Franklin D. Roosevelt Library in Hyde Park, New York; and the Woodrow Wilson Collection, Firestone Library, Princeton University.

To our editors at the Duke University Press, Ms. Valerie Millholland and Ms. Pam Morrison, and to the rest of their staff, we owe thanks for their patience and careful guidance on this project.

A very special debt of gratitude is owed to Mrs. Shirley M. Roberts, who typed (and retyped) an embarrassing number of drafts with intelligence and usual good humor.

Finally, we dedicate this book to our wives, Marge Crispell and Mimi Gomez, who read and reread many drafts and whose constant encouragement and support made this book possible—and all the more enjoyable.

Illness and History

An Overview

██████ In 1960, shortly before John F. Kennedy appointed him secretary of state, Dean Rusk published an article in which he constructed the following hypothetical scenario:

> Picture two men sitting down together to talk about matters affecting the very survival of the systems they represent, each in a position to unleash unbelievably destructive power . . . one is impulsive in manner, supremely confident . . . and possibly subject to high blood pressure; the other . . . weighted down by a sense of responsibility for the hundreds of millions who have freely given him their confidence . . . a man with a quick temper and a weak heart.[1]

Later commentaries on Rusk's imaginary meeting identified Nikita Khrushchev and Dwight Eisenhower as these two world leaders. Rusk avoided specific names to argue more generally against the sort of personal diplomacy that had become so popular following World War II. What is most intriguing about Rusk's position, however, is that he mentions the medical weaknesses of his two mythical leaders in this context. Rusk went on to warn that by circumventing the logical, impersonal machinery of foreign offices and departments of state, governments were gambling too much on imponderables, namely the personal idiosyncrasies of their leaders. Among the most insidious and least predictable of these characteristics, Rusk pointed out, was a leader's health. He went on to speculate on the "extent to which the course of world affairs may have been affected by illnesses among those holding high public office," later adding that "the international list of those who have carried great responsibility while ill is a long one and there are fleeting glimpses of decisions which good health might have turned another way."[2] The most dire decision one imagines in this context concerns the use of nuclear weapons, a decision that would have irrevocable consequences.

We need not raise the specter of a sick man poised over the trigger of a nuclear arsenal to point out the influence which one's medical condition might have over one's capacity to make reasoned decisions. The word "might," moreover, is too speculative and tentative, for history presents us with an abundance of instances in which illness converges with power—often absolute power—and often with dire consequences.

We need only go back as far as the early 1970s to find examples of men who wielded incredible power while beset by illness. In Yugoslavia, for instance, the machinery of government practically ground to a halt while Marshal Tito hung on tenuously to life, obstinately refusing his physician's warnings that his leg needed to be amputated. Generalissimo Francisco Franco was essentially catatonic for months (perhaps longer) as the government continued to insist to Spain and to the rest of the world that he was still in control of his faculties. Georges Pompidou's death shortly after leaving the French presidency confirmed the gravest suspicions about his health during his last year in office. In China both Mao Tse-tung and Chou En-lai died while still in power and while they were negotiating perhaps the riskiest transition in that country since the Communist Revolution.

Later in the decade a troubled Israeli state would be further troubled by Prime Minister Begin's unexplained absences from state functions and his increasing (and ominous) complaints of chest pain, leading to his eventual resignation. Far from Israel the Soviet Union would also suffer the uncertainties of an ailing and unstable leadership. Leonid Brezhnev, after a prolonged period of poor health, would die while still in office. The subsequent deaths of his successors, Yuri Andropov and Konstantin Chernenko, within months of each other further confused the already weakened leadership in the Kremlin.

One need not look abroad to find instances of illness in high office. Indeed, the focus of this study is the possible impact that hidden illness has had on the occupants of the White House. Before we turn our attention to presidents who were ill while in office, however, we offer the study of a political aspirant whose medical problem prevented him from reaching his goal. The case of Senator Thomas Eagleton is offered as both a cautionary tale and as an introduction to our subject.

Eagleton and an Illness Made Public

In the summer of 1972 Senator Thomas Eagleton from Missouri, the Democratic vice presidential nominee, saw the focus of a vigorous campaign against President Richard Nixon shift from the president's policies to Eagleton's medical condition. On July 25, twelve days after he had been nominated for the vice presidency, Eagleton held a press conference from George McGovern's retreat in South Dakota and told an astonished group of reporters that he had been hospitalized for "fatigue and nervous exhaustion" three times during the prior twelve years.[3] Responding to a reporter's pointed questions, Eagleton outlined his history of psychiatric hospitalizations.

In 1960, following his successful campaign for attorney general of Missouri, Eagleton had voluntarily checked himself into Barnes Hospital at Washington University's Medical Center in St. Louis and had spent "almost all of December" of that year receiving psychotherapy, chemotherapy, and electroconvulsive treatments (ECTs) for depression. Four years later, again following a successful campaign, this time for the lieutenant governor's office, Eagleton entered the Mayo Clinic to be treated for depression. Finally, in 1966 he again went to the Mayo Clinic to be treated for recurring depressive episodes. Eagleton stated that he had received the ECTs during two of the three hospitalizations and that in each instance the treatments had been successful.[4]

Amid the immediate speculation that this revelation would disqualify Eagleton from office, Senator George McGovern was quick to assert that Eagleton would remain his running mate. At that same press conference, McGovern stated that "there is no one sounder in body, mind, and spirit than Tom Eagleton."[5] Although not told of Eagleton's condition at the time the vice presidential slot had been offered, McGovern claimed that the information would not have changed his mind. Eagleton said that he had not purposely obscured information from McGovern, but that he had considered these breakdowns no more serious than "a broken leg or a broken arm." The McGovern-Eagleton campaign then issued a statement contending that this revelation would have no effect on the campaign and that the two candidates would continue with their previously planned itineraries.

All the major news networks carried the Eagleton story that evening, and by the following morning workers in McGovern's campaign were disabused of their optimism. The *New York Times*, the *Washington Post*, and other major daily newspapers ran the Eagleton story on their front pages, including verbatim transcripts of the press conference. Hoping to staunch speculation about Eagleton's being forced to resign, McGovern then issued his now infamous "1000 percent" endorsement of Eagleton, adding that he was proud of his running mate's candor. As a counter to the murmurings from the opposition, McGovern's campaign manager, Gary Hart, called for all candidates to disclose information regarding their health.

The issue became further muddled, however, by a column Jack

Anderson published that same day, in which he claimed not only that Eagleton had a history of mental illness, but that he was a chronic alcoholic who had once been arrested on charges of reckless driving. Despite McGovern's attempts to repair the damage, Anderson's column escalated the histrionics of the debate. Though Anderson provided no documentation for his charges (he could not—they were subsequently proven false), McGovern and Eagleton found themselves answering questions regarding this matter long after they had hoped to put it to rest.

On the following day the *New York Times*, which had previously welcomed Senator Eagleton to the ticket as an "intelligent, conscientious, and compassionate legislator," called for the vice presidential candidate's withdrawal: "We believe that the only way the campaign can be turned back into a true test of the programs and leadership qualifications of President Nixon and his Democratic rival, Senator McGovern, is through the voluntary withdrawal of Senator Eagleton from the McGovern ticket. . . . it would be a helpful contribution not only to the McGovern candidacy but to the health of the American political process."[6] And yet as gamely as the McGovern camp tried to steer the debate around to other issues, it found itself unable to redirect the torrent of questions regarding Eagleton's health problems.

Two days later, on July 30, Eagleton made a final effort to save his candidacy by appearing on the CBS News program "Face the Nation." McGovern's once firm "1000 percent" endorsement of his running mate was steadily giving way to qualified, tepid statements about Eagleton. "To a great extent," McGovern confided "casually" to some reporters, "it's up to Tom whether or not he stays on the ticket." During his television appearance Eagleton strongly asserted his determination to stay in the race, saying that even if McGovern asked him point-blank to resign, "I'll listen respectfully and attentively, and I'll weigh his words," but declining to blindly do McGovern's bidding. Eagleton contended that "my health is not really the issue," that he was fully competent to discharge his duties if elected, and that the matter would soon die down.

Eagleton met privately with McGovern in Washington the next day and during a joint press appearance with McGovern announced his voluntary withdrawal from the ticket. To the end, however, both of these men insisted that the problem was not Eagleton's health. McGovern stated that Eagleton's move was a noble gesture, done for the sake of the party, and that "I am fully satisfied that his health is excellent. In the joint decision we have reached tonight, health was not a factor." Both the *New York Times* and the *Washington Post*, which had also called for Eagleton's resignation, took up the "health was not a factor" cry. In its commentary on the resignation, the *Washington Post* said that the matter "was not some sort of referendum on mental health, a question, as so many persisted in putting it, of whether a person who once sought psychiatric care was to be forever denied a part in the political process. This is not and never was what the issue was about." The *New York Times* echoed the same sentiments, arguing that "the withdrawal of Senator Eagleton from the Democratic national ticket was an admirable act of self-abnegation designed to permit the Presidential campaign to proceed on the issues, rather than in a sterile debate over his own capacity to stand the rigors of the Presidency in an emergency."[7]

One wonders, if "health was not a factor," what, then, was a factor? Several critics complained that Eagleton had mishandled the affair by not being more forthcoming during his initial encounter with McGovern during the Democratic Convention. Others stated that the American public was not yet ready to discuss the issues of mental illnesses rationally and compassionately. Perhaps a more candid (and partisan) assessment came from one "highly placed source in the White House," who told a reporter: "The people simply aren't going to want to put a mental patient in charge of the nuclear arsenal."[8] And, indeed, had McGovern been elected and had he subsequently died in office, Eagleton would have been his constitutionally designated successor. The image of a decompensated Thomas Eagleton in charge of the nuclear arsenal—irrespective of how sophisticated and compassionate the voters might have been—was a frightening one that could not be easily repressed. It was a possibility, however distasteful, which had to be considered.

It was precisely this possibility which McGovern and his advisers preferred not to consider. Despite their claims that Eagleton had come forth with his statement in order to be completely candid and "to educate the public" on mental illness, McGovern's operatives had known about Eagleton's past maladies for six days before they went public with the information. Tipped off by a friendly reporter, McGovern had learned that both Knight newspapers and *Time* magazine were piecing together final details of this story and were imminently ready to publish their own accounts. Even before a definitive account appeared in the press, there were rumors circulating about Eagleton's alleged drinking problem.[9] McGovern, Eagleton, and their aides debated the matter for another six days before concluding that they could salvage most of their political capital by airing the matter publicly before the press did. Nowhere in any record does it appear that the question of Eagleton's possible incompetence, based on his medical history, dominated the discussion. If at all, the competency question arose because Eagleton had not been candid about his hospitalizations when he was offered the nomination, which seems less a matter of competency than of candor and political savvy.

McGovern was more forthcoming in his political memoirs, *From Grassroots*, when he stated that he was prepared to run with Eagleton until he consulted Dr. Karl Menninger. The eminent psychiatrist had no hesitation as to McGovern's proper course of action: "For the sake of the nation . . . you can afford no risks and I would therefore hope that you would ask Mr. Eagleton to resign."[10] What McGovern fails to mention, however, is that he took no action until it became obvious that Eagleton's public revelations were having a disastrous effect on his standing in the polls.

Even while the debate over Eagleton's resignation was raging, there were some sober voices expressing concern, not over the specific tragedy of Thomas Eagleton's illness in relation to the campaign, but over the larger tragedy of a political process which left questions of this sort to be answered so haphazardly. One of McGovern's supporters, Matthew J. Troy from the New York Democratic Committee, noted that Eagleton would have failed the physical examination for less demanding or responsible positions in the armed forces and in industry. How, he asked, could we possibly allow this man to have come so potentially close to being in charge of the country's nuclear decision-making process? Mortimer Rostow, president of the Psychoanalytic Research and Development Fund, noted that "I have always contended that an individual who has been mentally ill should be denied no opportunity for advancement. However, to positions in which reliability is a major factor, he [Eagleton] brings a significant degree of risk. . . . This country is not so poor in administrative talent that in order to obtain brilliant leadership, it must also accept a risk of this order of magnitude."[11]

Perhaps the most cogent explanation of the problem came from James Reston, who wrote the following shortly before Eagleton resigned: "The Eagleton Case demonstrates once more the need for a coherent policy of checking the medical records of men and women who are being considered for positions of great power. Senator Eagleton is not the cause but only the latest example and victim of a much more serious problem."[12] Reston noted that every other American institution which had some larger public responsibility regularly checked and rechecked its leaders' health. Citing instances in recent history in which an American leader had either died in office or had been incapacitated by illness, Reston asked, "Why do we forget the elemental lessons of the past? Why rely in such important matters on the valuable but accidental and often imprecise disclosures of newspaper reporters or the reassurances of Eagleton and McGovern, who are obviously more concerned with the political than with the medical facts?" Again, Reston was not necessarily faulting McGovern and Eagleton (though he had few kind words for the way they handled this matter). Rather, he was bewildered by a political system which seemed to forget the harsh lessons of its own past.

Illness, Power, and the Gambles of History

Reston's analysis of the Eagleton case provides a concise introduction to this study, for he argues forcefully for a reform of the way the current political process handles this problem:

> This is the fault of the system, a system that is very compassionate to human beings whose age and health interfere with the efficient execution of their work. . . .
>
> Maybe the Republic can bear this human compassion in the Supreme Court and the Congress—even though there it is highly questionable—but at the level of the Presidency and the Vice Presidency in this age of atomic weapons abroad and human violences and political assassinations at home, the present system is wildly out of date.[13]

What is at once so intriguing and frightening about this topic is that in the modern West we have invested a great deal of power in the ideal of rationality: rational belief, rational politics, and rational causes and explanations. Perhaps this notion provides the tacit motivation for many of the postassassination theories. It is easier to believe, for example, that Lee Harvey Oswald was part of a larger conspiracy, however sinister, than to believe that his act of violence resulted from a deranged mind. To assume otherwise is to admit to a certain amount of randomness and chaos, to admit to the possibility of irrational acts that escape our defenses. Yet the concept that an undetected sickness in a powerful man can alter the course of history falls within the realm of irrational politics.

Many of the recent writings in history revolve around the twin concepts of causality and predictability. Indeed, at least one political scientist, James David Barber of Duke University, lays claim to the idea of predictability in presidential politics. One has to understand, he says, that "the crucial differences in the presidency can be *anticipated* by an understanding of a potential president's character, his world view, and his style."[14] What we will suggest in this study borrows, in part, from Barber's notion of character, yet in extending that term to include a president's documented illnesses, we will see the idea of character not as an organizing principle or concept but as a source of randomness and unpredictability in history.

We have chosen as the focus of our study three case histories of American presidents: Woodrow Wilson, Franklin D. Roosevelt, and John F. Kennedy. Each of these studies illuminates a particular facet of the problem of presidential illness.

The most substantive study in this book deals with President Franklin D. Roosevelt. We focus on Roosevelt for a variety of reasons. First, the fact that he died in office makes it—at least at the outset —more plausible to assume that he was in ill health for at least a portion of his term. Moreover, through the Freedom of Information Act, we were able to obtain enough direct and indirect medical evidence to document Mr. Roosevelt's health problems. Secondly, Roosevelt was president during a time of economic crisis and war, a time in which this democracy conceded a great deal of power to the executive office, some of which it has since taken back. Thus, Roosevelt's hand in the affairs of state is perhaps more clearly seen than in the other cases we describe. Thus, we begin with a figure in history through which we can at least begin to substantiate our thesis that it is at least *plausible* that illness had some bearing on history.

We begin our study, however, with Woodrow Wilson. If the Roosevelt health history presents to us a case of a man who—though dying a slow death—was still minimally effective up to the actual point of his death, Wilson's history is a sadder study of a man who languished in office even after a stroke rendered him demonstrably incompetent to discharge his duties. Moreover, the facts in Wilson's case bring more sharply into focus the perplexing questions surrounding the nature of the doctor-patient relationship. What, for example, are the duties of a physician to a patient who refuses to resign from a sensitive position, even after the patient can no longer function effectively in office? Put another way, does the physician's pact of confidentiality with the patient ever take into account the larger needs of society in its covenant? The relationship between President Wilson and his physician, Dr. Cary Grayson, is an excellent example of the dilemma which any doctor may encounter when treating a public official.

Lastly, we turn to the case of President John F. Kennedy. So far as we have been able to determine, Kennedy was relatively in good health throughout his tragically shortened term in office. Yet the story of his path to the White House, coupled with the documentation of his chronic illnesses, raises several questions about not only the role of physicians *as* physicians, but about physicians who exercise power outside the bounds of their profession. That John Kennedy survived the illnesses of his early years is a testament to the wonders that modern medicine has wrought—and, in all fairness, to Mr. Kennedy's courageous determination. It is also a testament, however, to the power of politics to co-opt the prestige and respect of the medical profession for its own purposes. Kennedy's case history demonstrates the lengths to which politicians go to hide their medical problems and the degree to which physicians, either wittingly or unwittingly, cooperate in the deception. Mr. Kennedy's story raises once again the question of the proper role of the physician.

Having outlined the evidence we have gathered, we hope, finally, to conclude with a discussion of the legal and ethical implications of this problem. Lest we be accused of being naive, a study of this sort raises difficult questions, many of which, perhaps, will frustrate our best attempts to solve them. Yet in addition to bringing to light a problem which could, as Reston noted when discussing the Eagleton case, "have the direct and most final consequences for us all," we hope to present at least some partial solutions, solutions which are well within our power to effect.

2

Woodrow Wilson

Strokes, Versailles, and the Pathology of Politics

▬▬ And so, instead of making peace, we make war, and are going to reduce Europe to ruin. The smaller nations are all mad. They want credit, not for food, for their starving population, but for military expenditure. It is enough to reduce one to complete despair. Poor old Europe, the mother of civilization.—Jan Smuts, Versailles, April 1919

The author of this letter, General Jan Smuts, was no squeamish observer. A veteran of the Boer War in South Africa, Smuts had come to Paris as a member of the British negotiating team in the fall of 1918. As a seasoned military man, Smuts was not given to the histrionics that usually accompanies a war. The rebellion against Britain in the early 1900s had given him a taste not only of the horrors of a conventional battle, but of the added misery and destruction of guerrilla warfare. And yet, even as inured as he was, the carnage and wreckage of World War I left him aghast. The surface statistics were grim enough: of the sixty-five million men who had been mobilized between 1914 and 1918, at least eight million had died by the beginning of the Versailles Conference. An additional twenty million soldiers had been crippled, maimed, or wounded. The added, modern twist to this old theme was the engagement of civilians; twenty-two million were either killed or permanently handicapped by the war, making them as active and immediate in the battles as the soldiers themselves.[1] This loss of life was unprecedented: there were ten times more soldiers killed per day in World War I than in the American Civil War; twenty-four times more than in the Napoleonic Wars; and five hundred and fifty times more than in the Boer conflict, the very war which Smuts had directed. Even after the guns were silent, a defoliated European countryside was incapable of sustaining enough agricultural production to feed its natives. Weakened by malnutrition, exposure, and the unsanitary conditions, another eight million civilians died in the two years after the war from a raging epidemic of influenza.[2]

Into this apocalyptic landscape stepped Woodrow Wilson, the first historical figure in our study. When the president walked onto the dock at Brest, France, on December 13, 1918, he carried with him specific proposals to wake Europe from its collective nightmare.[3] Earlier in the year, he had articulated his famous "Fourteen Points" proposal, which called for the end of the war, and for the restructuring of the European governments which had led to the war. In October the embattled and dispirited Germans had secretly sent a message to Wilson asking him to negotiate a treaty among the belligerents.[4] The German leadership saw Wilson and his plans as the only way to salvage a decent future from the wreckage they had helped create. Wilson's humane and idealistic program, they hoped, would serve to temper what they perceived as the vengeful ambitions of the leaders of the Entente and would ultimately evolve into a peace proposal which they could accept. So desperate at this point were the Germans that they undiplomatically acceded to Wilson's plans even before the negotiations began and wrote to the president that "The German Government accepts as the basis for its negotiations the program laid down by the President of the United States."[5] By the time the formal sessions began in January of the following year, Wilson and his ideas began to take on mythic proportions, and the Germans began privately to refer to him as their "savior." Yet the man in whom the

Germans and many other Europeans placed so much of their trust, and whom they hoped would breathe new vitality into their decaying continent, was a cripple, both politically and physically.

Wilson had made his foreign policy the central theme in the previous month's congressional elections and exhorted the electorate to return a sizable Democratic majority to Capitol Hill so that he would be in a strong bargaining position in Paris. Either his pleas did not work or the electorate had other concerns, for the Republicans won twenty-five out of forty contested senate seats.[6] While those gains only gave the Republicans a slim majority, it did give them effective veto power over any treaty legislation; more importantly, the Democrats lost the chairmanship of the Foreign Relations Committee to Henry Cabot Lodge, an avowed and vociferous isolationist.[7] When the formal negotiating sessions began in January 1919, Wilson faced the difficult task of selling the other leaders on a program which commanded little political domestic support. It was a point that was not lost on France's Clemenceau, Britain's Lloyd-George, and Italy's Orlando.

The president, however, was beset with another problem which had pursued him all his life: his health. By the time he arrived in France to undertake the most arduous and dangerous political task of his life, Woodrow Wilson was suffering from the sequelae of a series of maladies which have been diagnosed as both neurological and psychosomatic in origin.

The subject of Wilson's health came under the scrutiny of William Bullitt and Sigmund Freud in the 1920s, who collaborated on a psychological study of the president.[8] Their interpretation of the symptoms and events in Wilson's life suggests that the president was severely impaired at critical times in his life by neurotic illnesses, which bordered on the psychotic and pathologic. Their study, which did not come out until after Mrs. Wilson's death, paints the disturbing picture of an ambitious man driven by unconscious and conflicted desires. An alternative diagnosis, described and analyzed by Dr.

Edwin Weinstein, suggests that the president suffered from severe neurological impairment. In his original study, Weinstein chronicles at least six separate episodes in Wilson's life which can be described as strokes, including the final one which killed him in 1924.[9]

As Weinstein points out in the introduction to his study, any diagnosis of Wilson is going to be hampered by "the paucity of medical records, by the state of medical knowledge in his time, and by the unique circumstances connected with the Office of the President of the United States."[10] In many ways, the particular case of Wilson is even more difficult to assess, for Wilson's malady involves an area of human physiology and anatomy which, even today, remains much of a mystery to the medical profession. The relationship between the physical, organic component of behavior and the unconscious, dynamic component of behavior is still the subject of a heated debate among physicians. Wilson's case is even more complex, as Weinstein points out, because the president "was not hospitalized; case records were not kept (or they may have been kept and subsequently destroyed); no technical procedures to define the exact location and extent of the brain lesion were carried out; and no tests to evaluate mental function were made."[11] And yet Weinstein and other researchers have done a commendable job of piecing together the available data to come up with a compelling medical interpretation of Wilson's political problems. In this section, we will trace the development of Wilson's health problems from birth until the end of his tenure as president; we will try to correlate medical crises in Wilson's life with his political mistakes.[12]

The drama of Wilson's handicapped presidency, however, adds one further dimension to our discussion, which we hope to highlight in this section. If a president is grossly and demonstrably incompetent to discharge the duties of his office, but refuses to relinquish his power, what can, or should, be done? And what happens when that question acquires a particular urgency, as in the case of the Versailles negotiations? Rather than being idle speculation, the case of Woodrow Wilson demonstrates the political system's defenselessness against the ravages of disease.

The Early Medical History

Woodrow Wilson's early medical history has been the subject of a great deal of misdocumentation and misinterpretation. The consensus of his initial biographers was that he was a frail, sickly child, whose delicate constitution made him prey to an exorbitant number of diseases.[13] Nothing could have been further from the truth. Born in 1856 in Staunton, Virginia, to the family of a Presbyterian minister, Wilson was, for ten years, the youngest child in the family and, as such, was the prime focus of his parents' lavish and often smothering attentions. As a child, Wilson engaged in a full complement of athletic activities, including horseback riding and baseball. According to Weinstein, "there is no evidence of any illness in childhood and no record of any behavior that would indicate that he was frail or sickly. Even someone as health conscious as his mother could recall no illness or 'weakness of any kind' in his childhood."[14] The correspondence between Wilson and his parents during his early adolescent years further indicates that he traveled widely throughout the South during his summer vacations and that his activities were in no way curtailed by any serious maladies.

The confusion concerning young Wilson's health arises from a number of quarters. As a child, Wilson seems to have had a great deal of difficulty in his studies, particularly reading and writing. One biographer, noting that Wilson was basically illiterate until age nine, inferred that some illness or series of illnesses hampered Wilson's early education.[15] In fact, Wilson did have an "illness" in the formal sense of the word, but it was some form of learning disability, most probably dyslexia. Unaware of his handicap, Wilson's parents attributed the boy's slow learning to "willfulness" or laziness. Through sheer effort and practice, Wilson would learn to read, albeit quite slowly and with great difficulty.[16] It would continue to be a problem for which he eventually compensated quite well but would never completely overcome until he reached full maturity. Thus, despite his dogged efforts to keep pace with his peers, Wilson would continue to be plagued by his poor reading skills throughout college, in his graduate studies, and up to his early faculty years. What his contemporaries interpreted as Wilson's "languid" approach to his studies, as one classmate put it,[17] and what biographers would infer was a physical malady, was actually the result of a condition that even today is difficult to diagnose and treat.

Wilson himself also contributed to the confusion surrounding his early health. Ashamed of his erratic academic record, including his sudden and unexplained leaves of absence from Davidson College and, later, the University of Virginia Law School, Wilson would vaguely allude to his associates that he had been quite ill as a child and once even specified his illness as scarlet fever.[18] To Dr. Cary Grayson, his physician in the White House, Wilson said that he had suffered from measles in childhood, which Grayson would later claim "permanently weakened his physique."[19]

Finally, it has been pointed out that the prevailing medical theories of the day also influenced what biographers in the 1920s and 1930s would say about Wilson. It was believed at that time, for example, that all diseases, including infectious ones, affected only people who had a "constitutional predisposition" for them. Wilson's subsequent neurological problems made many biographers, including Dr. Grayson, suspect that there was some hidden pathology to be discovered in Wilson's childhood, and this assumption subsequently colored their analysis. Adding to this general misconception was the widespread notion that intellectually gifted people were necessarily sickly. Wilson's multiple and varied accomplishments in academia and his aloof, professorial appearance made many suspect that he was more subject to illness than the common man.[20]

A careful reading of the available materials documenting Wilson's early life, however, contradicts all of these theories of his physical infirmity. At the same time, these documents do suggest an image of a troubled, anxious young man who was so remarkably driven and harsh with himself that he often did, in fact, make himself sick. Wilson's early letters and entries in his journal suggest that he set unrealistic goals for himself and became frustrated and depressed when he failed to attain them. Moreover, his private memoirs also show a tendency toward harsh self-analysis, often couched in religious terms. One particularly grim entry in his journal from 1874 illustrates this facet of his personality: "I am now in my seventeenth year and it is sad, when looking over my past life to see how few of those seventeen years I have spent in the fear of God, and how much time I have spent in the service of the Devil."[21]

This emotional self-flagellation was apparently more than Wilson could bear. Having successfully completed his first year at Davidson College in 1873 (after a great deal of strenuous effort), Wilson abruptly decided not to return the following fall. Wilson would later suggest to Ray Stannard Baker, his first biographer, that illness had kept him from returning to Davidson. Yet Wilson spent an active and full year pursuing myriad interests while he "convalesced" at home, which has led later researchers to conclude that the combination of his anxieties and the separation from home provoked an emotional crisis.[22] Once he decided not to return to Davidson, his lethargy and melancholia disappeared. Other historians have also suggested that Wilson had only intended to stay at Davidson long enough to prepare himself academically to enter Princeton. This theory has merit, inasmuch as Wilson spent most of 1874 studying and practicing his writing. His diligence paid off; he was accepted at Princeton and matriculated there in 1875.[23]

The anxiety crises that had plagued Wilson while at Davidson seem to have been resolved by the time he entered Princeton. Weinstein suggests that Wilson had matured sufficiently to be able to handle the separation from his parents.[24] Certainly the range of activities, both athletic and academic, in which Wilson participated suggests that he was fully involved in college life. He worked at his studies with vigor, joined a debating club, and as if to compensate for his earlier writing handicap, authored several long, involved essays for school publications. His letters home from this period also indicate that he seemed relatively content and at peace.

Despite the tranquillity of his college days, Wilson began to struggle with his choice of a career. By the time he entered Princeton, he had definitely ruled out a career in the ministry. His memoirs from this time show that he aspired to a literary life and, indeed, devoted much of his effort outside of the classroom writing on varied and unrelated topics. At the same time, Wilson developed a passion for polemics and debate which, combined with a lifelong interest in history, kindled a desire in him to study law, possibly as an initial step toward political office. By the end of his senior year he decided to act on these interests and subsequently entered law school at the University of Virginia in 1880.

After four years of uninterrupted good health at Princeton, Wilson was suddenly beset with a host of ailments when he began his law studies.[25] He had been in Charlottesville less than a month when he wrote to his father that he was feeling ill; in his letter he complained of vague symptoms and of "fits of the blues." Reverend Wilson's reply suggests that he felt that Woodrow's symptoms were self-inflicted, for he advised his son to be less "introspective and self-conscious and more studious." Young Wilson, however, continued to send a stream of complaints back home, including a description of a "cold" that persisted throughout the winter and well into the spring. By April the self-diagnosis became dyspepsia, and Wilson's mother feared that he would leave his stomach "ruined for life" if he did not take better care of himself.[26]

Like Wilson's father, Weinstein is skeptical of the organic nature of Woodrow's complaints: "To judge from the nature of these symptoms, and with the knowledge of Wilson's subsequent medical history, his ailments were due not to bad climate or poor food, but were clearly a psychosomatic response to emotional tension."[27] The sources of anxiety and unhappiness that triggered these psychosomatic responses in Wilson are many and varied. Probably the greatest source of stress on Wilson at the time was his ambivalence toward the study of law. Just after he had announced his intention to pursue a legal career, he began to speak of his choice in dreading tones, and during the summer after his graduation from Princeton he complained to a friend about his unease at tackling the "dry dust" of the law. Although Wilson would later show great interest in the history and development of legal codes, he found the practical and rigorous application of law to specific cases to be tedious and at times overwhelming; he often wrote to his father about the "excessive" amount of work required, and his slow reading habits certainly contributed to this problem.

Further compounding the misery of Wilson's first year at Virginia, and contributing yet another factor to his psychosomatic illness, was a one-sided love affair he tried to carry on with his cousin, Harriet Woodrow. Though he had known her most of his life, he suddenly came away from a visit to her house after his graduation from Princeton with the conviction that he was fully and madly in love with her. As Wilson would later describe his emotional state during this time: "I was absolutely hungry for a sweetheart . . . I went to Virginia with a deep sense of the inconvenience and discreditableness of my condition. . . . Seriously, I was in *need* of a sweetheart."[28] Even in retrospect, Wilson's description of his desire for female companionship does not seem to have been exaggerated, judging from the numbers of letters (unanswered) he sent to Hattie and visits (unreciprocated) he made to her home in nearby Staunton. Despite Hattie's marked indifference, Wilson continued to pursue her throughout the rest of the year and in the process missed so many lectures that the dean of the law school threatened to dismiss him. Though Wilson carried on in his pursuit of Hattie, he managed to attend enough classes to avoid expulsion and to pass all of his courses with satisfactory grades.

Though he spent a rather healthy and quiet summer traveling around the South (including another vain visit to Hattie's home), Wilson's medical troubles returned with the commencement of the new school year in the fall of 1880. Wilson's father first detected the change in his son's mood in Woodrow's letters and told his son that in them he saw "a face of solicitude" and heard "sighs of anxiety." By November of that year Wilson's symptoms manifested themselves in the form of another persistent "cold." When Wilson continued to complain, his parents insisted that he return home to convalesce. Wilson initially refused; then suddenly, on Christmas Day 1880, he departed Charlottesville—and his law studies—without taking leave of friends or faculty. Shortly after he settled back into his home, his health improved dramatically. To concerned law school friends who inquired after him, he later gave out contradictory information, telling one that he had suffered from "a very severe cold" and another that his "digestive organs" were "seriously out of gear." After a brief respite of good health, Wilson's digestive troubles began again as the date of his bar examination drew closer (it was still possible in those days to sit for the bar without taking a formal degree from a law school), and he postponed taking the examination for another year.[29]

We bring up these early episodes in Wilson's life and discuss them in some detail because they make later diagnoses of Wilson's medical condition complicated and ambiguous. At least on the surface there seems to be a correlation between Wilson's early medical problems and his emotional state; in particular, his attitude towards his studies and his profession. For example, after Wilson passed the bar exam the following year, he again suffered from digestive problems as the time came for him to set up his practice with a friend in Atlanta. He spent several lonely and unprofitable months at this practice, intermittently suffering from a variety of minor somatic complaints, chiefly concerning his stomach, which suddenly disappeared when he decided to give up the practice of law and begin graduate studies in political science at Johns Hopkins in the fall of 1883.[30]

As we discussed earlier, the relationship between psychodynamic factors and organic factors in a person's health is still the subject of heated debate. With some exception, specialists on either side of the issue concede that both are important contributing factors: whatever we mean by "thought" and "emotions" does appear to affect our health and, conversely, our organic and physiologic characteristics necessarily constitute our health. The rub of the question is a matter of hierarchy and precedence: which plays a greater contributing role in a patient's disease, and which occurs first, an emotional or a physiological breakdown?

While most recent medical interpretations of Wilson's early life suggest that his health problems as a child were psychosomatic, there is wide divergence in the analyses of his later, and more serious, afflictions. Wilson's repeated and often severe breakdowns can become so much grist for the debate between physiologists and psychologists. Rather than playing advocate to alternative interpretations, we hope to present the medical documentation as clearly as possible to demonstrate how an illness could have affected the course of history.

Academia and the Onset of Illness

Having dismissed a career in law as both tedious and uninteresting, Wilson entered a graduate program in political science at Johns Hopkins in 1883. Despite his continued reading difficulties, especially with the German articles required by the curriculum, Wilson spent two remarkably successful and productive years at Hopkins. In addition to his own heavy course work, he also completed a manuscript late in 1884, which was published early the following year to general critical acclaim. Wilson's book, *Congressional Government*, established him as a promising scholar in his field and, despite his having foregone completing the requirements for his Ph.D. because of his troubles with German, helped him secure an appointment as professor of history at Bryn Mawr in 1885.[31]

The next few years in Wilson's life were characterized by both domestic and professional happiness. Despite occasional complaints of intestinal trouble, Wilson's letters indicate that this was also a relatively healthy time for him. Shortly after accepting the position at Bryn Mawr, Wilson married Ellen Axson, whom he had courted with characteristic intensity since meeting two years previous. Encouraged by both the dean at Bryn Mawr and his former professors, Wilson submitted his recently published *Congressional Government* as his doctoral dissertation, studied enough German at night to pass his qualifying examinations, and was belatedly awarded his doctorate in 1886.

Although Wilson had initially been delighted with securing any academic appointment, his growing reputation and his ambitions soon motivated him to look beyond the confines of Bryn Mawr. Thus, in 1886, when Wesleyan College offered him the Hedding Chair in History, he sought and was granted release from his contract at Bryn Mawr and moved his family to Middletown, Connecticut. Though Wilson seemed happy and healthy at Wesleyan, his most cherished private hope was to return to Princeton as a member of the faculty. To this end, he worked prodigiously on scores of scholarly enterprises. The result of these efforts was another significant work in political history, *The State*, published in 1889, which along with Wilson's brilliantly written and delivered lectures, added to his growing reputation and eventually led to an appointment at Princeton as professor of political science in 1890.

It would be difficult to underestimate the enormity of Wilson's accomplishments since he left law school in 1883 as a disappointed, troubled young man. In seven years he had resolved many of the inner doubts and turmoil that had probably led to most of his physical symptomatologies and had certainly frustrated many of his personal relationships. He had completed not only a rigorous doctoral program, but had published significant works in his field, and, finally, had distinguished himself in the classroom as an able and engaging teacher, leading to his appointment at Princeton.

Beginning in 1895, however, Wilson's mood and temperament began to change subtly. Although he was still exceedingly productive and active, he began to complain again of stomach problems. When the pains persisted, he visited a New York doctor, who suggested that his patient's troubles were caused by excess stomach acid. His treatment was to have Wilson wash his stomach out with water forced through a long rubber tube, then siphon out the contents. A potentially dangerous—and now outdated—technique, the treatments did little to alleviate Wilson's condition and may have exacerbated it: in one particularly painful episode the siphon broke just after Wilson had pumped his stomach full of water, and he had to rush, with a distended belly, to the doctor's office to have it drained. The severity of Wilson's symptoms increased throughout the rest of 1895, and his physicians, at a loss as to the origins of his illness, could find no manner of treatment to lessen his pain.[32]

One contributing factor in this apparent relapse was Wilson's schedule. Having recently bought a house in Princeton to shelter his growing family, Wilson found his professor's salary too meager and began seeking outside income as a speaker and lecturer. His efforts paid off financially, as he made as much from his lecture fees as from his teaching in 1895, but the arduous routine may have wreaked havoc with his health. Between the spring term and Christmas 1895, Wilson spoke at alumni gatherings and commencements in Princeton, Virginia, Oberlin, and Wesleyan; delivered eighteen out-of-town lectures in New York; and wrote six serialized articles for *Harper's Magazine* on the life of George Washington. In January 1896, though he delivered a series of lectures at Johns Hopkins, his routine may have caught up with him. His intermittent complaints about his stomach suddenly developed into, in his words, "a sharp attack of indigestion," which forced him to take to bed. The physician who had prescribed the stomach pump thought that the tube may have nicked the small intestine, causing inflammation, and advised that Wilson discontinue its use. The pain, nevertheless, continued, yet Wilson kept up his routine, rising from his sick bed in late January to give his annual lectures on government at Hopkins.[33]

The stress of this schedule, along with the chronic stomach pains, began to affect Wilson's behavior and demeanor. His friends and colleagues, noting how tense and uneasy Wilson seemed, pressed him to cancel some of his engagements and take a vacation. His physician, suddenly alarmed at Wilson's rapidly deteriorating condition, suggested he leave for an extended stay in Europe as soon as possible. Wilson pointedly disregarded all of this advice, yet he must have looked quite worn and haggard, for his father, noticing a nervous facial tic which Wilson had suddenly developed, worried to a friend, "I am afraid that Woodrow is going to die."[34] In May of that year the medical disaster which Wilson's physician and family had been fearing finally occurred. According to his most recent medical biographer, Wilson suffered the first of a series of incapacitating strokes.[35]

The diagnosis of a stroke is disputed in a number of articles and biographies.[36] Indeed, Weinstein himself, who first ventured this diagnosis, is careful to allow for alternative possibilities. Nevertheless, Wilson's symptoms are highly suggestive of a stroke. Wilson suddenly found that his right hand was weak, the tips of his fingers numb, and that he had lost most of his dexterity. Moreover, he experienced sharp, but transitory pain in his right arm, extending from his wrist to his shoulder. Weinstein submits that the nature of the symptoms and the sudden onset of the disease indicate "that (Wilson) had suffered an occlusion of a central branch of the left middle cerebral artery. This vessel supplies the regions of the left cerebral hemisphere that control movement and sensation for the contralateral extremities. The subsequent course of the disease suggests that the branch was blocked by an embolus from the left internal carotid artery."[37] Simply put, what Weinstein suggests in his diagnosis is that one of the cerebral arterial branches, which carry oxygenated blood to the brain, was blocked, depriving the region of the brain serviced by that artery of oxygen. In the absence of oxygen the function of cells becomes impaired, and if the deprivation is prolonged, they die. In Wilson's case the specific groups of cells that were affected controlled the right side of his body; more specifically, they controlled the function of his right hand and apparently also involved his right arm. When the embolism (blockage) occurred, it manifested itself as an impairment of Wilson's writing ability and decreased the mobility of his right arm due to pain.

Weinstein further suggests a causal relationship between Wilson's life-style and his subsequent disease. He notes, for example, that Wilson may have suffered a milder form of a stroke in 1891 when, in Wilson's words, he "had a temporary illness (slight but immediately concerning my nerves)" that affected his right hand and made it painful and difficult for him to write. Weinstein continues: "The usual cause of strokes in young persons (Wilson was then only 40 years old) is hypertension, which Wilson later showed; however, in 1886, accurate measurement of blood pressure was not yet a part of the medical examination."[38] As for the etiology of the disease, Weinstein seems convinced that Wilson's stressful schedule and his intense, nervous personality significantly contributed to the disease:

> The question of whether emotional stress (such as that which Wilson underwent in 1895 and 1896) has a connection with high blood pressure and strokes is an enormously complicated one. While many clinicians, from their experience, believe that there is a relationship, there are no verified prospective studies to support this belief. The problem in large part is a methodological one, since it is difficult to define and quantify stress. The occurrence of Wilson's stroke in 1896, after a prolonged period of intense stress, appears more than coincidental.[39]

Indeed, in retrospect we can see this tendency in Wilson toward demanding, hypercritical performance since boyhood.

Wilson's response to this particular incident, however, is curious. In contrast to what we had earlier suggested were psychosomatic symptoms, about which Wilson loudly and repeatedly complained, he tried to make light of—even to deny—his present malady. He did, however, find the illness painful enough to seek a consultation with W. W. Keen, one of the foremost neurologists of his day. We have none of Dr. Keen's clinical notes to indicate what his own diagnosis was, but we can surmise that Keen too dismissed the gravity of the illness, for he did not ask to see Wilson again and did not think it necessary for Wilson to curtail his activities. Wilson's own attitude toward his illness may have contributed to Keen's apparent lack of concern. Despite the continued pain in his right arm and the weakness of his right hand, Wilson continued to work apace. Rather than ceasing his writing altogether, he would peck out his notes and speeches on a typewriter or have his wife write them out longhand from his dictation. In time, rather than succumbing to this handicap, Wilson learned to write with his left hand, and a number of surviving letters from this period show a marked change in Wilson's script.

This aspect of Wilson's personality would become increasingly important as his health deteriorated and as his power and influence increased. Even to his closest friends, Wilson refused to admit that he had suffered anything serious. By way of explaining his sudden use of the typewriter in personal correspondence, he joked to his friends that "[I] have been threatened with an attack of writer's cramp." Weinstein notes the paradox of Wilson's behavior: "The stroke was a far more stressful experience for Wilson than his psychosomatic ailments had been. His digestive disturbance and headaches had been self-limited and manageable: they appeared when he was lonely, depressed, and under pressure, and they had departed promptly with relief of tension."[40] The pain and weakness in the entirety of his right arm, however, were not transient and persisted for well over a year.

Even when the more acute aspects of his disease disappeared, Wilson would continue to be troubled by intermittent weakness in the affected limb.

Wilson's denial of his illness, claims Weinstein, was "an integral part of his personality and the expression of an important cultural value."[41] It is a valid point. Wilson had been trained by his father to believe that health was a result of clean, moral living, and any severe illness necessarily indicated "some moral weakness or dereliction of duty." Tied up with this moralistic formulation of disease was also Wilson's own sense of work and accomplishment. The severity and sudden onset of this disease hit Wilson just as he was becoming something of a celebrity at Princeton in his academic circles. Having worked so diligently to achieve his place in the sun, Wilson was naturally reluctant to let personal problems interfere with his advancement, especially when he believed that this problem was probably self-inflicted, a result of some vague misdeed and thus solvable by sheer force of will. Hence, Wilson began to speak about his affected limbs in the objective case: diseased appendages were routinely referred to in his letters as "the hand" or "the arm," rather than "my hand" or "my arm." Fully believing, as Weinstein notes, that "the body was the servant of the spirit, and . . . that the mind could control the body," Wilson began to tell his wife that he had to learn how to teach his body "to behave."[42]

In time, Wilson would be able to temporarily compensate for his illness. In fact, he advanced his career magnificently during the next few years. He continued to teach a complete load of classes, delivered even more extracurricular lectures than previously, and published a substantial number of scholarly articles. A number of observers, however, detected a definite change in Wilson's behavior. For example, Stockton Axson, his brother-in-law, noted that Wilson became even more driven than before and that he was "less relaxed."[43] He became more critical of people, less tolerant of their weaknesses and mistakes, and rarely offered praise to his colleagues and students. As if to compensate for the time he had missed because of the stroke, Wilson gave up most forms of recreation and put himself on a strict schedule that left little time outside of his scholarly activities.

Whether or not this change was due to the stroke or to Wilson's psychological reaction to the stroke is difficult to tell. It is always possible that a neurological impairment affecting motor functions could also affect behavior. Nevertheless, because of subsequent events in Wilson's life and his reaction to those events, it is important to take note of his curious, and somewhat unrealistic, way of reacting to his disease. As we shall see, in time Wilson's denial of illness becomes even more important than the illness itself.[44]

———

The First Presidency and the Second Stroke

Though Wilson's recovery from his stroke in 1896 was slow and incomplete, he continued to act as if nothing had ever happened to him. Throughout 1896 and into most of 1897 Wilson was bothered by transient episodes of weakness and pain. These symptomatic recurrences in the right side of his body were jokingly dismissed by Wilson, and when the problems in his right hand became too pronounced, he would simply switch to writing with his left (at which he had become remarkably adept). Even in the worst of times Wilson never broke stride in his hectic routine and continued to produce writings and speeches at a remarkable clip.[45]

The frenetic quality of Wilson's work habits was no doubt due, in part, to his more ultimate ambitions of becoming president of a major American university. This ambition might also account for Wilson's consistent denials of illness. This first stroke came at a time when Wilson's reputation as a scholar had come under attack, and Wilson felt compelled to respond to his critics by increasing his already prodigious output. Moreover, Wilson began to take a greater interest in the administration of Princeton, and in speeches to alumni gatherings around the country he began to advance proposals for revamping the educational system at the school.

As Wilson's reputation for innovative thinking grew, he became identified with a cadre of young faculty members who were agitating for dramatic reforms in the school's curriculum. Until 1900 Princeton's advancement as an elite, respected university had been frustrated by its lack of a graduate school and by the haphazard and inconsistently applied requirements of its students. Despite repeated appeals on the part of the school's most distinguished faculty members (many of whom had left the country to complete their graduate education), the conservative members of the board of trustees, along with the school president, balked at any innovation. Citing the school's origins as a Presbyterian seminary, the old guard claimed that the expansion of its secular humanities and science programs would ruin Princeton's essentially religious character. The younger professors, including Wilson, were eager to refashion Princeton on the European models and contended that Princeton was lagging behind the rest of the world's scholarship.[46]

These battles over educational philosophy effectively polarized the Princeton community and left the progressive faction, which was ill-represented on the board, feeling disenfranchised and dispirited. Wilson was one who most acutely felt the disappointments. Having nominated Frederick Jackson Turner, the eminent historian, for a chair, Wilson found that Turner was not even considered because the scholar was a Unitarian. So despondent was Wilson at one point in these battles that he seriously considered accepting an offer from the University of Virginia to become that school's first president. In fact, Wilson would have accepted the offer had it not been for a group of wealthy alumni who appealed to Wilson's loyalties and, perhaps more importantly, raised a small endowment to supplement his salary. The offer from Virginia also seemed to energize sympathetic Princeton alumni to take a more active role in the school's affairs. By 1902 enough of Wilson's supporters had been placed on the board to bring matters to a head, and they suddenly demanded that President Patton, who still refused to sanction any major changes in the university, either resign or turn over his duties to a faculty committee. Faced with the dilemma of either destroying the power of his office or stepping down, Patton reluctantly tendered his resignation on the condition that Wilson be named in his place. It is ironic to note that Patton would insist upon the election of the one man who was most responsible for forcing him out of office. In this academic battle Wilson first displayed the political tact and skill which would later serve him well in public office.[47]

Wilson's election to the Princeton presidency met with wide approval in scholarly circles across the country. His inauguration was an event of the first order, with representatives from academia, industry, and politics in attendance. Wilson began his term with a flurry of activity. A few weeks after his installation, he announced his plans to the board of trustees to restructure Princeton completely. The core of Wilson's plan involved a change in what he called the "outdated and unworkable" lecture system, modeled after the undergraduate programs at Oxford and Cambridge, with preceptors, or tutors, in charge of the education and development of a small group of students.

As with many grand plans, ambition outran economic possibilities; Wilson estimated the cost of his program at a staggering $12.5 million. To a skeptical and fiscally conservative board Wilson confidently predicted that he would raise the entire sum from wealthy alumni who supported the new regime at Princeton.[48]

A man with little tolerance for compromise, who inevitably recast differences of opinion into pitched moral battles, Wilson found himself and his plans consistently frustrated by his colleagues, the financial constraints of the university, and his own rigidity. During the eight years that Wilson was president of Princeton, he was able to implement many of his programs, but at a terrific cost to his health and his sense of personal esteem. Previous interpretations of Wilson's tenure at Princeton note the vanity of many of his struggles, but they fail to take into account the possibility that Wilson's deteriorating health may have played a part in the failure of his academic program and may ultimately have led to his resignation from Princeton to enter politics. For example, Wilson seems to have acted irrationally and at cross-purposes to his goals in three incidents which coincided with what appears to be a recurrence of neurological disease. In each of these Wilson displayed poor judgment and an inability to separate personal concerns from his duties as president.[49]

The first two of these episodes occurred in 1904, just after Wilson began to manifest increasing symptoms of neurological pathology. Having successfully overcome the embolus in 1896, Wilson spent the next eight years in relatively good health. Although he would experience some pain in the right half of his body on occasion, the duration of the episodes was short-lived, and Wilson more than compensated for them. Moreover, his bouts of depression and self-absorption became less frequent. Having accomplished one of the major goals in his life, namely presiding over a university, Wilson found himself for a time at peace and contented.[50] In letters to his wife and friends Wilson's rhetoric and language convey the impression of a happy man. In the summer of 1904, however, he had another recurrence of his old symptoms that were more acute and lasting. The details of the illness are sketchy, and one has to infer a good deal to make sense of the incident. In a letter dated July 23 Wilson mentioned to the correspondent that he suddenly found himself unable to use his right hand and apologized for typing out the letter. Wilson's mention of this symptom is significant, inasmuch as, so far as we know, it was the first recurrence in eight years that was severe enough to occasion the use of a typewriter. To the recipient of the letter Wilson then excused his illness by explaining that "I find real difficulties now-a-days in using the pen, because of an immoderate use of it in the past."[51] Weinstein notes that, characteristically, Wilson used the third-person objective in referring to a personal possession, which is indicative of the degree of denial on Wilson's part. Moreover, the use of the phrase "now-a-days" suggests that the episode lasted longer than previous ones.

Shortly after the onset of this symptom Wilson became involved in two incidents which suggest that the pain in his right hand may have been neurological in origin. The first involved a professor of French, Arnold Cameron, who was a fixture at Princeton. Although his academic credentials were suspect, Cameron was a favorite of the Princeton students. His bizarre and unorthodox behavior in the classroom kept students amused, and he was voted the outstanding teacher at Princeton three times, despite the fact that his students would later admit that they learned next to nothing in his classes. When Wilson assumed office, he immediately appointed one of Cameron's junior colleagues to head the department. Though Wilson had long considered Cameron "a charlatan" and "a mountebank," he expected that he would be able to take care of the problem by removing any administrative powers from Cameron.[52]

Following the weakness in his right hand, Wilson suddenly decided that Cameron had to go. To that end Wilson began to gather specific data on Cameron's performance and had his friends on the faculty inform him of any particularly unusual behavior. When Cameron one day made the comment to his class that women were good "only for raising bread, babies, and hell," Wilson seized on the remark as an opportunity to rid Princeton finally of Cameron.[53] What could have been settled as a relatively painless administrative decision developed into a nasty, personal battle between the two men. When Wilson informed Cameron of his decision to dismiss him with a year's grace of employment, Cameron used Wilson's depiction of him as a "charlatan" to claim that the action was personally motivated. Cameron's remark so incensed Wilson that he withdrew his offer of the extra year's employment and ordered Cameron to be gone by the end of the academic term. The exchange between Wilson and Cameron soon degenerated and spread beyond the confines of the president's office. At one point, Wilson's handling of the matter seemed so overtly vindictive that the students and faculty, who were sympathetic to Cameron's claim that he was being forced out for reasons unrelated to his teaching, planned a protest march on the president's residence. Though Wilson averted this public challenge to his power by again extending Cameron an extra year's employment, the incident unnecessarily gained Wilson the enmity of many alumni and students. Though one could argue that Wilson was well justified in dismissing Cameron, the president's clumsy handling of the affair betrayed how much he let personal consideration interfere with his professional judgment.[54]

A few months later, Wilson again found himself at odds with the university community over a relatively trivial issue. Citing the number of tourists who intruded upon his family's privacy in the president's residence, Wilson ordered the construction of an iron fence around his house during the summer of 1904. When the students returned in September, they raised an outcry over the "unnecessary and unsightly" fence which destroyed the beauty of "a spot which has been the pride of undergraduates." In one editorial the students suggested a compromise by making the fence portable so that it could be removed after the tourist season. Wilson refused the compromise and further refused to discuss the matter, saying that "when a man was right, he need not make explanation." The students' reaction to Wilson's studied indifference to their demands was more than the president could have anticipated. One night, a group of undergraduates destroyed a portion of the fence with picks. Wilson's only action was to have the fence repaired. A few weeks later, Wilson was satirized in the annual student parade by having a pig with his name around its neck dragged on a cart, a symbol of what the students considered to be Wilson's selfishness. When Wilson failed to respond to even that affront, another group of students incited a minor riot in one of the dormitories, breaking windows and chandeliers in their rampage. It finally took the delicate diplomacy of two of Wilson's alumni friends to suggest that the portion of the fence which bordered a sidewalk frequently used by students be taken down. Though Wilson finally acceded to this compromise, he refused to explain his actions and instead had one of his friends insert a notice in the student newspaper suggesting that the construction of the fence was undertaken at the suggestion of the Buildings and Grounds Committee, which was patently untrue.[55]

As minor as these incidents seem, they are part of a pattern of symptoms which, taken together, indicate at least the possibility of some neurological impairment. The fact that these two unpleasant episodes in Wilson's tenure came close on the heels of a definite physiologic impairment (the pain and weakness in his right hand) may be a coincidence, but a curious one. Wilson's handling of these two affairs may, in fact, simply indicate his inexperience. Yet his behavior during the Cameron affair and the fence incident is not consistent with the self-possessed, politic demeanor that had won the Princeton presidency for Wilson. His unbridled anger at Cameron and the manner in which he mishandled the students protesting the construction of the fence indicate at the very least some underlying and unresolved emotional conflict. Dr. Weinstein goes even further in his appraisal of these incidents, and suggests that "possibly neither the Cameron nor the fence incidents would have occurred, at least in the form they took, had not Wilson had his stroke in 1904."[56] Though at least one other medical researcher contests Weinstein's categorical assertion that Wilson had a stroke in 1904,[57] there seems to be some agreement among Wilson scholars that these two incidents are in some way connected with the pain and unease Wilson was feeling during the summer of 1904.[58]

In the light of subsequent events, however, the suggestion that Wilson suffered a stroke in 1904, or at least had the first premonitory signs of some neurologic disease, becomes all the more convincing. On May 28, 1906, Wilson awoke completely blind in one eye. Compounding the horror of this discovery, Wilson also found that the old pain and weakness in his right arm had returned. This episode in Wilson's medical history is one in which most physician-researchers seem to be in agreement.[59] Weinstein describes the illness thus: "The clinical neurologist would say that stroke in 1906 and his previous history clearly defined the nature of his illness. The combination of sudden blindness in one eye, and episodes of weakness and paresthesia (sensations of tingling or numbness) in the opposite upper extremity is characteristic of disease of an internal carotid artery."[60] The carotid artery, which Weinstein mentions in his diagnosis, has one branch, called the ophthalmic artery, which supplies blood to the eye on the same side; the rest of the artery supplies most of the blood to the rest of that hemisphere of the brain. Weinstein's diagnosis suggests that Wilson's carotid artery became "sclerotic and narrowed," and that ulcerations formed.[61] When blood platelets sweep along the scarred surface, they tend to aggregate and form clumps, further aggravating the already narrowed passage. What is even more dangerous, however, is that in time some of the pieces of this solid mass may break off from the larger body, be carried along the various branches in the neurovascular system, and completely block one of the smaller channels. In Wilson's case Weinstein suggests that the ophthalmic artery was substantially blocked by this solid matter, depriving the nerve tissue in the eye of blood, and eventually blinding him. Weinstein continues: "In Wilson's earlier strokes anterior branches of the left middle cerebral artery—itself a continuation of the internal carotid—were occluded and resulted in weakness and impaired sensation in the opposite arm. In 1906, the left ophthalmic artery was also blocked. The weakness of the right hand cleared, but after some initial improvement, there was permanent visual loss."[62]

The gravity of this situation was too much for even Wilson to deny. A few days after the onset of these symptoms Wilson went to Philadelphia to see Dr. George de Schweinitz, an ophthalmologist, and Dr. Keen, who had seen Wilson during his stroke in 1896. Although there is no record of Keen's diagnosis, de Schweinitz apparently was the first to inform Wilson that his blindness was symptomatic of a much larger, generalized condition and that it was probably the result of a blood clot. Although his family despaired at the news, Wilson's friends relate that he was, paradoxically, "calm, even gay."[63] Despite the definitiveness of de Schweinitz's diagnosis, Wilson continued to consult with other physicians, possibly in the hope of receiving a more favorable prognosis. A few weeks after the visits with Keen and de Schweinitz, Wilson went back to Philadelphia to see an internist, Dr. Alfred Stengel, who gave Wilson a guardedly optimistic report:

> I find a very moderate grade of arterial trouble and of a character that does not suggest any progressive course as likely in the future. You were fortunate in having the local (ocular) trouble because it called attention to the general condition which would otherwise have passed unnoticed. I feel entirely confident that a rest of three months will restore you fully. Of course 50 year old arteries do not go back to an earlier condition, but I expect that you will be as well as you need be for any work you can reasonably wish to undertake next fall. The warning simply indicates that excess of work is dangerous. You have doubtless done too much in the last few years.[64]

Writing in this same vein, Wilson's wife provides an interesting, if unscientific, insight into one of the possible causes for Wilson's stroke: "It [the stroke] is [a result of] hardening of the arteries, due to prolonged high pressure on brain and nerves. He has lived too tensely. . . . It is, of course, the thing that killed his father . . . it is an awful thing—a dying by inches, and incurable. But Woodrow's condition has been discovered in the very early stages and they think it has already been arrested."[65]

Both Stengel and Mrs. Wilson suggest that Wilson's disease may have been precipitated, if not caused, by his driven work habits. As noted earlier, the relationship between tension and stress and subsequent neurovascular and cardiovascular disease is a tenuous one

and has defied current attempts to quantify and describe it. Nevertheless, Wilson's life-style and the inner turmoil his letters reveal are
suggestive of a very tense, overwrought temperament. It is difficult to
decide, however, whether environment and lifestyle are causal factors in this type of disease or if in fact the proposition has been stated
backwards. To illustrate this ambiguity, we turn to the most damaging incident in Wilson's career at Princeton, the so-called Quadrangle Plan incident.

The events between Wilson's major stroke in 1906 and his resignation from Princeton to enter the New Jersey gubernatorial race in
1910 are a chronicle of turmoil and ill will. They may, in fact, mark
the unhappiest time in Wilson's life, as he saw his dreams for Princeton
shattered and his health seriously deteriorate. Though Wilson's plans
surely suffered at the hands of contending and powerful factions
within the university, Wilson's own bizarre and self-destructive behavior also played a part in their demise. In fact, a more skillful, self-
possessed administrator might have been able to achieve what Wilson could not. It ultimately cost Wilson a number of friendships and
his esteem within the university, finally forcing his withdrawal from
the president's office. It also provided the impetus for his entry into
American politics.[66]

The events leading up to Wilson's resignation began five years earlier in 1905 when the preceptorial system he designed was finally
put into place. The board of trustees had given Wilson the power to
hire fifty new tutors who, as full members of the faculty, substantially
diluted the power of the older, established professors. With this cadre
of new, receptive instructors in place Wilson hoped finally to implement the college system he had seen while traveling in Europe. A
year after the inauguration of the tutorial system Wilson suddenly
(and quite unexpectedly) presented to the board a new plan to build
an undergraduate college. The so-called Quadrangle Plan provided
living and dining facilities for both students and faculty, along with
classroom space for instruction for which Wilson requested two mil-

lion dollars from the board. Despite the enormity of the sum, the board was so taken aback at the proposal that they acquiesced with little discussion or dissent.

When word of Wilson's proposal leaked to the rest of the university community, it elicited an immediate outcry. The plan offended two powerful factions at Princeton. The first was the fraternal supper clubs, elite social organizations for the sons of the very wealthy. Sensing that Wilson's quad plan would dilute, if not completely eliminate, their control over much of undergraduate life, they waged an active campaign among their more powerful alumni members to have the plan reconsidered. The second, even more powerful, group offended was the Graduate College Committee, headed by the popular classics professor Andrew West.[67] During the lackadaisical administration of the previous president, West had been given an amazing amount of power by the board as a way of bypassing President Patton's lethargic administration. In addition to having full control over the graduate school curriculum, West had also wrangled the power to hire new faculty without consulting Patton and at one point even had it within his province to grant degrees. West had been one of Wilson's earliest supporters and had obtained from Wilson his promise to give the proposed graduate college top priority. When West heard of Wilson's Quadrangle Plan and the astronomical sum involved, he felt betrayed by Wilson and began to agitate among his wealthy alumni friends.

The uproar over the Quadrangle Plan took Wilson by surprise, and his dismay at the reaction to his proposal was indicative of how ill-prepared he was. When he made his proposal to the board in December 1906, barely five months had elapsed since his stroke in May of that year. Even though some of the overt, physiologic symptoms had eased, Wilson showed signs of acute depression and emotional instability. His reaction to all of this criticism, for example, was excessively emotional and charged with intense personal animosity. To a friend who noted that the faculty would probably vote down the plan, Wilson wrote: "The faculty (above all the faculty) has 'deprived me of hope.' I can only hope that you are mistaken. If what you suppose to be the prevailing sentiment and purpose should turn out to be so indeed, I shall stand isolated and helpless."[68] As with previous policy disagreements, Wilson reformulated this conflict into a moral battle and considered those who opposed his ideas to be his enemies. Rather than attempting some negotiation with his critics, Wilson felt compelled to launch a defense for the purity of his plan as "a man convinced of duty," even if the tactic doomed his plan to ultimate defeat. Thus, in what one friend described as a "nervous and excitable mood," Wilson brought the matter before the faculty and delivered a stirring, impassioned speech. With the help of the younger faculty, many of whom Wilson had just recently appointed as preceptors, the motion carried the day. Wilson was delighted over the faculty vote, but it was to be a Pyrrhic victory. In the interim between the initial proposal and the faculty vote the chairmanship of the board of trustees had changed hands from Grover Cleveland, who had honored Wilson with a White House dinner when elected president of Princeton, to Moses Pyne, a wealthy alumnus who was an old friend of Andrew West. Shortly after the faculty vote Pyne reopened the matter in a board meeting and skillfully guided a motion which withdrew the board's support for Wilson's proposal. In his despair over this unexpected defeat Wilson wrote out a letter of resignation and was only dissuaded at the last minute from submitting it to the board.

While the power politics of West and Pyne certainly played a major role in the defeat of the Quadrangle Plan, Wilson's emotional state after the 1906 stroke cannot be overlooked. His sloppy, impolitic presentation of the plan, as well as the arrogance and anger with which he responded to his critics, may well have had something to do with affective changes brought on by Wilson's neurological trauma. Some of Wilson's contemporaries, for example, noted at the time that he was more irritable than usual. More ominously, Wilson began to reminisce about his own father's rapid descent into senility just before his death, leading some people to believe that Wilson was worried about dying before his goals were accomplished.[69]

Despite the apparent vanity of these struggles, Wilson continued to pursue his plans with ardor. In February 1907 Wilson's wishes seem to have colored the reality of the situation. In a talk before the alumni club of Philadelphia he made a rousing speech in which he claimed that Princeton was on the verge of receiving an enormous donation which would make it "the greatest seat of learning and research in the world." The comment may have been an excess of rhetoric, but it sounds delusionally euphoric. He had to retract the statement four days later and then even went so far as to rationalize the disappearance of these imaginary funds by saying that "the receipt of such 'munificent' funds would cause a growth 'which would not be healthy.'" Wilson's inflated, intemperate speech-making continued through 1907, even when he was told that he was making bitter enemies among the board members, who by now were tired of the matter and furious with Wilson for refusing to drop it.

Wilson, however, had become so wrapped up in his cause that it would have been impossible for him to dissociate from what he now saw as a "holy" struggle. To a friend who tried to get Wilson to desist, he retorted that "The fight is on, and I regard it not as a fight for the development, but as a fight for the restoration of Princeton. My heart is in it more than it has been in anything else, because it is a scheme of salvation."[70] Clearly, Wilson's interpretation of the problem was incommensurate with the facts of the situation. In November 1907 Wilson had another recurrence of his symptoms, though their precise onset is uncertain. He again began to complain of pain and weakness in the right hand and apparently felt poorly enough to stay away from his office during part of December. The observations of his wife and his friends suggest that in addition to the physiologic symptoms Wilson was also emotionally and physically exhausted by his struggles.

Despite the board's demonstrable hostility to Wilson's plan, they were unable to muster enough support from either the faculty or from wealthy alumni to develop a counterproposal. Certainly, Wilson's machination did not help, and there are several instances recorded in which he actually obstructed a possible solution. The Quadrangle Plan dragged on throughout 1908 and into most of 1909, with factions on both sides of the issue desperately scrambling for funds that would tip the scales decisively in their favor. In this test of financial connections Wilson was at a decided disadvantage compared to Andrew West and the rest of the board members, who made a conscious effort to socialize with the wealthy of Princeton so they could solicit funds from them. Late in 1909 a wealthy benefactor in England died, leaving his entire estate, valued at several millions of dollars, to Princeton. While it was welcome news for the expanding university, it also signaled Wilson's final defeat: a codicil to the will stipulated that West be made executor of the trust. With West in control of such vast funds, Wilson realized that he was beaten.

Though he tried to find some way around the estate's stipulations, the conditions were quite clear. In one last futile attempt to retain control, Wilson ludicrously suggested that the board might not want to accept the gift because it limited the university's freedom to act. Following the board's vote to accept the gift, Wilson typed out a note which effectively signaled the end of his career at the school. In near suicidal language he ended the letter with these despairing lines: "The acceptance of this gift has taken the guidance of the University out of my hands entirely, and I seem to have come to the end."[71] That year, Wilson tendered his resignation and ended his career in academia. Feeling beaten and betrayed in his chosen field, Wilson cast about and decided to enter another. In September 1910 he launched his entry into politics.

Wilson and the Wages of Politics

At first glance, Wilson's entry into the state politics of New Jersey seems something of an anomaly. For years the legislature and the governor's mansion had been nests of corruption. Although the Republicans had held effective power in the state since 1896, historians have noted that the greed and graft of the state's politicians knew no political boundaries; Democrats and Republicans alike profited from the unscrupulous dealings of their respective party's leaders.[72] New Jersey in 1910 was the fiefdom of powerful business interests, leading Weinstein, among others, to note that it was little more than "a boss-ridden, corporation controlled state, dominated by the railroads and a public utilities monopoly."[73] It was out of this cesspool of corruption that the New Jersey Democratic party first extended an invitation to the embattled president of Princeton University.

The offer to Wilson to run in the Democratic gubernatorial primary was a stroke of minor genius on the part of party boss James Smith and was also an exercise in opportune timing. With Smith's support Wilson was nominated on the first ballot during the Democratic convention in September 1910 and immediately dashed Smith's hope of having a puppet in the governor's mansion. In his acceptance speech Wilson pointedly divorced himself from the party machinery, saying that he owed his nomination to no one and that he would support unreservedly the entire reform platform approved by the convention.

Wilson's excellence as an orator, coupled with his spotless record and the machination of the Democratic party, left the Republicans at a distinct disadvantage. In November 1910 those factors not only propelled Wilson into the governorship of New Jersey, but gave the Democrats control of the legislature for the first time in several years.

Wilson's victory in New Jersey was just a part of a much larger Democratic tide that had lifted the party into control of the Congress

for the first time since 1894. Buoyed by their success in the congressional elections, the Democrats finally saw a possibility to retake the
presidency in 1912.[74] Although William Jennings Bryan had long
dominated national Democratic politics, a succession of three defeats
at the presidential polls had sapped whatever support he might once
have had. With Bryan out of serious contention and a liberal electorate ready to assert its newly found voice, the Democrats looked to
their rank of freshly elected leaders. Wilson had barely been in office
a few months before his name began to circulate throughout the party
councils as a possible contender in 1912. What started as a whisper
among New Jersey politicians in 1910 became a roar in May 1911,
when Wilson made his first political foray outside of New Jersey.
Disregarding Wilson's virtual lack of political experience, many Democrats saw him as the front-runner in the nomination fight. Wilson
accepted his rocketing reputation with delight and saw the fight for
the presidency as a challenge worthy of his skills. In one remarkable
year he had gone from being a broken, dispirited academician to
being a leading contender for the presidency of the United States.

Wilson had responded quite well to the stresses of gubernatorial
campaigning, but the burden of the presidential race, added to his
duties as governor, provoked another bout of severe abdominal pains.
Stockton Axson, Wilson's brother-in-law, noted that the "physical
vigor" he displayed during the 1910 race now seemed dissipated.[75]
Wilson's wife worried to a friend that he was working under "fearfully
high pressure."[76] Even the state newspapers, which had previously
been uninterested in Wilson's health, noted in October 1911 that
Wilson seemed fatigued.

During these pressure-filled months of campaigning, when his
health suffered, Wilson's speeches were again filled with metaphors
relating to health and disease. One particularly notable example compared the scandals over public corruption to a disease and its
treatment: "The world for years suffered from inflammation of the
bowels, but one day a doctor discovered that it was due to appendici-

tis. Now hundreds of lives are saved yearly and when you are cautiously opened and the difficulty is removed, there is no trouble thereafter. It is the same with us; the outbursts are only the evidence of the recrudescence of the public conscience."[77] A few months later in December 1911 Wilson had another recurrence of what appeared to be neuritis. He complained of cramping and pain in his right hand. More ominously, Wilson began to suffer from bouts of severe headaches, and in one instance Wilson had an episode of dizziness while speaking before an audience, causing him to interrupt the talk. All of these symptoms, coming either concurrently or close to one another, lead Dr. Weinstein to suggest that Wilson was suffering from a "transient ischemic episode," that is, a temporary deprivation of blood to the brain.[78] These symptoms were alarming enough to Wilson for him to have a physical examination. Although the examination revealed that Wilson's blood pressure was normal and failed to detect any pathology, his physician suggested that, once again, Wilson's frenzied schedule was affecting his well-being. Wilson, however, took the physician's statement to mean that he had no overt organic problem and kept up his hectic pace.

What Wilson would later term "a miracle"—his winning the Democratic party's nomination for president—and some historians have called an amazing stroke of luck continued into the general election of 1912. Theodore Roosevelt, the progressive former president, decided to challenge the incumbent and unpopular President Taft over the protests of other Republicans who feared that it would split the party. Their worst fears were realized when Roosevelt, failing to capture the nomination, decided to run on the third-party Bull Moose ticket. Although Wilson failed to win a popular majority, Roosevelt and Taft so split the Republican vote that Wilson not only won a great victory in the electoral college but also helped the Democrats tighten their grip on Congress.[79]

Wilson began his first term in office in good health. His daughter, reminiscing on those promising first days in the White House, noted that Wilson "looked extraordinarily well and vital. . . . I noticed that his walk had acquired more than its usual buoyancy. His eyes were strikingly clear and bright, and there was a sort of chiseled keenness in his face. He was finer looking in those days than ever before."[80] The first years of Wilson's presidency, perhaps not coincidentally, were also his most successful and productive. True to his campaign promises to battle entrenched business interests, Wilson coaxed and cajoled Congress into passing a series of tariff reform measures which broke the near monopoly many business conglomerates had previously enjoyed. In 1913 he negotiated with Congress on a series of measures that led eventually to the Federal Reserve Act, and in 1914 he forced Congress to repeal a number of monopolistic practices concerning the Panama Canal. The noted Wilson scholar Arthur S. Link contends that Wilson's activities and performance during these first two years in office constitute "one of the most extraordinary displays of leadership in his entire career."[81]

The political and personal success and peace of Wilson's first two years were soon to end, however. Although Wilson had been relatively untroubled by any event as severe as his stroke in 1906, he had had a number of portentously ominous episodes. A few months into his first term Wilson suffered a recurrence of his old neurological symptoms, but this time they were on the opposite side of his body. To a friend Wilson wrote that since April 11 "there has been a recurrence of my old enemy, neuritis [emphasis added], as nasty a beast as ever attacked poor human flesh. . . . Maybe, this time, it is only a touch of cold."[82] In his study Weinstein notes that Wilson's neuritis lasted, uncharacteristically, for several weeks, and suggests that it was, in fact, a stroke."[83] To support his diagnosis Weinstein points not only to the duration of the episode, but to the short acute depression into which it cast Wilson. Weinstein also notes the added seriousness of this event:

The episode which affected Wilson's left arm was particularly ominous from a clinical standpoint. The most likely diagnosis is that he had developed an ulcerated plaque in his right carotid artery, from which an embolus had broken off. This meant that the cerebral circulation has been affected on the right, previously unaffected, side of the brain. This evidence of bilaterality of involvement not only increased the risk of further strokes, but also created the possibility that enduring changes in behavior might be based on insufficient blood supply and impaired oxygenation of the brain.[84]

Weinstein further supports his contention by noting that these "neuritis" attacks continued for at least six months. Moreover, Wilson's behavior took a turn for the worse in the middle of the crisis. The historian Link, for example, notes that during a trip to New Jersey to patch up some political infighting, Wilson appeared "haggard, worn, and short-tempered."[85] More importantly, his speech was disorganized and incoherent, and the excessively emotional delivery of the talk was disproportionate to the task at hand.

Since coming to the White House, Wilson had been treated by Cary Grayson, a Navy physician to whom Wilson soon became very attached. Grayson seems to have attributed many of Wilson's symptoms to overwork, and his sparing use of drugs, along with the admonition that Wilson needed to take more exercise, suggests that he felt that many of Wilson's maladies were psychosomatic in nature.[86] Certainly Grayson seems to have ruled out any neurological involvement in Wilson's illnesses, and in his memoirs Grayson dismisses these episodes as either a result of stress or fails to mention them altogether. Curiously enough, Grayson does mention the fact that at least one physician, the neurologist Silas Weir Mitchell, had claimed as early as 1912 that Wilson suffered from some neurological disease and had publicly claimed that Wilson would never finish out his first term.[87]

As with other presidents' physicians, Grayson may well have fallen prey to the glamour surrounding his famous patient. Moreover, Wilson was likely a difficult patient to diagnose because of his tendency to hide his symptoms or, once they were revealed, to deny them. By 1914 the declining health of Mrs. Wilson further complicated an already complex medical situation. Although President Wilson and others had noted Ellen Wilson's declining health since at least 1913, they tended to attribute it to her grief over her brother's recent death and over her concern for her husband's own health. In fact, she was most probably suffering from chronic nephritis, which was further compounded by a succession of infectious diseases over the next two years. On March 1, 1914, Mrs. Wilson probably entered renal failure and collapsed in a faint in her room.[88]

The situation facing Dr. Grayson now became exceedingly difficult, as he was physician to both the Wilsons, but with an overarching responsibility for the president's well-being. Biographers have noted that by this time Grayson was virtually a member of the family and had become one of Mrs. Wilson's confidantes. Yet his sense of duty to the president and his persistent worry over the state of Wilson's emotional stability may well have prevented him from being as forthcoming with the president over Mrs. Wilson's illness as he might have been. Indeed, Grayson may have taken this duty too far, for he failed to call in any specialists to consult on the case until the very end, possibly for fear of alarming the president. Grayson's attitude seems also to have affected the president, for Wilson denied the severity of Ellen's illness until a few days before her death.[89] In a particularly revealing letter written just a month before Mrs. Wilson's demise, Wilson said that "there is nothing at all the matter with her [Ellen] organically. It is altogether functional, and the doctors assure us that all with care will come out right."[90] As bravely as Wilson continued to hope, his wife's illness was having an impact not only on his mental state, but on the conduct of American affairs.[91]

In one particularly alarming incident Wilson may have misdirected his anger over his wife's illness at the Mexican dictator General Huerta.

Wilson's previous covert efforts to depose the Mexican usurper had been unsuccessful. Seizing upon a relatively minor breach of international law, Wilson ordered a detachment of troops to invade Mexico and seize a customhouse at Veracruz.

This blatant aggression on the part of the Americans was violently resisted by the Mexicans, who killed nineteen U.S. soldiers in the battle. When Huerta broke off diplomatic relations, Wilson blindly ordered another contingent of soliders to Veracruz and mobilized another unit along the Texas-Mexican border. Wilson's indiscriminate actions did little more than unite the warring Mexican factions and almost provoked a full-scale war. Seeing the folly of his actions, and overcome with guilt over the unnecessary deaths of the American soldiers, Wilson suddenly ordered the mobilization halted. In a particularly painful press conference held immediately after the incident, one observer noted "how preternaturally pale, almost parchmenty, Mr. Wilson looked when he stood up there and answered the questions of the newspaper men. The death of the American sailors and marines owing to an order of his seemed to affect him like an ailment. He was positively shaken."[92] To attribute Wilson's rash behavior in this matter solely to his grief over his wife's condition may be stretching the connection too far, but it may well have played a significant factor. Shortly after his wife's death in August, Wilson wrote out a memo to his secretary of war in which he completely reversed his previous position regarding the Mexican government.[93]

The death of Wilson's wife plunged him into a prolonged depression, the severity of which can be deduced from many of Wilson's despairing, almost suicidal remarks. To his children Wilson apologized for Ellen's death by saying that his political ambitions had killed her. He wrote to an old friend of Mrs. Wilson's that "God has stricken me almost beyond what I can bear."[94] In comment to his aides he made references to feeling like a machine which has run down. Most ominously, Wilson noticed that his normally orderly thought processes had been disrupted and that his memory was suffering. These symptoms, he said, made him unfit to be president because he could no longer "think straight," to use his own words. In a final grim admission he confided to his closest friend, Colonel House, that his life was over and that he wished someone would kill him.[95]

As the depression lingered throughout the rest of 1914 and into the early months of 1915, Grayson noted with alarm his patient's deterioration. Although Wilson continued to work his regular schedule, he postponed making definitive decisions and failed to give order and structure to events in the White House. Even the outbreak of war in Europe in 1914 failed to concentrate Wilson's mind; as bravely as he tried to make sense of the situation and to prepare the American response, he confided to another friend that he could not focus on the matters at hand because the "affairs of state were no substitute for the intimacy of a dear one."[96]

Grayson correctly sensed that unless he acted, Wilson's mood would become even more somber and self-absorbed and in an act of creative medical therapy decided to schedule a series of social events to distract and entertain the president. Wilson's mood did, in fact, seem to improve as Grayson coaxed him into the informal gatherings. Sensing that the outings lifted Wilson's spirits, Grayson apparently arranged for a "chance" meeting between the president and Edith Galt, a widow who shared Wilson's southern heritage.[97] Wilson's reaction to Mrs. Galt was electric. Invitations to tea and dinner followed the initial encounter, and within two months Woodrow Wilson and Edith Galt were engaged to be married. In the words of one observer, "none of Dr. Grayson's prescriptions ever had a more salutory or instantaneous effect."[98] On December 18, 1915, the president and Mrs. Galt were married.

Wilson's elation in 1915 over his new bride was tempered by the horrifying war reports coming from Europe. After the outbreak of the European hostilities Wilson and his secretary of state, William Jennings Bryan, tried to maintain a policy of strict neutrality in an effort to avoid America's being drawn into the expanding war. Breaches of maritime law by both the Axis powers and the Entente were stoically ignored by the American government. In May 1915, however, the sinking of the British liner *Lusitania*—which caused the deaths of hundreds of Americans—shocked Wilson and the rest of the country out of their anxious detachment. Although Wilson's harsh diplomatic note stopped just short of a declaration of war, it seemed that the United States was being drawn into a war which neither its president nor its citizens relished.

The quickening war spirit in America coincided with another series of medical maladies for the president. Colonel House, a sort of minister without portfolio who enjoyed Wilson's complete confidence, notes in his diary on January 13, 1915, that Dr. Grayson had confided to him that Wilson's "kidneys were not functioning."[99] Although Grayson was not more specific, Weinstein asserts in his own study of the problem that "the same disease process which affects the vessels of the brain and retina may also involve the kidneys."[100] Following this account of some sort of renal failure, Wilson again began to experience transient weakness in his right arm. Additionally, he had another recurrence of what has been described as "blinding headaches," the most severe of which lasted for four days. Weinstein suggests that the episodes indicate not only the emotional tension of Wilson's response to these world events, but also high blood pressure and the progression of Wilson's cerebral and retinal disease.[101]

In support of this diagnosis Weinstein offers the following pieces of evidence. An entry in Colonel House's diary on March 25, 1914, relates the following:

> I had a long talk with Dr. Grayson. He tells me everything concerning the President in the most minute detail in order to get my advice. He alarmed me somewhat by saying that the Philadelphia oculist [Dr. de Schweinitz], who has had the President under his care for ten years or more, told him, Grayson, there was

some indication of hardening of the arteries. The President does not know this, neither does any member of his family.[102]

In another entry dated October 20, 1914, House writes that he had heard secondhand that Grayson did not think the president would survive another term in office. The most interesting piece of medical information comes from Dr. Edward S. Gifford, who wrote the following letter to Weinstein:

> When Dr. de Schweinitz died in 1932, his records passed to Dr. Alexander G. Fewell, who had assisted Dr. de Schweinitz in his office . . . When Dr. Fewell retired in 1961, Dr. Fewell's records and practice came to me.
>
> But some time in the fifties Dr. Fewell destroyed the de Schweinitz records, which pained me considerably because I know those records contained historical material about many prominent people. Before destroying those records, however, Dr. Fewell read that of Woodrow Wilson and talked to me about it. According to Dr. Fewell, Woodrow Wilson suffered from a very high blood pressure and his fundi showed hypertensive vascular changes with advanced angiosclerosis [arteriosclerosis], angioplasticity [spasm of the arteries], and exudates [which appear as white spots on the retina resulting from vessel damage]. . . . These observations were made while Wilson was President.[103]

Weinstein goes on to note that the observations made by de Schweinitz were "harbingers of cardiac, renal, and diffuse cerebral disease," all of which could have had a profound impact on Wilson's demeanor and mental state.[104]

The period from mid-1915 until Wilson's declaration of war on Germany in April 1917 remains medically ambiguous. Although we know that de Schweinitz continued to visit Wilson regularly at the White House, there are no extant records, and Dr. Grayson is remarkably reticent on the subject in his memoirs. We do, however, have several indications that Wilson continued to suffer from painful symptoms. On several occasions, for example, Wilson suddenly canceled speaking engagements or cabinet sessions due to what Grayson referred to as "colds."[105] Yet these absences were marked by the almost complete seclusion of Wilson in his room for days at a time, suggesting that his illnesses were rather more severe than Grayson's bland statements imply. We get an even more graphic picture of Wilson's distress from Mrs. Wilson's memoirs, where she writes at one point:

> In the coming years [from 1916 on] when every nerve was tense with anxiety during the War, and burdens on his shoulders enough to crush the vitality of a giant, there would come days when he was incapacitated by blinding headaches that no medicine could relieve. He would have to give up everything, and the only cure seemed to be sleep. We would make the room cool and dark, and when at last the merciful sleep would come, he would lie for hours this way, apparently not even breathing.[106]

In the midst of what seems to have been immense personal pain and increasing signs of severe physiologic pathology, Wilson made the decision to seek a second term, apparently with Grayson's tacit, if not explicit, consent. Though Wilson's renomination was a virtual certainty, his race against Republican Charles Evans Hughes turned into a bitter political brawl.[107] Both candidates ran on a progressive peace platform. Since the campaign lacked controversy over substantive policy issues, it quickly degenerated into ad hominem attacks and slanderous statements. These tactics seemed to favor the Republicans, for up until the election on November 8, 1910, most of the newspapers were predicting Hughes to be the winner. The race turned out to be so close that it was not until two days later that Wilson received the news that he had been reelected in a minor upset.

The end of the election may have somewhat lessened Wilson's duties, but it brought no respite from his medical troubles. Continual headaches and colds were unaffected by Grayson's ministrations, and the president finally acceded to Grayson's request that he relent in his hectic pace. After his inauguration in 1917 Wilson rarely, if ever, returned to his office in the afternoons after lunch and, instead, either returned to his bedroom to sleep or played golf with Grayson or one of his aides. Even this abbreviated schedule, however, failed to alleviate Wilson's symptoms, and he spent several days in March 1917 in bed with what appeared to have been severe headaches. During this most recent medical relapse Wilson received word that the Germans had torpedoed three more American boats. Sensing that he could neither placate a growing national sentiment for retribution nor reason with the Germans to negotiate a treaty of neutrality, Wilson roused himself from his sickbed to deliver a war message to Congress, which both houses passed on April 2, 1917.

Despite delivering a rousing speech calling America to arms, Wilson approached the war in Europe with great ambivalence. Although he saw no rational alternative, Wilson was aghast at the carnage the war had produced. After a speech denouncing German aggression, Wilson turned to a young State Department official and asked: "Wasn't it horrible? All those Congressmen and Senators applauding every wretched little warlike thing I had to say, ignoring all the things for which I really care. I hate this war! I hate all war, and the only thing I care about on earth is the peace I am going to make at the end of it."[108] Moreover, Wilson saw no clear justice in either side's cause. Though he entered America on the side of the British, French, and Italians, Wilson had grave misgivings about the Entente's ultimate aims and feared they would try to impose an unjust peace on the Germans. As if to distinguish his aims from those of the leaders of the Entente, Wilson designated the United States as an associated power, rather than an ally, and refused to integrate the American military command with the rest of the Entente's organization.[109] By the time the United States was formally and practically engaged in the war, though the hostilities raged on, the contending armies were at a virtual stalemate. No great territories were lost or captured, and

thousands of soldiers on both sides died trying to defend or recapture
—literally—a few feet of territory. Even the addition of American men
and matériel did little to affect the battle scarred geography of Europe.

The American declaration of war in 1917 seems to have catalyzed
Wilson into action, but by early 1918 he again began to show signs of
fatigue. Colonel House indicates in his journal that Wilson spent a
good deal of time away from the Oval Office in February and March
1918. The diary of the White House head usher, in which are recorded
the president's whereabouts at all times, also shows Wilson's increasing absences in April and May of that year.[110] Other observers note
disturbing changes in Wilson's behavior. Edmund Starling, one of the
Secret Service agents assigned to the president's detail, writes in his
memoirs of Wilson's heightened irascibility and of his mercurial,
inexplicable outbursts over trivial issues. Wilson himself seemed
vaguely aware of these changes: to one aide he suddenly commented
that he was growing absentminded.[111] He also confided to Colonel
House that he would forget decisions right after the conclusion of a
meeting and, in an interesting choice of language, said that his mind
was becoming "leaky."[112] Weinstein writes that all of these signs are
symptomatic of increasing pathology:

> Diminished emotional control, greater egocentricity, increased
> suspiciousness and secrecy and lapses in judgment and memory
> are common manifestations of cerebral arteriosclerosis. In Wil-
> son's case, these symptoms seem to have been brought on by a
> combination of his vascular disease and the extraordinary degree
> of external stress to which he was subjected. In 1918, events
> were growing more complex and unpredictable, and much of
> Wilson's behavior seems to have been a defense against feelings
> of incapacity and a sense that he was no longer in control of his
> environment.[113]

Indeed, Wilson's deteriorating condition seems to have affected his
handling of two vitally important issues in the summer of 1918: the

unveiling of the proposed League of Nations and the congressional elections.

Since its founding in June 1915, the so-called League to Enforce Peace had been a signal failure in its stated aim of forcing countries to arbitrate their differences before an international board rather than on a battlefield. Under the guidance of President Taft, however, the league had floundered due to its lack of international support and its inability to coerce concerned nations to abide by their decisions. Despite the league's shortcomings, Wilson forcefully embraced its ideals, hoping eventually to reconstruct the organization into an effective, universal judicial body. Any aims of this kind required open negotiations among the competing nations and their full support at every step of the way. Initially, Wilson had been open and forthcoming in his plans, consulting with every possible interested party before deciding an issue. After 1918, however, Wilson's attitude changed perceptibly. In the words of Weinstein he became "more proprietary about the league," refusing to share information and ideas with other participants. Furtive cables and memoranda replaced open dialogue.[114] One might argue that Wilson's secretiveness was born of concern about matters of national security, yet he refused to be candid not only with "loyal opposition" Republicans, but with his own ministers and envoys. A streak of paranoia began to manifest itself with Wilson's dark, cryptic muttering about senators who would destroy his plans.

Wilson's lack of emotional control and his misreading of the political situation also caused a terrific blunder during the congressional elections in the fall of 1918. Fully realizing that any efforts at an international peace would be blocked by isolationist Republicans, Wilson decided to issue an appeal to the American electorate on October 15, 1918, to return a workable Democratic majority to Congress. Yet Wilson cast the appeal in terms of support for his programs, at one point implying that the Republicans would scuttle his peace plans:

> The return of a Republican majority to either house of the Con-
> gress would, moreover, certainly be interpreted on the other side
> of the water as a repudiation of my leadership. Spokesmen of the
> Republican party are urging you to elect a Republican Congress
> in order to back up and support the President . . . [but] it is well
> understood . . . that the Republican leaders desire not so much
> to support the President as to control him.[115]

The tacit message in Wilson's speech was that the Republicans were
undermining his office and in doing so were disloyal. The tactic
backfired and may have kindled enough fire in discontent midwestern farmers, who voted in huge numbers, to return the Republicans
to power in both houses of Congress. The Democrats not only lost
control of the legislative purse strings but, more crucially, lost the
chairmanship of the Foreign Relations Committee to Republican
Henry Cabot Lodge, who was politically at odds with Wilson, and
whom the president had gone out of his way to insult.

Finally, then, the year 1918, which saw Wilson in such alarming
declining health, also brought an end to the active hostilities in Europe
and brought an attempt to impose some order to the chaos across the
Atlantic. It was a task that would consume Wilson's last reserves,
take him to Paris, and do him in. It is a story which brings us back
full circle to the end of our first case history.

---

*Wilson at Versailles: The Politics of Power
and Paranoia*

The events surrounding the signing of the Treaty of Versailles had all
the flavor of a morbid carnival. The German document of uncondi-
tional surrender, which they transmitted directly to Wilson, had
brought a collective sigh of relief from the continent and made Wilson an instant international hero. His idealistic call for a new "world
moral order," which would scrupulously observe the sovereign auton-

omy of all nations, played well in beleaguered Europe. When Wilson landed in France in the middle of December 1918, the adulation of the crowds reached near hysterical proportions. A long motorcade down the streets of Paris brought more of the same: the crowds of Parisians threw bunches of flowers at the president, chanting his name over and again. Wilson was euphoric. The demonstrable good-will of the people gave him hope that the plan he had articulated earlier in the year in his famous "Fourteen Points" would eventually carry the day.[116]

Yet the events on the Paris boulevards were really a vain sideshow. Even before Wilson arrived in Europe, the leaders of the three Entente powers, Clemenceau, Lloyd-George, and Orlando, were already stip-ulating damaging amendments to the treaty. The ravaged European countryside also belied Wilson's sense of optimism; no treaty would be able to repair with speed the horrors that four years of unlimited war had wrought on the Continent. And despite the finely flourished speeches, which called for a just and lasting peace, most of the Entente leaders really had vengeance on their minds. In this war there had been winners and losers, and the winners wanted their pound of flesh. Wilson's hope for a humane peace, in which the Germans would be active and complete partners, was a dead issue even before he could present it to his European partners.[117]

Diplomatic historians have argued for years over the vital factors which led to the ultimate defeat of Wilson's plan. Some have sug-gested that Wilson, in his idealism, refused to grasp the basic power politics at play in the negotiations. Each nation was seeking to advance its own parochial interests, and any call for a collective, common goal would be rejected out of hand by competing powers. Other historians have argued that Wilson, whose political base had been destroyed by the congressional elections, was an unskilled negotiator and, lacking the power to enforce his plan, refused to compromise on less important issues, which eventually led to the defeat of his entire plan. Whatever the many merits of these analyses, they all fail to take into account that the man who represented America's interests, the putative leader of the Western powers, was a frail, ailing man who was clearly below form. There are several instances in which Wilson's failing health and the bizarre behavior which followed seem to have affected the course of events at Versailles.

Upon his arrival at Paris, Wilson fell into his old pattern of working a murderous schedule. One observer noted that while the other leaders relied on an array of aides and diplomats to cull and synthesize information, Wilson generally handled the details of the negotiations himself, with the occasional help of one or two trusted men.[118] The flavor of this routine is captured well by one of the members of the British delegation, who noted that the president "is a quaint bird. This afternoon he came from the Conference Room and gave instructions for someone to telephone for his typewriter. . . . The typewriter was placed in a corner of the Conference Room and the President proceeded to tap out a long memorandum, the purpose of which had been decided by him and his colleagues. It was a strange sight to see one of the greatest rulers in the world working away in this fashion."[119] Working without an adequate staff, Wilson would spend hours by himself, looking over the details of the other parties' proposals, then single-handedly typing out the American response. Compounding the problem was an aggravation of Wilson's tendency not to consult with anyone before presenting a proposal for fear of being betrayed or undercut. Within a few weeks, this routine began to take its noticeable toll.

A member of Wilson's inner circle, Ike Hoover, grew alarmed when the president developed a continuous nervous twitch in his face. Others in the president's entourage noted that Wilson quickly grew thin and pale, and his hair whitened perceptibly. Wilson further added to the strain of his isolation by giving up most forms of outside recreation; during his infrequent moments of relaxation he would put away his papers and play solitaire for hours at an end. A shift in Wilson's demeanor accompanied these physical changes: "[Wilson's] temper grew short, he would refer to Lloyd-George and Clemenceau as 'madmen' and bitterly say that the Irish petitioners for home rule were devoted only to 'miserable mischief making.'"[120] The normally composed Wilson would suddenly give way to incoherent outbursts when he reached a breaking point, as one observer would record in his diary: "'Logic! Logic! I don't give a damn for logic!' he burst out. He seemed worn and old and his only exercise came when Grayson would stand him before an open window and grasp his hands to pull him vigorously to and fro so that at least a little color would come to his cheeks."[121] By the end of March, Wilson seemed to have reached his limit. Ray Stannard Baker, an aide who would later write a biography of Wilson, notes Wilson's terrible appearance: "Sometimes . . . I went up to see him in the evening after the meetings of the Four . . . he looked utterly beaten, worn out, his face quite haggard and one side of it and the eye twitching painfully."[122] Worn down by the persistent and intransigent demands of the other leaders, as well as his own painful condition, Wilson suddenly conceded several points to his European partners on March 27.

And yet the following day brought a near disruption of the entire proceedings. In the middle of one heated discussion Clemenceau accused Wilson of harboring sympathies for the Germans. Wilson's stinging reply and the ensuing altercation brought a threat of resignation from each of the participants. Only a last minute apology from Wilson prevented the dissolution of the conference.

On April 3 Wilson finally succumbed to the strain of the events. Grayson records Wilson's own description of the symptoms: "I am feeling terribly bad. My equatorial zone was considerably upset soon after lunch but I was anxious to proceed with the afternoon conference, which I was barely able to do owing to intense pains in my back and stomach and head."[123] Grayson made the diagnosis of influenza, which was endemic in Europe at the time. By that evening Wilson's temperature had shot up to 103 degrees and hovered around 101 degrees the rest of the following day. His "racking" cough developed into what Grayson called "asthmatic coughing" and nocturnal dyspnea.[124] With help from Grayson's ministrations, which included breathing exercises, bed rest, and the administration of an expectorant to help with the cough and congestion, Wilson's temperature returned to normal in three days. In a characteristic denial of the severity of his illness Wilson insisted that the proceedings continue. Over Grayson's strenuous objections a series of negotiations were held in a sitting room adjoining Wilson's bedroom. Though the president was absent from the actual dialogue, he sent Colonel House as his emissary. House would sit in on the meetings for a time, excuse himself, then take a hidden hallway into Wilson's bedroom to apprise the president of the situation and to receive further instructions.[125]

Although most biographers seem satisfied with Grayson's diagnosis of the flu, the diagnosis remains questionable, and there are several facts that argue that Wilson actually was much sicker than Grayson suspected. For example, in his memoirs Ike Hoover categorically states that he was told by Dr. Albert Lamb, physician to the American delegation in Paris, that Wilson actually suffered from an infection of the prostate and bladder. Supporting Hoover's contention is a letter written by Dr. Lamb, in which he writes to a friend that Grayson asked him to obtain a vial of urotropin, an antiseptic that was then used for urinary tract infections.[126] Additionally, Wilson's long history of cerebrovascular disease suggests the possibility that Wilson may have also suffered another stroke. As Weinstein notes, patients with influenza tend to feel weak and lethargic.[127] By contrast, Wilson's mood seemed perceptibly heightened after the onset of these symptoms. On April 6, Grayson says that Wilson looked as though he did not "have a care in the world." Even in the middle of the acute phase of the illness, Wilson told Grayson that he felt "first-rate."[128]

One might possibly dismiss Wilson's exclamations as part of a brave front, but the president's bizarre behavior following these episodes suggests that there was at least some neurological involvement. For example, Wilson suddenly became obsessed with the idea that the French servants in his quarters were really spies who spoke perfect English. To Lady Northcliffe he apologized for not answering her questions because he "had discovered that one of the servants spoke English 'perfectly' although he addressed the Americans in French only."[129] Acting on his suspicions, Wilson ordered Hoover and the Secret Service men to investigate. Although Hoover reported back that they found only one servant who could speak English —and only a few words at that—Wilson refused to be convinced. He ordered security arrangements tightened, acquired a safe for his papers, and had a Secret Service agent guard his room when he was away. In another strange incident Wilson became obsessed with the arrangement of the furniture in his suite. As Dr. Grayson records the event, Wilson made an abrupt declaration one day:

> I don't like the way the colors of this furniture fight each other. The greens and the reds are all mixed up here and there is no harmony. Here is a big purple, high-backed covered chair, which is like the Purple Cow, strayed off to itself, and it is placed where the light shines on it too brightly. . . . And here are two chairs, one green and the other red. This will never do. . . . Over in the right-hand corner at our meetings are the British together; in the left-hand corner are the Americans; in the middle the French are seated. Now . . . we will harmonize them as much as possible.[130]

Dr. Grayson reports that after rearranging the furniture with his wife and some aides, Wilson suddenly became very relaxed and contented.

Dr. Weinstein collects these data together to suggest that these two strange incidents not only indicate the severity of neurological impairment in Wilson's illness, but are also highly symbolic representations of Wilson's inner conflicts and hostilities.[131] The "French spy" affair might well have been a projection of Wilson's anger and animosity towards Clemenceau—who spoke perfect English—and who continually frustrated Wilson's peace plans. Similarly, Wilson's sudden obsession with the "disharmony" of the furniture in his suite betrayed his own unhappiness with the friction over the peace settlement, and his attempts to "harmonize" the furniture in the room may have been a way of regaining order and control over the proceedings.[132]

Another indication of the degree to which Wilson's behavior was affected by his illness was the sudden reversal of his negotiating stance. Before the onset of his symptoms in April Wilson had been adamant about not putting the German kaiser on trial because of the "horrible precedent" it would set and because it offended his own personal sense of charity and forgiveness. After the acute symptoms disappeared and Wilson returned in person to the negotiating session, however, he suddenly drafted an amendment to the treaty which provided for the kaiser to be tried for "a supreme offense against international morality and the sanctity of treaties." Another sign of his deteriorating mental state was his exultant mood after this amendment was approved: Wilson believed he had won a great concession from the French (even though they were the ones who had originally proposed the trial) and told Grayson that "we made progress today, not through the match of wits, but simply through my hammering and forcing them to decisions." In fact, Wilson did not realize (or would not admit) that it was he who had capitulated on this issue.[133]

Wilson's curious and inconsistent behavior was noted by a number of participants at the conference. Prime Minister Lloyd-George, who lost a point he had been contesting with the French after Wilson suddenly changed his position, commented that the president had "suffered something like a stroke" and complained to some of the American delegates that their leader was completely under Clemenceau's control.[134] Others noticed that Wilson seemed less alert. Herbert Hoover, for example, noted that after the illness in early April, Wilson's normally quick mind had to "grope for ideas."[135] The president's memory also seemed to have suffered. Toward the end of the conference he confided to Grayson that he was having trouble in the evenings remembering what had happened just that afternoon. In his diary Baker writes this alarming confession: "have never seen the

President look so worn and tired. A terrible strain, with everyone against him. He was so beaten out that he could only remember with an effort what the council had done in the forenoon."[136]

Perhaps the most disastrous outcome of Wilson's sickness was not that he was unable to see his plan to victory, but that he deluded himself into believing that he had, in fact, won. On almost every major point about which the president had been adamant, from the League of Nations to postwar reparations, Wilson had either acceded or compromised. The treaty which they would eventually sign in June pleased no one and further damaged the Germans. Yet Wilson acted as though he had, in fact, won a great victory. Dr. Weinstein notes the curiosity of this transformation:

> The effects of Wilson's illness on his behavior can be compared to the effect of electroshock therapy, another form of stress to the nervous system. . . . The depressive mood is replaced by euphoric and sometimes paranoid attitudes. . . . Wilson's illness "cured" him of his depression, [but] furnished a neural milieu for a new relationship to events. Formerly, Wilson expressed the hope that his Fourteen Points might be carried out. Now he believed they had indeed been fulfilled.[137]

Wilson's damaged mind and the virtually unworkable treaty he signed left him in a vulnerable position when he returned home in the summer of 1919. Even though the acute symptoms of his illness had disappeared, Dr. Grayson notes that the president was still "below par," and, more seriously, that Wilson had "trouble arranging his thoughts."[138] Wilson's indecision over how to win Senate ratification for the Treaty of Versailles was also the product of the hopeless political corner into which he had forced himself. Despite his outward enthusiasm over the merits of the proposal, Wilson must surely have been plagued by doubts over the final plan. The treaty was a far less humane document than he had earlier hoped it would be. Moreover, several of the specific provisions it contained—such as

America's participation in the League of Nations—were bound to offend the politics of the midwestern Republicans who held the balance of power in the Senate.

Wilson found himself in a political wasteland when he returned home, and his first appearance before the Senate confirmed just how bleak his political landscape had become. When Wilson entered the chamber, two Republican senators refused to stand; others refused to applaud. Though serious breaches of decorum, they accurately manifested how unwelcome the president's policies had become during his absence.[139] In a subsequent appearance before the Senate Foreign Relations Committee, Wilson tried vainly to deflect the hostile, almost insulting questions from antagonistic senators and at one point even lied about his knowledge of previous agreements.[140] Yet all these indications of certain defeat notwithstanding, Wilson decided to forge ahead.

Against the expressed wishes of his wife and the warnings of his physician, Wilson decided to take his case "to the people."[141] If the Senate would not ratify his treaty, perhaps the general public would. As patently naive as this plan now seems, Wilson was convinced that the great masses in America—isolated from what he took as the petty bickering of Washington politicians—would ultimately approve his plan. Wilson's idea took the form of a great cross-country speaking tour. Traveling by train, Wilson planned to make dozens of stops along the way, exhorting his listeners to pressure their senators into supporting him.

The trip was a disaster from the outset. The sweltering heat of the western sun and the trip's breakneck schedules taxed Wilson's already depleted strength. Even at the outset of the trip his speeches were rambling, punctuated now and again with metaphorical allusions to diseased organs and ill health. At one point, for example, he defended a particular clause in the treaty, which the isolationist senators wanted to delete, in the following manner: "Without that clause the heart of the recent war is not cut out. The heart of the recent war was an absolute disregard of the territorial integrity, the political independence of smaller nations. If you do not cut the heart of the war out, the heart is going to live and beat and grow stronger."[142] Wilson's language in this instance is self-referential and revealing. Within a few days of beginning his trip he showed signs of cardiac decompensation; episodes of persistent, painful coughing were followed by such labored breathing that he had to sleep upright at night.

Shortly thereafter, Wilson began to complain of severe headaches and then had several episodes of double-vision, which may have been indicative of a stroke involving the ophthalmic region of the brain. Mrs. Wilson and Dr. Grayson tried vainly to get Wilson to end the speaking tour in light of these new and alarming symptoms. The president, however, was beyond persuasion at this point, claiming that if he cut short his trip, Senator Lodge would consider him a "quitter" and would defeat the treaty.[143]

What neither Grayson nor Mrs. Wilson could accomplish, a near fatal stroke did. On September 25, 1919, Wilson showed the first signs of a massive embolism. Speaking before a large crowd in Pueblo, Colorado, the president stumbled and allowed himself to be aided to the lectern by a Secret Service agent. A few minutes later, Wilson halted in the middle of his speech and looked around dazedly, as if he had forgotten his lines. He began again, then faltered. Finally, he came to the emotional ending of the talk and suddenly burst into tears.

A few hours later, Mrs. Wilson noticed that the president was holding his left arm awkwardly, but made no comment. However, Wilson's secretary, Joseph Tumulty, noticed the same thing, and recognized that the president's entire left side was paralyzed. The following morning brought no improvement; Wilson still could not move his left arm, and now his speech was beginning to be affected.[144] Although Wilson argued that he should finish the trip, the symptoms were too severe for even Wilson to deny. Dr. Grayson ordered the train back to Washington.

When the president's entourage arrived back in the Capital, Wilson's condition had improved sufficiently for him to walk to his car. This slight improvement, however, was ephemeral. On October 2 Wilson suffered an even more severe stroke.[145] Though accounts surrounding this event are sketchy, Wilson had apparently tried to walk to the bathroom by himself when he collapsed, unconscious, and cut his face badly on either the sink or the toilet as he fell to the floor. Grayson rushed in after he heard the president's fall and, when he emerged a few minutes later exclaimed, "My God, the president is paralyzed!" For three weeks Wilson lay in bed, practically immobile. His condition was further complicated by an enlarged prostate which caused a urinary obstruction. The condition grew so severe at one point that a urologist from Johns Hopkins, Dr. Hugh Young, was called in for consultation.[146] Though Dr. Young entertained the notion of operating to relieve the obstruction, Wilson's weakened condition persuaded him that the president would probably not survive the operation. The situation finally resolved itself when the obstruction cleared naturally and Wilson was able to void.

The severity of this final stroke left President Wilson completely paralyzed on his left side, with left-sided homonymous hemianopsia (that is, blindness in the left fields of both eyes). Moreover, this stroke, coming as it had on the heels of previous cerebrovascular accidents, permanently damaged Wilson's vision. It also affected the musculature of his face, tongue, and mouth, making his speech labored and indistinct. According to several observers, Wilson would never regain the measured cadence that had once made him such an effective speaker. Prone to long, severe depressions, the president was wont to cry without apparent provocation, and he found it increasingly difficult to sustain the intricacies of a long argument. Lastly, his impaired vision made it impossible for him to read reports with any accuracy.

In this crippled enervated state, the president of the United States lingered throughout the rest of his term. How the country responded to his condition is a sadly curious story, one which throws into relief the political question we asked at the beginning of this chapter: how should the government respond when an incapacitated president refuses to relinquish power?

___

Conclusion: Wilson and the Sequestered Presidency

The case of Woodrow Wilson's last year in office, which we summarize below, highlights one of the problems posed at the outset of this study. The problem lies not so much with illness, or the effect illness has on policy, but with the defenselessness of the presidency against the ravages of disease and the ineffectiveness of the current constitutional remedies. Wilson's last year in office is a classic study of the interplay between human frailty and ego and the larger societal responsibilities which an office of the magnitude of the presidency imposes.

Wilson was afflicted with what appear to have been successive neurological diseases since at least 1906, four years before he assumed public office and six years before he assumed the presidency. Between 1906 and 1920, when Wilson's second term ended, Dr. Weinstein chronicles, with commendable exactness and fairness, at least six separate medical episodes which affected the president's performance. We find his documentation of these incidents clear and compelling. The most potentially damaging of these occurred while the president was in Paris. Perhaps no one could have possibly salvaged a workable peace out of Europe's hateful wreckage in 1919, but Wilson was less than adequate to the challenge—not because of any lack of talent or courage, but because of a debilitating illness. Similarly, the Treaty of Versailles and America's participation in the League of Nations were probably preordained to failure, but a dying Wilson surely hastened their demise. In the midst of this deteriorating situation, however, there were, and are, no effective procedures to relieve a president of his duties. Part of the problem is clearly a function of a constitutional system that is specifically designed *against* sudden and frequent discontinuities of power. But another part of the problem has to do with the proprietary hold presidents seem to develop over their office. It is a question to which we turn again in subsequent chapters.

In Wilson's case this aspect of presidential power has a peculiarly sad quality to it. For four weeks the President saw no visitors. In the interim he found that when he tried to smile, the exertion accentuated his paralysis, and in an apparent attempt to hide his weakness Wilson grew a beard and moustache for the first time in his life. On October 31, when the president finally decided to admit the visiting king and queen of Belgium, Mrs. Wilson and his aides went to great lengths to hide the president's disability. Wilson was propped up in bed, and the sheets were drawn up to his head, with only his right arm showing. The curtains in the bedroom were drawn, the lights dimmed. When the visitors entered the room, they were ushered to the right side of the bed so that they could not clearly observe the extent of the paralysis on the president's left side. At all times, either Mrs. Wilson or Dr. Grayson remained in the room, ready to interrupt if the president began to ramble. This technique initially worked quite well, and the Belgium royal couple told waiting reporters that the president was fine.[147]

Mrs. Wilson and Dr. Grayson continued to shroud the true extent of the president's illness in secrecy. The First Lady, for example, refused White House aides access to the president for months and often took the responsibility for presidential business into her own hands: several times she responded to policy questions by writing instructions in the margins of documents, ostensibly after consulting with the president.[148] Grayson, too, was an active participant in this charade. At a cabinet meeting called just after the president's last stroke, Grayson told the secretaries that Wilson had suffered "a nervous breakdown, indigestion, and a depleted nervous system."[149] At the same time Grayson specifically forbade the cabinet members from

"bothering" the president because "any excitement might kill him."
When Secretary of State Robert Lansing mentioned to Grayson that
the Constitution provided for the vice president to assume the duties
of the president in case of some incapacity on the chief executive's
part, Grayson became incensed and said that he would never certify
that the president was disabled.

The activities of other politicians and the press in this matter were
curiously lethargic. For days the bulletins to the public continued to
present only a vague picture of the president's condition. Even the
vice president was kept totally in the dark. He eventually learned of
Wilson's condition through a reporter who was dispatched by Tumulty
to tell him only that the president could die at any moment. The vice
president was visibly shaken by the news because he had little working knowledge of the government. He himself declared that it would
have been a tragedy for him to assume the duties of president and an
equal tragedy for the American people. Although some New York
papers circulated rumors that the president was dead, sending stock
prices plummeting, most papers remained quiet and did not pursue
the story. Most of their articles were limited to expressions of good-
will and hopes for a speedy recovery.[150]

What emerges from the record of Wilson's final White House days
is that, in the words of one historian, "our Government has gone out
of business." Bills were left unsigned, policy left undecided. Mrs.
Wilson and Dr. Grayson's complicity in this matter is well documented. As the president's condition weakened, and it became obvious that he would never recover full function of his affected limbs,
Mrs. Wilson made the remarkable decision that Woodrow Wilson
would continue as president and that she would do all she could, as a
doctor suggested, to keep the burden of government from hindering
his recovery. Slowly she took over the reins of government and
attempted to run things as best she could, her ultimate goal being not
to take on the power of government, but to protect her husband. As
Mrs. Wilson stated on one occasion, "I am not interested in the

President of the United States. I am interested in my husband and his health." While stage-managing the president's meetings, and screening out important documents that might upset him, Mrs. Wilson instructed Dr. Grayson to continue issuing his reassuring, and patently false, press releases. All the while, Wilson was led by Grayson and Mrs. Wilson into believing that he would recover: "Mrs. Wilson believed that it would be therapeutic to conceal the seriousness of his illness from him, and that his recovery would be hindered if he was presented with matters which might tax his recovery. She and Dr. Grayson were also concerned that, if the nature of Wilson's illness was known, his authority would be impaired."[151] While one might excuse Mrs. Wilson's actions on the grounds of wifely loyalty, Grayson's behavior during these days exceeded the bounds of physician responsibility. Grayson was using the office of the president of the United States as therapy for his patient. Certainly Grayson was well aware of the devastation the stroke had visited on the president's mind. To Breckenridge Long, a confidante in the State Department, Grayson confided that "the President is still in grave danger" and asked that he and Long's colleagues do everything in their power to alleviate the president's burdens.

All the while, Wilson's administration was falling apart. Without the president's leadership, Senate Democrats who had tried to salvage the League of Nations Treaty were thrown into disarray; in November the treaty was defeated. Yet even after this defeat Grayson continued his effort to keep the president in power. At one point Wilson himself realized the full extent of his incapacity and called Grayson in for a talk: "My personal pride must not be allowed to stand in the way of my duty to the country. If I am only half efficient, I should turn the office over to the Vice President. If it is going to take much time for me to recover my health and strength, the country cannot afford to wait for me. What do you think?"[152] Grayson's reply, unbelievably, was to dissuade Wilson, arguing that the president was still in touch with the political events of the country and would in any case be a more effective leader than the vice president. After this pep talk Wilson gave up any notions of resigning.

Throughout the rest of the year Grayson and Mrs. Wilson gamely managed to keep the rest of the country in the dark about the president's true condition. When a group of senators began a whisper campaign to the effect that the president had lost his mind, two of them were selected to visit the president to determine his mental status. All morning long Dr. Grayson and Mrs. Wilson prepped the president for the encounter. When the delegation arrived, they were led, as before, into a darkened room; Wilson was lying in bed with Grayson and Edith Wilson on either side. The interview was kept brief, the questions specific. Apparently the ruse worked. After the meeting the two senators reported to waiting journalists that the president was "in fine form mentally and physically."[153] A few months later, right after Wilson had been dissuaded from resigning by Grayson, the physician arranged a cabinet meeting. As each secretary entered the room, he was loudly announced by Grayson or Mrs. Wilson, leading one observer to wonder, in horror, if the president could not remember the names of the very men whom he had entrusted to run the government. In fact, President Wilson could not. Brief moments of lucidity were followed by chaotic, incoherent ramblings. At one point the charade reached its apex when Grayson asked Dr. Young to make the following statement to the press about the president's condition: "The slight impairment of his left arm and leg have improved more slowly. . . . At no time was his brain power or the extreme vigor and lucidity of his mental process in the slightest degree abated. . . . The President walks sturdily now, without assistance and without fatigue. . . . As to his mental vigor, it is simply prodigious."[154] Dr. Young ended this glowing report with this remarkably inaccurate statement: "Indeed, I think in many ways the President is in better shape than before the illness came. . . . His frame of mind is bright and tranquil and he worries not at all. . . . You can say that the President is able-minded and able-bodied, and that he is giving splendid attention to the affairs of state."[155] Even as Dr. Young spoke, the president was sitting in a wheelchair, in a darkened room, wondering out loud to Dr. Grayson when he would recover the use of his legs.

In this depressed, semiparalyzed state the president of the United States would wait out the rest of his term and even make an abortive attempt at a third-term nomination. In March 1921, after the Democrats lost resoundingly in the 1920 presidential election, Wilson held his last cabinet meeting. In a shaky, emotion-filled voice he bade farewell to his staff and made the first public admission of his illness: "Gentlemen, it is one of the handicaps of my physical condition that I cannot control myself as I have been accustomed to do. God bless you all."[156] Wilson—and the United States—survived this last presidential term, though it was more a matter of good fortune than of good statesmanship. Wilson would linger for another four years and to the very end would deny the severity of his illness. He died on February 3, 1924, broken physically and mentally, convinced that he had failed, convinced that if fate had helped, he might have succeeded.

3

Franklin D. Roosevelt

The Diagnosis of an "Unexpected" Death

■■■■■■ The widely beloved American politician who awoke one spring morning in Georgia was the most powerful man on earth, the first American president who could plausibly make that claim. The armies he commanded stretched around the globe and were proving themselves victorious in every direction they struck. The economy he headed had risen from near ashes to roaring vitality. Available to the wartime commander-in-chief at the slightest beckoning were the best minds in all America, many of them also the best in the world. Yet, for a man in his early sixties, Franklin Delano Roosevelt was gravely, irrevocably ill. And hardly anyone outside of his own close circle, certainly not the American public, had any such idea, so secret had been the state of Roosevelt's health for many months now.[1]

Just the year before, unknown to the electorate looking ahead to the 1944 elections, Roosevelt had been forced to absent himself from the White House for weeks at a time, to reduce his work load drastically, even take to bed, all because of ill health. Suffering from extremely high blood pressure that resisted treatment, from congestive heart failure and concomitant hypertensive heart disease, Roosevelt was an alarmingly sick man even then, more than a year before his visit to Warm Springs, Georgia, in April 1945.[2]

The most critical period of Roosevelt's medical log begins in late

1943, in the final months of his third term in office. At that time the Allies had not yet landed in Normandy. In addition to a wartime president's daily duties at home, Roosevelt had made two exhausting trips abroad to confer with his fellow Allied leaders—to Casablanca in January 1943 to meet with Winston Churchill and to Tehran in November for a conference with Churchill and Josef Stalin.

On both trips the traveling president's personal physician, Navy Admiral Ross T. McIntire, had insisted that Roosevelt's plane fly at surprisingly low altitude. For the flight to North Africa in January, McIntire ordered a top ceiling of nine thousand feet, despite normal wartime precautions dictating a flight path of thirteen thousand feet. Then, for the journey to Tehran late in the year, McIntire demanded an even lower ceiling. When the president's son Elliott asked why, McIntire tersely replied, "Nothing over 7,500—that's tops."[3]

Later, on the flight home from Tehran, McIntire went further. Even though the presidential flight path would take the White House party fairly closely to Axis-held territory, the Navy doctor ruled out any attempt to seek protective cloud cover. That would place them at an altitude of about eight thousand feet, which McIntire thought too high. Clearly, the doctor was treating the president as a patient who should not run the risk of oxygen-thin air.

Roosevelt endured the latter flight without known incident, but by the end of 1943 he was physically depleted. The two trips abroad had lasted a total of thirty days, not only in travel but in conference with one, and then two, of the world's political titans. With a world-wide conflict raging, Roosevelt's schedule at home had been no light burden either; by any man's standard he had kept up a remarkable pace.

White House physician McIntire had suggested several times during 1943 to Roosevelt's staff that his work load be curtailed, but Roosevelt rarely would keep to an abbreviated schedule. Then in December he contracted what he himself diagnosed as a "bad flu," an illness that this time had greater impact on him than similar bouts of the past. The fever and associated symptoms were soon gone, but through January and February 1944 Roosevelt admitted to fatigue, "abdominal distress," and general malaise.[4] From time to time the president began to sweat profusely for no apparent reason. Over a two-week period in February he suddenly lost ten pounds.

Though McIntire expressed no alarm, others did, among them former Postmaster General Jim Farley, who still maintained access to the White House despite his abortive attempt at the Democratic presidential nomination in 1940. "From the time of his return from Tehran in December," Farley later wrote, he heard "disturbing" reports on Roosevelt's health from persons high and low in official Washington. Roosevelt looked bad, his mind wandered, his hands shook, his jaw sagged, he tired easily, and his familiar voice on the radio had "lost much of its vitality," summed up Farley.[5]

Even though McIntire still appeared outwardly unperturbed, Roosevelt did begin to take time off, a week here and there, for restful sojourns at his family estate at Hyde Park, New York, possibly at McIntire's own insistence. By the end of March 1944 Roosevelt's condition had visibly worsened. He now looked ashen, his breathing became labored at the slightest exertion, and he was tired all day long irrespective of the previous night's sleep. "This latest cold has taken lots out of him," wrote William Hassett, a White House press aide, in his diary on March 24. Worse, when asked in the morning how he felt, Roosevelt's characteristic reply had become "rotten" or "like hell."[6]

Just days later, Roosevelt ran a slight fever one morning, but by evening had a temperature of 104. Observed Hassett: "Boss looks ill, color bad."[7] Eleanor Roosevelt and their daughter Anna were concerned enough to ask McIntire to examine the president more thoroughly. One historian has reported that McIntire did so, then blandly reported the president simply suffered from flu and bronchitis and was "overworked." For the first time Mrs. Roosevelt now rejected the Navy doctor's diagnosis and insisted upon a second opinion.

Roosevelt was taken to the National Naval Medical Center in Bethesda, Maryland, to be examined by Commander Howard G. Bruenn, a Navy cardiologist, a choice that is interesting in view of McIntire's diagnosis given the previous day that Roosevelt suffered from nothing worse than the flu. It also was a fortuitous choice in view of Bruenn's belated findings.

The man wheeled into Bruenn's examining room at the Navy hospital was well known to the world as a polio victim whose legs were paralyzed. For years he had favored the semimobility afforded by leg braces, but the Roosevelt whom Bruenn now met had given up all such pretense. He readily allowed himself to be lifted bodily from his wheelchair. He could not move without pain. The slightest effort gave him marked difficulty in breathing.[8]

The medical history that Bruenn now began to uncover also was alarming, much of the data unknown to either the president's staff or his family. In 1941, for example, Roosevelt had suffered from bleeding hemorrhoids and severe anemia. Even now, the concentration of hemoglobin in his blood was a low 4.5 grams per milliliter, compared to a normal 15.0 grams per milliliter. There is no record of any x-ray examination of Roosevelt's stomach and intestine to determine the cause of his anemia, its severity unusual for bleeding hemorrhoids alone. Nevertheless, he had been given iron tablets (ferrous sulfate), the treatment of choice for anemia blamed upon prolonged blood loss.

The president's medical charts that McIntire gave Bruenn also disclosed a steady rise in Roosevelt's blood pressure readings from 1935 to 1941, the date of the admiral's last complete entry in the medical records. During that period Roosevelt's blood pressure had gone from a tolerable 136/78 to 188/105, an obvious sign of severe hypertension. As Bruenn further noted, an EKG tracing done in 1941 showed a "slight abnormality." When Bruenn asked McIntire about previous EKGs, the White House physician responded that they were "all normal." McIntire thus failed to mention a noteworthy heart tracing taken in 1931, before Roosevelt came under his charge, before Roosevelt even was president.

Aside from the history, Bruenn's own reading of the patient's vital signs disclosed a man in acute distress. Roosevelt's face was "very gray," with a bluish discoloration of his lips. His blood pressure was high, about the 1941 level (186/108). His coughing was persistent and painful, with labored breathing afterwards, and he was running a slight fever. Bruenn took his own EKG of the president. The tracing again showed abnormality in the T-wave, suggestive evidence of early enlargement of the heart. And indeed fluoroscopic viewing of the chest showed the left side of the heart to be enlarged and distended. In all, Bruenn's tentative diagnosis of the man before him was hypertension, hypertensive heart disease, congestive heart failure, and acute bronchitis.

The Navy commander urged aggressive therapy, none of it surprising under the life threatening circumstances. He called for administration of the heart stimulant digitalis; two weeks of bed rest to relieve stress on the heart; a light, salt-free diet for the hypertension, and codeine to suppress Roosevelt's painful cough. But McIntire rejected both the diagnosis and projected treatment—the presidential schedule would not permit that kind of therapy. After further discussion, though, he did agree to give Roosevelt cough syrup containing codeine and ammonium carbonate. Clearly worried, the senior Navy doctor also assigned Bruenn permanently to the president.[9]

The next morning Bruenn appeared at the White House to see the president, and found no significant change in his condition. The following day, after still no significant response, McIntire allowed Bruenn to initiate some further treatment, to curtail Roosevelt's activity, and to limit his heavy smoking to six cigarettes a day. Bruenn now discontinued the codeine and prescribed fifteen milligrams of a mild sedative (phenobarbital) three times a day. But those steps still were not enough; four days after Bruenn's initial examination, Roosevelt showed no improvement. In fact, Bruenn adds in his clinical notes, even without benefit of x ray he could tell that Roosevelt's heart was "grossly enlarged to the left, with a heavy systolic impulse palpable at the apex." Once more he urged McIntire to give Roosevelt digitalis.[10]

By now, with no response by Roosevelt to the mild therapy, McIntire became alarmed enough to call in two civilian specialists— Dr. James A. Paullin, an eminent internist from Emory University in Atlanta, and Dr. Frank Lahey, the famous surgeon who founded the Lahey Clinic of Boston. Reporting to the White House the very next day, March 31, Paullin and Lahey tentatively agreed with Bruenn's diagnosis, but Paullin was reluctant to try the heart stimulant without more evidence as to degree of heart failure. Bruenn argued forcefully that Roosevelt's paralysis from polio made it impossible to develop the usual history of diminished heart reserve. Admitting the absence of such conclusive evidence, all laboratory and functional data nonetheless pointed to congestive heart failure. Paullin finally dropped his reservations, and all three then recommended the digitalis therapy to McIntire. Reluctant still, he acceded.

Bruenn began the therapy immediately and within a week achieved stunning results. By April 4 EKG tracings in the heart showed fewer abnormalities, while Roosevelt's chest x rays showed a marked decrease in heart size from the week before.[11] Still a concern, however, was the president's unresponsive blood pressure, now dangerously higher than ever. Even as the bronchial infection cleared, his blood pressure continued to rise—from a systolic reading of 180 during his first examination by Bruenn to 210 within the next two weeks. By April 3 the reading was even higher, 220/118, yet Roosevelt now claimed to feel fine and was notably improved in appearance.[12]

Two weeks after the digitalis therapy was begun, all four doctors met in conference again, with Bruenn presenting the medical case. Almost all symptoms had disappeared. Roosevelt's coughing, no longer painful, was occasional; the lungs were clear; color had returned to his face. The heart tracing was still slightly abnormal, but Bruenn saw in it "changes towards normal, that is, less deep inversion of the T-waves in the precordial leads." That would mean that the heart was decreasing in size toward normal. Also, an x-ray film showed a smaller heart size. Bruenn did not make note for posterity as to whether the group discussed Roosevelt's continuing high blood pressure, now fairly constant at an alarmingly high 210/120, with no sign of abatement. The consultants agreed the heart stimulant had been successful, though, and it was decided to maintain him on a dosage of 0.1 gram of digitalis per day.

Now, however, as the wartime Allies girded themselves for the historic assault upon Normandy in just a few weeks, Roosevelt's schedule of daily appointments was further restricted, on Bruenn's recommendation. The notes entered in the presidential appointments calendar kept by his aide, General Edwin Watson, show fewer and fewer visitors in late March and early April 1944, until the pages essentially became blank.[13] Indeed, by late May, with the Normandy invasion only days off, Watson stopped keeping a calendar altogether. Before that Watson's notes disclose only occasional meetings with Army officials, and even those were restricted to an hour or less. The White House excused Roosevelt's cancellations with vague statements about pressing war business.

Twice, though, he did see political leaders—each time, Watson scribbled on the margin that those interruptions were authorized by Dr. McIntire. Bruenn remained worried about the president's blood pressure, still high despite his patient's overall improvement, and about the possibility of a relapse. Although outside visitors were banned, the president's aides and other White House officials continued to have access to the president. Bruenn wanted an even stricter regimen of rest and lobbied for a complete, two-week vacation away from Washington and its demands. Roosevelt would have liked deep-sea fishing off Guantánamo Bay in Cuba, but the state of his health —and fear of Nazi submarines—ruled that out. Instead, he accepted financier Bernard Baruch's invitation to visit Baruch's estate in Hobcaw, South Carolina. Bruenn and McIntire went with him.

For the first two weeks of the sojourn, Roosevelt again was much improved. At the combined persuasion of both presidential doctors and various aides, Roosevelt had agreed to a light, relaxing schedule. He would be awakened at 9:30 or 10 o'clock in the morning, have breakfast, then undergo examination by one of the two White House physicians. The rest of the morning would be devoted to reading newspapers and to the presidential correspondence. Roosevelt then would have lunch, take a short nap, and end his afternoon with a brief fishing excursion aboard a Coast Guard cutter, closely followed by a detail of Secret Service agents. Just before dinner, the president reviewed the latest contents of the White House mail pouch flown in daily from Washington, signed necessary papers, or even met on occasion with necessary politicians or military officials. Dinner invariably ended early, with the president himself giving the signal to retire at about nine o'clock.

While this regimen seemed beneficial for two weeks or so, Bruenn then began to note a disquieting change in Roosevelt's blood pressure readings. On his awakening in the morning the figures shot up to an alarming 230/126; by bedtime they had declined again to about 190/90. Bruenn again prescribed the sedating phenobarbital and increased Roosevelt's dosage of digitalis. He was puzzled by the fluctuation in blood pressure, for there seemed no correlation between the various readings and Roosevelt's daily activity.

A week later, his blood pressure still high, Roosevelt began to have severe stomach pains. Bruenn relieved the pain with codeine, while diagnosing the abdominal distress as an acute cholecystitis—an inflammation of the gall bladder. That complication disappeared in a couple of days, but by the beginning of May Roosevelt's blood pressure mounted still again—to 240/130 at one point. For the first recorded time, too, Roosevelt complained of a dull pain in the back of his neck and of a throbbing sensation throughout his body. Bruenn does not say so in his notes, but the pain and throbbing were symptomatic of Roosevelt's unchecked hypertension. In the absence of any other effective therapy Bruenn canceled the president's activities for two days and sent him to bed. When Roosevelt returned to Washington on May 26, his acute symptoms had disappeared.[14]

By this time, previously undisclosed records show, Roosevelt had been absent from the White House for a total of nine weeks in the first five months of 1944, the lost weeks spent in his recuperative trips either to Hyde Park or South Carolina.[15] Even that figure is deceptive, for throughout March Roosevelt had been so acutely ill that he rarely left his bedroom. Thus, between January and the end of May the president, unknown to his public, had been absent from the Oval Office roughly half the time. That such absences did not generate undue publicity was a result of various factors, among them Roosevelt's special relationship with the press.[16]

When Roosevelt reentered political life in the 1920s, after his bout with polio as a young man, the press treated him with a deference that would seem amazing today. By the rules that tacitly were adopted, Roosevelt never was to be photographed from the waist down. Thus, almost all published photos of Roosevelt show him seated or standing behind some sort of lectern. The taboo went back to his campaign for governor of New York in 1928 and in part was instigated by Roosevelt himself. The morning of his election that year he arrived at Hyde Park Town Hall to vote and of course noted the gaggle of newsreel and newspaper photographers ready to begin clicking the moment he left the car. "No movies of me getting out of the machine, boys," Roosevelt chided. "And, indeed," reports one journalist-historian, "they turned away until he had alighted, adjusted his braces and taken a pose."[17]

The self-censorship not only lasted throughout Roosevelt's political career, but it applied to articles and cartoons as well. For example, when Roosevelt lost his footing and toppled off the ramp leading to the rostrum at the Democratic National Convention of 1936, no photos were published, no cartoons drawn, no word appeared in the papers. More generally, the few references ever made in the press to

FDR's "shriveled legs," or his "hobbled body," elicited such a storm of protest from readers that editors from then on deleted any mention of Roosevelt's infirmity from their news stories.[18]

In the White House years there was a policy close to enforcement of certain rules. For one, there were no candid shots allowed of the president. Then, too, before any photo session presidential press secretary Steven Early gave Roosevelt's Secret Service detail a memorandum outlining the session's "ground rules." Any eager cameraman who broke the rules would find access to Roosevelt even further restricted; they might be denied entrance to his chambers or placed in a disadvantageous camera position. Early's memos were so detailed they sometimes listed rooms, even objects within rooms, that could be photographed. Moreover, close-up shots were made difficult by Secret Service enforcement of a minimum distance between photographers and their presidential subject. Looming above all other strictures, though, was the one unwritten law, seldom necessary to enforce: never show any part of Roosevelt from the waist down.[19]

By the time Roosevelt was completing his third term as president, wartime censorship (and a sense of patriotism) had joined other notions of good taste as a further gag upon the press. If the president's agenda went unexplained for the moment, the White House press office could claim security considerations for its reticence—a point that often was true. It was fairly simple to deflect probing questions with enigmatic phrases suggesting military deliberations, and in those wartime days of public patriotism few reporters were ready to challenge the word of their own government officials. Thus, any detailed investigative reporting of the president's health would have been difficult, could have run afoul of the unstated rules, and could even have raised security issues, in view of Roosevelt's added role as commander-in-chief of the United States military. Newcomer Bruenn never met with the press, while McIntire's few appearances before the White House scribes were occasion for prepared state-

ments about the president's generally robust health, with only infrequent reference to a "cold" or sinusitis. Reporters as a rule were not
admitted to Roosevelt's retreats. Indeed, few persons outside his inner
circle really could know whether he was vacationing or secretly
arranging some monumental plan with someone on the order of
Winston Churchill.

As we now know, in the months after Roosevelt first contracted his
stubborn flu of late 1943, the Allies of World War II had prepared,
then mounted, their largest and most crucial military operation of
the entire war, the invasion of France on June 6, 1944. In that year
also the war in the Pacific against Japan was pressed forward largely
by Roosevelt's American forces, with the Japanese now stubbornly in
retreat.

In November 1944, meanwhile, the same Roosevelt who had fallen
so ill the previous spring ran for an unprecedented fourth term as
president of the United States. He of course won handily, the state of
his health unknown to the general public. Then, early in 1945, as
one of "The Big Three," the same hollow figure of a once robust man
conferred in the distant Crimea with Churchill and Stalin—a conference in which the three world leaders carved out a new, postwar
Europe affecting the destiny of millions.

And then, on April 12, 1945, two months after Yalta, Franklin
Delano Roosevelt, sixty-three, awoke at 9:15 A.M. in Warm Springs,
Georgia, to his last day. In six hours, victim of a massive cerebral
hemorrhage, he was dead.[20]

Polio, Politics, and Roosevelt's Early Years

Franklin Delano Roosevelt's early history reflects nothing untoward
in his health. Born to an aristocratic family in upstate New York in
1882, the young Roosevelt was reared by the patrician norms of the
day. He attended Groton in his teens, then went on to Harvard. He
attended Columbia Law School, did not take a degree from there, but

eventually did pass the New York State bar exam admitting him to practice. In 1905 he married his distant cousin Eleanor Roosevelt and began a career in law and business, with indifferent success.[21]

Roosevelt's natural inclination toward politics found expression in 1910 when as a Democrat he was elected to the New York State Senate. His first experience with a serious illness came two years later, in the midst of his campaign for reelection to the Senate seat. He came down with typhoid fever, but successfully overcame the potentially dangerous disease—and his Republican challenger, whom he defeated without campaigning in person. A year later, President Woodrow Wilson appointed Roosevelt assistant secretary of the Navy in Washington, a job and locale in which Roosevelt's fascination for the sea merged with his interests in politics and business.

By all accounts, young Roosevelt was an avid sportsman in generally excellent health. His energy seemingly boundless, he found time for many interests, a growing family, and high political ambition. In 1920, at the urging of the party leadership, he stood for election as vice president on the Democratic party ticket headed by presidential nominee James Cox. The cause that year was hopeless, as Roosevelt knew, but he recognized the opportunity to build both his reputation and power base within the party. After the expected debacle at the polls Roosevelt stepped out of active politics for the moment; he worked on Wall Street, happy to have paid some important political dues, pleased for now to enter the relatively quiet, more lucrative world of business. He became vice president of a Manhattan bank and with friends founded a law firm, where he worked in his spare time.

His new tranquillity was to be shattered a year later, however. On a yachting excursion to Campobello Island, New Brunswick, in August 1921, Roosevelt took a swim in the icy waters of the Bay of Fundy. Shortly afterwards, he felt a chill, and soon fever set in. He at first dismissed the episode as nothing worse than a bad cold, but his condition rapidly deteriorated. In a short time Roosevelt felt dull pain, then numbness in his legs. A local doctor called in for consultation was alarmed by the speed and severity of the infection and by the ominous paralysis striking the young man's lower body. He turned for more expert advice to W. W. Keen, an elderly physician vacationing nearby who had been a pioneer of American neurosurgery. Keen first diagnosed Roosevelt's debilitating illness as a spinal thrombosis. As the illness grew worse and real paralysis took hold, Keen amended his diagnosis to "inflammation of the spinal cord." A few days later the grim truth became apparent as a third doctor, Robert Lovett, made the definitive diagnosis of polio.[22]

Once that was established, Roosevelt's family spirited him away from Campobello in secret and isolated him at Hyde Park to recuperate in all possible comfort. Then began a family crisis, for in her son's new handicap Sara Roosevelt evidently saw opportunity to reestablish some of the control over his life that she had lost when he married Eleanor. Consequently, she now counseled a life of retirement for her invalid son in the apparent hope that he would passively live out his days close to her in the seclusion of the family estate at Hyde Park. Such motherly thinking did not quite suit Eleanor, who long had chafed under her mother-in-law's heavy-handed attempts to run the young couple's affairs. Joining forces with Roosevelt's assistant Louis Howe, Eleanor pressed her stricken, dispirited husband to throw himself into his physiotherapy program, the hope being that he soon would be fit enough to resume a more public life. In this test of domestic wills, Roosevelt's own inner strength would tip the scales. By January 1922 the indefatigable Roosevelt was back at work in his New York law office.[23]

His crippling disease now had a paradoxical effect. He always had pursued a range of interests with uncommon vigor; now his handicap seemed only to multiply those interests and drive him to achieve their fulfillment with greater energy than ever. In the two years after his illness Roosevelt continued as vice president of his bank, maintained his law practice, chaired fund-raisers for numerous charities, became a trustee of Vassar College, served as president of the Navy

Club, collaborated in organization of the Woodrow Wilson Foundation, and served on the president's National Crime Commission. He
also embarked on at least a dozen business ventures—none of them
destined for success, despite his own best efforts.

Eleanor and former newspaperman Howe, in the meantime, still
collaborated in their own plans to see Roosevelt return to politics.
Roosevelt himself had not completely given up his political ambitions, but his highly visible physical handicap understandably did
dampen his enthusiasm for a public role. Further, more than anyone
he realized the difficulties of a political campaign for a man of limited mobility. He long since had discarded the hated wheelchair for
leg braces, supplemented by a cane or crutches—but walking for
him still was an arduous task.

Roosevelt at the same time had developed strong interest in polio
rehabilitation, a new field of research. Shortly after his illness he
began to travel to Warm Springs, Georgia, sharing the belief of many
that the spa's waters had a special medicinal effect. He eventually
bought land there with dreams of building a preeminent polio treatment center. Stoking these fires was the ubiquitous and fiercely loyal
Louis Howe, always ready to encourage any interest of Roosevelt's.[24]
Howe helped Roosevelt raise funds for the project—a plan to finance
a whole series of spas all the way up the eastern seaboard to Lake
Placid, New York. Predictably, the idea never went beyond animated
discussion between Roosevelt and Howe, but the planning and fund
raising kept Roosevelt happily occupied for the moment.

His absence from the political scene from 1920 to 1924, in fact, was
a result not only of his polio setback, but also of his own keen reading of the public mood. Following the disarray of Woodrow Wilson's
idealistic grand alliances so soon after World War I, Roosevelt sensed
the country's self-absorbed mood of retrenchment, with little patience
for the crusades that recently had characterized the Democratic party.
Roosevelt anticipated the Republicans would be in power for at least
two presidential terms.

This is not to say that Roosevelt had abandoned his earlier interest; on the contrary, both he and Howe mapped out various avenues for Roosevelt's eventual return to political life. While not quite as ebullient as Howe, Roosevelt indulged him in strategies for reaching the White House, and to that end Howe had suggested that Roosevelt avoid the internecine struggles of the Democratic party throughout the rest of the 1920s. Let Al Smith and others carry the Democratic banner to inevitable defeat, Howe counseled, while Roosevelt continued with rehabilitation, business, and charitable affairs at home. Howe's projected timetable had Roosevelt rejoining the political wars for the 1932 governor's race in New York, where Roosevelt already enjoyed a broad and solid base of power.[25] Upon winning that race, and its follow-up in 1934, Roosevelt could then challenge the Republicans for the presidency, after a predicted two terms in the office for Herbert Hoover. So battered were the Democrats that Howe was conceding the Republicans sixteen years in power before they would be vulnerable to Democratic challenge.

For all his careful, quiet planning, Howe failed to take into account Roosevelt's remarkable recuperative powers and impatient ambition. The faithful aide also failed to consider the quirks of Democratic politics and Roosevelt's sense of duty to his party. Because he was a man of influence in New York State, a rare enclave of remaining Democratic strength at the time, Roosevelt's endorsements, advice, and aid were sought by various candidates for public office. It therefore was not too surprising that fellow native son and governor Al Smith should seek out Roosevelt in 1924 for an active role in Smith's bid for the party's presidential nomination. Smith asked Roosevelt to nominate him at the Democratic National Convention that presidential year. Roosevelt naturally had some misgivings, for it would be his first major public appearance since he had been stricken by polio, but he acceded to the request.

When the moment came on June 26, 1924, Roosevelt was rolled to the convention's podium in his wheelchair. He then rose unaided, struggled to the lectern on crutches, and delivered a stirring speech (calling Smith the "Happy Warrior") that brought the delegates roaring to their feet. It was a dramatic moment, even allowing for the tendency of convention audiences to cheer anything, for Roosevelt's own prowess as a speaker, or for sympathetic reaction to his determination to persevere over his handicap. The spectacle of hundreds of party regulars cheering this crippled man was a scene to be etched indelibly in Howe's mind, making all his planning seem so less fanciful.[26] Roosevelt had shortcut Howe's elaborate timetable by the action, but it soon became apparent that neither had misread the country's political mood. The Democrats were defeated soundly in the 1924 elections, and Roosevelt again turned to his business ventures and his treatments at Warm Springs.

In the years that followed Roosevelt became so much a part of the Georgia community that he had a regular column in the local newspaper called "Roosevelt Says." For his efforts on behalf of a polio treatment center, townspeople came to address him as "Doctor Roosevelt," while Roosevelt came to see himself as quite an expert on the disease. He even corresponded occasionally with doctors treating other victims of polio. In one such letter, dated October 11, 1924, he freely offered his advice on the treatment of a patient to William Egleston, a physician in South Carolina. With the caveat that he was no doctor himself, Roosevelt went on to say: "I am very glad to tell you what I can in regard to my case, and as I have talked it over with a great many doctors can, I think, give you a history . . . which would be equal to theirs." The rehabilitative program that he then outlined was as assured and detailed as any clinical chart.[27]

Roosevelt might have finished out the 1920s so engaged with his various enterprises, in his shuttling back and forth between New York and Hyde Park, in his regular travel to Warm Springs—all by Howe's timetable. He might have but for another interruption by Al Smith in 1928 when Smith was gearing up for another run at the presidency. In a frantic call to Roosevelt at Warm Springs, Governor

Smith expressed fears that absenting himself from New York state politics would hand his governor's mansion to the Republicans. Would Roosevelt please consider running for governor?

Alarmed, and of course closely attending, Howe pestered Roosevelt to decline Smith's offer. The timing was still premature, Howe felt, and Roosevelt was not yet strong enough for a full campaign. Sensing his aide's anxiety, Roosevelt quipped to Smith, "You're asking me to run, Al, but I can't even walk!"[28]

Undeterred, Smith persisted. Would Roosevelt say no if he were spontaneously drafted for the party's gubernatorial nomination? When Roosevelt momentarily fell silent, it was Al Smith who hung up the phone, who immediately began to implement *his* plans for Roosevelt. Howe at first was stunned—he had not planned for Roosevelt to reenter the fray quite so soon. But he soon saw that if Roosevelt ever were to win the presidency, the governorship of New York would be the best platform from which to launch a national campaign. In the end, then, Roosevelt aggressively sought both the gubernatorial nomination and, that fall, election to the post. He carried the day in both instances and now could begin planning for the national elections that would come again in 1932.

First, though, Roosevelt's health did become a factor in his political career. Personally reconciled to his invalid status by 1928, Roosevelt nonetheless worried that he might appear too incapacitated to discharge his duties in public office. As one result, he waged a gubernatorial campaign in 1928 vigorous enough to wear down many a younger, physically whole man. He made dozens of speeches a week as he crisscrossed most of New York State, many of his stops consisting of rallies carefully arranged to minimize any appearance of handicap.

Roosevelt won the governorship in 1928, in spite of the fact that his party's national ticket, headed by Al Smith this time, again bowed to the Republicans. He then won reelection as governor in 1930 by a landslide. It appeared that Roosevelt was a winner, paralysis or no paralysis.

By the middle of his second term as governor, however, rumors about his health began to surface as a price apparently to be paid for growing success. Now preeminent among the Democratic hopefuls for the presidency, Roosevelt had attracted the attention of the national press, and some of its members became irritatingly curious. One writer, for instance, editorially suggested that it was one thing for a Governor Roosevelt to take the waters at Warm Springs with no detriment to state government, but another to consider the same luxury for a President Roosevelt. Furious, Roosevelt wrote back that he knew perfectly well how to allocate his time and order his priorities. The innuendoes continued, however, and at one point he took pen in hand to protest an editorial in the *Butte Standard* (Montana) that ran under the headline, "The Wheelchair in Albany."[29]

The economic depression that had begun to take hold under Herbert Hoover's Republican administration made prospect of a Democratic victory all the more likely for 1932, but Roosevelt and his aides were at a loss over the health question. While he undeniably was a cripple, they felt constrained to show that his illness was behind him, that it now had no adverse effect other than the paralysis of his lower body. But how to do so demonstrably, other than by stage managing his public appearances and encouraging his bent for vigorous campaigning? One interesting tactic the Roosevelt camp then hit upon was a medical examination and public release of its findings. The outcome silenced all but the most persistent critics, even though the report made public was clinically inconclusive.

The notes of the examination showed a forty-nine-year-old man with total paralysis of both legs but partially mobile when using a cane or crutches. Among other selective data made public were a blood pressure reading of 140/100, a mild but significant elevation above the norm (120/80), and an abnormal heart tracing by electrocardiogram (EKG) indicating enlargement of the left side of the heart and displaying an inversion of the T-waves in Lead 3, usually meaning a decrease in blood flow to the heart. No other details of the EKG tracing were released; no other details of Roosevelt's cardiovascular system, either from clinical observation or laboratory tests, were elucidated.[30] The clinical report in fact was incomplete, and the data it did present suggested potential health problems unrelated to polio. Yet so much attention had been focused upon Roosevelt's crippled status that no reporters followed up on the real shadow the data had cast. Indeed, charges that Roosevelt was sick now rang hollow; those who questioned his health were characterized by the Roosevelt entourage as mean-spirited or low-handed. From then on, Roosevelt's political operatives could point to the unchallenged (also undefended) medical report and chide his detractors for impugning a courageous man who happened to be crippled. It was a tactic they would employ over and over again, ultimately to succeed in deflecting any serious inquiries into Roosevelt's health at any time.

Those early health signs, of course, pointed to a man suffering from essential hypertension, cause unknown. The enlargement of one side of Roosevelt's heart was evidence of incipient hypertensive cardiovascular disease. Unabated, such illness can lead to a narrowing of the blood vessels in the brain and a stroke; it can lead also to blockage or narrowing of the blood vessels in the heart and to heart attack. If untreated, chronic hypertension (of course often treatable today by drugs) in time will lead to the failure of proper heart function, with accumulation of fluids in various vital organs (for example, the lungs) and the lower extremities as a result. This end stage of the disease, called congestive heart failure, is characterized by weakness, fatigue, loss of appetite, shortness of breath. Should the patient develop severe anemia, as Roosevelt later did, his struggling heart is forced to work all the harder to provide the rest of the body with an adequate supply of oxygen. For the heart disease patient, such a development can be a major factor in the onset of acute heart failure.

In 1932 there was no known treatment for high blood pressure other than a mild sedative (such as phenobarbital) given to reduce anxiety or tension, but that step was more a palliative than a cure. In the 1940s the medical community discovered that a salt-free diet worked as a partial treatment but was difficult to impose because of the typical patient's distaste for saltless food. Fortunately, even if the basic causes of hypertension remain unknown, drugs introduced in the 1950s now effectively control high blood pressure and prolong life. They, too, do not exactly cure, but they are effective in a high percentage of cases.

In 1932, however, there were drugs, most specifically digitalis, that could relieve symptoms of heart failure. Although the exact mechanism is not perfectly understood even today, digitalis does make the heart action more effective—a result that serves to clear the body organs of accumulated fluids and relieves the most distressing symptom, shortness of breath. Again, the drug is a palliative and not a cure, and as the heart disease progresses, digitalis becomes less and less effective.

Sadly enough, a Franklin Delano Roosevelt at age forty-nine today would enjoy an excellent chance for effective control of his high blood pressure. In 1932, though, he stood at the brink of significant health problems with no such medical help available—and he wasn't even president yet.

In view of the medical expertise that *was* available in the 1930s, however, two issues arise. First, we can question whether it was to Roosevelt's personal benefit to seek the presidency, a stressful job compared to most occupations open to a man of his background. Certain palliative steps were known to the medical community, and for his own, personal well being Roosevelt might have been best advised to find himself a life of little stress, opportunity for rest, and light but regular exercise. There can be no assurance that such a relaxed regimen would have enabled Roosevelt to live beyond age sixty-three. Moreover, he is held in high regard by a large number of American historians, who rank him as one of the ten most effective presidents. Secondly, though, there is no doubt that the steadily declining state of his health prevented him from giving the presidency the energy and full attention that a healthier man could have. Further, the voting public did not know the condition of his health.

As the 1932 presidential campaign drew near, Roosevelt and his aides continued to develop his image as an assured, unimpaired, and capable candidate for the highest office in the land. A polished orator with booming voice, Roosevelt was given to speeches delivered from open cars or the caboose of his campaign train. He supported himself with one arm and gestured decisively with the other; his public appearances were almost always impressive. When he had to mount a rostrum before an eager crowd, he was in a wheelchair pushed along by an aide. But he often was so surrounded by others in his entourage that all the crowd saw was a clot of people moving towards the podium, Roosevelt himself still not visible. When finally the protective circle broke, FDR would pull himself out of the chair, stagger slightly to the lectern, and then stand straight up to deliver his speech while braced against the structure. Throughout his campaign in 1932 (in which he first wrested the Democratic party nomination from his old friend Al Smith), Roosevelt demonstrated time and again that he had adapted to his handicap, that it in no way interfered with his duties.[31]

The focus of too much concern, Roosevelt's famous malady may have had the same paradoxical and yet galvanizing effect on the voters as it had had on him. They themselves were victims—stricken, even afflicted, by economic disaster, the Great Depression. The sight of a physically crippled man who would be their leader may have struck a sympathetic chord. Once, when asked if her husband's polio had affected his mental ability, Eleanor Roosevelt, surprisingly, said yes. "Any person who has gone through great suffering," she explained, "is bound to have a greater sympathy [for] and understanding of the problems of mankind."[32]

Perhaps the voters felt the same way. For whatever reason, or combination of reasons, medical or political, Franklin Delano Roosevelt was elected thirty-second president of the United States in 1932.

———

World War II and the Strains of Office

One privilege that comes with the office of president is the service of a full time, personal physician as a member of the White House staff. Precedent dictated that Roosevelt's doctor should come from the medical corps of one branch or another of the Armed Services, but the choice otherwise was his. He remembered meeting a young Navy commander some years before through Woodrow Wilson's personal physician, Admiral Cary Grayson. Now, based upon little more than a pleasant conversation a few years back, Roosevelt appointed Ross T. McIntire as White House physician for the Roosevelt years.

The appointment, in retrospect, seems to have been hasty and ill-advised, but it appeared a logical choice at the time. Apart from his polio, which Roosevelt managed well by himself, the only other illness to which he regularly was subject was sinusitis. A heavy smoker, Roosevelt had endured a mild but chronic sinus condition for several years. As McIntire had been well trained in both otolaryngology and ophthalmology, he seemed a reasonable enough choice. In fact, Roosevelt soon formed a strong friendship with the genial McIntire, then gave him the additional post of chief of the navy's Bureau of Medicine and Surgery.[33]

With no medical crisis intervening for the first eight years of Roosevelt's tenure, McIntire's duties largely were restricted to administering the navy's medical corps and treating the president's occasional cold. Imperceptibly, though, Roosevelt was beginning to feel the strain of his duties, even while enjoying the fruits of political success.

The country in the mid-1930s still remained in an economic depression, but conditions did appear somewhat stabilized. Roosevelt was widely credited with checking a slide into an even deeper depression, a perception that served to keep him in office for eight years.

But then, as his second term drew near its close, the leaders of both parties guessed at Roosevelt's future plans. There seemed to be no Republican noteworthy enough to challenge an incumbent Roosevelt, and the Constitution did not preclude a third presidential term. Roosevelt remained coyly reticent while any number of ambitious Democrats blanched at the thought of awaiting their turn while Roosevelt took a third term.

Roosevelt, in the meantime, had been watching events overseas with growing anxiety, as first Mussolini, then Hitler, consolidated their holds over most of Europe. Before Roosevelt's tenure the Japanese had invaded Manchuria, and now they continued to prowl the Pacific Basin in search of oil and other resources for their rapidly expanding empire. The last months of Roosevelt's second term brought the situation in Europe to ugly climax. Hitler, now allied with Mussolini, annexed Austria in 1937 and shortly thereafter dispatched Czechoslovakia (1938) and Poland (1939). France fell within the year, and suddenly only the beleaguered British remained in opposition. Across the Atlantic in warily watching America, 1940 would be a crucial presidential election year.

Whether for those reasons, the economic storm he and his country had suffered, or simply normal strains of the job, President Roosevelt's friends had begun to note a decline in his appearance. As early as summer of 1937, for example, Secretary of the Interior Harold Ickes noted: "Roosevelt has paid a heavy toll during these last four years. His face is heavily lined and inclined to be gaunt . . . and he is distinctly more nervous."[34] Former Postmaster General Farley, now chairman of the Democratic party, also noticed a change. "I found the President looking tired and drawn," he commented after a meeting with Roosevelt. "He said he had not been feeling well."[35]

Farley's observations may have been colored by his ill-disguised ambition to succeed Roosevelt, but Ickes was a progressive Republican who had served Roosevelt's New Deal with fierce loyalty, and he continued to express worry. Noting in his diary in November 1937, he said there was no doubt that Roosevelt was showing the strain he had been through. "He looks all of fifteen years older since he was inaugurated in 1933."[36] Four months later in March 1938 Ickes returned to his diary after a cabinet meeting: "His face showed, perhaps more than ever, the terrific strain under which he has been working."[37]

As the deadline for the 1940 race approached, rumors of Roosevelt's ill health increased. Publicly, the president professed an indifference to his prospects for a third term. In the company of his more private advisors, such as Harry Hopkins, however, he seemed more determined than ever to continue as president.

Part of that resolve no doubt was born of a personal conviction that he was one of the few leaders in the country who clearly saw the imminence of war. Yet America still had not shed its isolationism; the public consistently balked at any suggestion of foreign entanglements. Despite the debacles suffered by the European democracies, it took all of Roosevelt's persuasive skill and political gamesmanship to convince Congress to abrogate the Arms Embargo Act of 1939 as a concession allowing him to aid Britain materially under the newly negotiated Lend-Lease Act and, later, to supply Russia under an amended version (1941) of the same act.

While Roosevelt was committed confidentially to a third term, he publicly said nothing and thus allowed potential rivals to criticize one another in hopes of striking a killing blow upon their divided ranks when he made his formal announcement. It was in this somewhat deceptive atmosphere, then, that fears of Roosevelt's declining health began to surface. The peripatetic Jim Farley continued to express his loyalty but quietly approached others with hints that a third term would have dire effects on both the president and the country.

In his boldest foray Farley went to the Capitol office of Vice President John Nance Garner one October day in 1939. They talked about the presidential election that would be in full swing one year later.

"I want to tell you exactly where I stand," Garner apparently said, "so that you can govern yourself accordingly." He went on to say he opposed a third term for Roosevelt. "It's bad for the country and bad for the party and bad for the Boss."[38] Garner, perhaps intending to draw Farley out into the open, said he did not know what Roosevelt would do, but noted, "he doesn't dislike third term talk, and he's doing nothing to discourage it." Farley did take opportunity to talk about an alternative candidate but was careful not to mention himself. Roosevelt, he also said, had spent twelve "long, trying years" in his stints as governor of New York (four years) and as president (eight). "I doubt if he can stand the strain of another four years, particularly war years," said Farley. "Those around him shouldn't ask him to put himself in a position where he would be shortening his days." However, while they both said that neither of them really wanted the job, they also agreed that a third FDR term was not best either. Garner said nothing of Farley's own transparent hopes.[39]

Shortly after, Roosevelt himself met with another potential rival, Ambassador Joseph P. Kennedy, back from his post in London for consultations with the president. Roosevelt in fact had summoned Kennedy back to Washington because the outspoken isolationist's views were creating problems for the nascent Anglo-American war alliance. Looking "terribly tired but cordial," Roosevelt received Kennedy while still in bed. Potential challenger Kennedy, a presidential favorite in isolationist circles, bluntly asked Roosevelt if he would run for a third term. "Joe, I can't," said Roosevelt at first blush. "I'm tired. I can't take it. What I need is a year's rest."[40] But then Roosevelt warmed to a theme that others had heard. "You do, too," he told the ambassador from London. "You may think you're resting at times, but the subconscious idea of war and its problems—bombings and all that—is going on in your brain. I just won't go for a third term unless we are at war."[41]

Despite the disclaimers and admission of fatigue, Roosevelt had conditioned his refusal on the nation's being at peace. To those who knew his belief that war was imminent, the little charade with Kennedy was clear signal that, yes, Roosevelt would run.

He did, of course, and a year after his reelection, the country indeed was dragged into the war that had engulfed Europe and the Far East. From the hour of the Pearl Harbor attack on December 7, 1941, through all of 1942 and long into 1943, however, the battle news was largely grim; the strain of conducting the war began to have an impact on Roosevelt. It would appear so from the fact that the gradual decline in his health now accelerated. In the past, he normally was able to shed the symptoms of his sinus attacks in short time. By early 1943, however, the episodes were more frequent; it took Roosevelt longer and longer to recover.

It is difficult to guess today just how much McIntire actually knew or suspected about the president's state of health. But it is curious that for the conference with Churchill at Casablanca in January 1943 McIntire should order the presidential plane to fly at low altitude. Even then, with the stricture of no higher than nine thousand feet, McIntire noted how pale Roosevelt became. McIntire states in his memoirs that he "naturally" feared for the president's heart but mentions no hidden cardiovascular pathology—nor does he expand upon the restrictive flight plans. There is not even a hint, either, of the president's visits to the Bethesda naval health facility under a series of pseudonyms in those war years.[42]

Later, in that spring of 1944 when Roosevelt was absent from the White House so much, the pending Normandy invasion was the focus of truly monumental Allied hopes. Ever since America's entry into the war, both the British and the Soviets had been pressing for a second front that would force Hitler to split his forces. Roosevelt had returned to Washington on May 26 from the last of his recuperative absences. The invasion, which had been painfully negotiated and planned among the Allied commanders for four years in all, finally began on June 6. Within the week, it became apparent that the military gamble involving massive numbers of American men and maté-

riel had succeeded in establishing a beachhead for the Allied armies
—but at painful cost, too. Yet, Dr. Bruenn in his memoir is strangely
silent about this critical moment in Roosevelt's presidency. Although
the American commander-in-chief must have felt the stress as he
watched the progress of the enormous military operation, Bruenn
merely comments that Roosevelt was generally asymptomatic during
the month of June, even if his blood pressure remained above
normal.[43]

As so happened, the dramatic staging and execution of the Normandy invasion coincided with Roosevelt's planning for a possible
fourth term—1944 again was a presidential election year, and November was not that far off. This time, though, there was far less speculation and subterfuge than four years before, for few expected Roosevelt
to step down in the middle of the war. To outside observers that
seemed a rational expectation; indeed, in the greater public's mind
Roosevelt seemed indispensable by now. He had safely carried the
nation through a succession of crises for nearly twelve years. Moreover, he was not simply president, but a commander-in-chief whose
armies just now were beginning to achieve dramatic results.

There might have been earnest and serious debate among his closest advisers, doctors included, but this fact was hidden from the
public. Even Roosevelt's doctors were influenced by their patient's
aura; theirs was not the usual doctor-patient relationship by any
means. As John Gunther, one of Roosevelt's earliest biographers, asks:
"What Navy doctor could have dared tell the Commander-in-Chief,
at the supreme climax of the war, that he had to quit?"[44]

Then, too, notes Gunther, the physician assigned to the president
might well ask himself: "Have I the right to alarm the President
further—is it my duty to make him stop work?" After all, with millions of men risking combat death their president perhaps should
run his own risks in order to win the war.[45] Thus, the normal ambiguities of a doctor-patient relationship in Roosevelt's case easily could
have been distorted by his very status as president, by the exigencies

of war, by the hesitancy of any doctor to categorically assert an unwelcome diagnosis. Further blurring the parameters of the decision facing the Roosevelt entourage was the fact that in the early summer months of 1944 the president was in much improved condition, encouragement of an almost mythic belief in his recuperative powers. Although Bruenn's reticence here is notable, McIntire seemed pleased with the idea of a fourth term for Roosevelt, only now and again adding enigmatic warnings about watching the president's "heart reserve."

A Rumor of Illness in the 1944 Presidential Campaign

So foregone was the political conclusion in 1944 that Roosevelt's renomination for the presidency barely required anything more than his assent; he did not even attend the Democratic party's national convention in Chicago. Any opposition from within party ranks would have been futile, despite evident concern over Roosevelt's health. "Everywhere I found delegates restless but resigned to the inevitable," later said the ubiquitous Jim Farley. The inevitable of course was a fourth term for Roosevelt. But Farley also took note of the accompanying phenomenon. "Everywhere the President's health was a major topic, though it was discussed largely in whispers."[46]

The small suspense of the 1944 convention came in maneuvering for the second spot on the national ticket, that of the vice-presidential nominee. For the first time in memory of most associates Roosevelt was uncharacteristically passive in the face of the debate over his proposed running mate. Just four years earlier, he had threatened to refuse his own nomination unless the party bosses accepted his choice of Henry Wallace for vice president. He then fought vigorously for Wallace; the ultimatum worked. Now in 1944, rather than even attend the national convention, he held a secret, late night meeting with party officials in which he quickly acceded to their wishes: Henry Wallace was off the ticket. Roosevelt signed a letter stating his willingness to run with either William O. Douglas or Harry S. Truman. It was Truman of course who got the nod.[47]

Whether because of the war, fear of dividing the party, or quite possibly his ill health, Roosevelt approached the 1944 presidential election in subdued fashion. One wonders if he himself expected to live through the all but certain outcome. To Joseph P. Kennedy he joked about his lethargy. "Yes, I am tired. So would you be if you had spent the last five years pushing Winston up a wheelbarrow."[48]

Roosevelt seemed to lack the zeal with which he always had pursued his political fortune. Gone were the countless meetings and political negotiations that marked his previous campaigns. Some observers believed that Roosevelt had "risen above" the sometimes petty fray of domestic politics, his statesmanlike concern only with winning the war, then settling the peace to follow. Others felt his reelection simply was so certain that it failed to excite him. Perhaps his aide and longtime confidante General Watson came closest to the mark with the observation, "He just doesn't give a damn."[49]

Publicly, Roosevelt announced that he was seeking reelection as a "good soldier." He bypassed the normal politicking of the summer altogether and began a cross-country trip that would take him also to the Pacific War Theater for a conference with General Douglas MacArthur and Admirals William Leahy and Chester Nimitz. As one concession to political protocol, his train detoured by way of Chicago, where he met with some party leaders—on the train. As a second concession, he stopped in San Diego on July 20 and, again without leaving his train, accepted the 1944 Democratic nomination over a live, nationwide radio hookup. Then he was off to meet his military chieftains.

Bruenn claims that Roosevelt was in relatively good health during this period, but others who saw him that summer thought otherwise. After their latest meeting, the first in some months, Joseph P. Kennedy confided to the New York Times columnist Arthur Krock, "The President looks sick." Kennedy in fact was shocked by the change since his last White House visit. He found the president pale and gaunt, despite his recuperative vacations of the spring, and Roosevelt's hands shook uncontrollably. Worse, the normally self-possessed Roosevelt wandered aimlessly in thought at times, while his face would take on a vacant, slack-jawed expression.[50] Kennedy wondered why a man so obviously ill would choose to run again, then answered his own question by blaming the "rabble" surrounding Roosevelt: "That crowd can put anything over on him. He hasn't the mental energy to resist."[51]

Out of grace with Roosevelt anyway, Kennedy broke their old political bond that autumn to endorse Roosevelt's Republican opponent, New York Governor Thomas E. Dewey. Since the advent of the New Deal, the conservative isolationist's alliance with the liberal activist in the White House had been an uneasy one. With Krock, though, Kennedy swore he personally bore Roosevelt no ill will. He did assert that the Roosevelt of 1944 was but a ghost of the man whom Kennedy had helped to win the presidency in 1932. "He's not the same Roosevelt I knew."[52]

And indeed, Roosevelt's health did, in fact, seem to be deteriorating. In one wrenching episode, for example, his own son James was witness to a sobering incident. James Roosevelt was with his father in his study one July day when Roosevelt "suddenly began to groan, his face took on an expression of suffering." The president clutched at his abdomen, the younger Roosevelt recounts, and bent sharply over. "Jimmy," he gasped. "I don't know if I can make it. I have a horrible pain."[53]

Naturally, young James's first thought was to get in touch with Dr. McIntire—immediately. But Roosevelt stopped his son, out of fear that any revelation would jeopardize his chances for reelection. Meanwhile, the pain quickly subsided; it appears that James Roosevelt let it go at that, in respect for his father's wishes. Neither McIntire nor Bruenn mentions the episode in his notes.

Roosevelt's recurrent abdominal pain is known and has been the source of considerable speculation in the past. Bruenn himself had noted his patient was susceptible to all manner of gastric disturbances; Bruenn once had diagnosed a particularly severe attack as gall bladder disease. Clearly, though, the gastric syndrome was less worrisome to both presidential physicians than his other problems, such as the high blood pressure. As in the incident reported by Roosevelt's son James, however, it may be that Roosevelt stoically kept some of his suffering to himself. Certainly, Bruenn did not aggressively treat the gastric discomfort, save for occasional pain medication or an alteration in diet.

Interestingly, it was Roosevelt's gastrointestinal tract that had struck Dr. Lahey as a source of professional concern ever since his initial visit to the White House at the end of March 1944. Bruenn says that after the consultant examined the president, "Lahey was particularly interested in the gastrointestinal tract, but submitted that no surgical procedure was indicated at the time."[54]

Since surgery had not been mentioned as a possibility before, the statement is more enigmatic than illuminating; it prompts speculation as to what so interested the Boston physician. The subsequent abdominal pain that Roosevelt experienced while visiting Bernard Baruch's estate in South Carolina did prompt Bruenn to order an x-ray examination of Roosevelt's stomach and gallbladder. The film did reveal gallstones, and their presence of course could explain the occasional attacks of acute abdominal pain.[55] Bruenn's therapy was to place Roosevelt on a low-fat diet of 1,800 calories, an accepted treatment for gallbladder disease that also could result in weight loss and thus relieve stress on his heart at the same time. The diet did not completely alleviate Roosevelt's pain, but it succeeded in trimming twenty pounds from his weight. Most probably it was the gallstones that moved Lahey to consider surgery, but the doctors attending the president may wisely have decided against major surgery because of his heart condition. Fortunately, he never did develop really serious gallbladder problems.

Roosevelt's trip to the Pacific in the summer of 1944, on the heels of his nomination for a fourth term as president, was without significant health difficulties. He toured naval installations in Hawaii and conferred extensively with his Pacific Theater commanders, then proceeded by ship to Alaska. He returned to the continental United States for a nationwide radio address to be delivered from the shipyards of Bremerton, Washington, and for that public occasion he resumed his leg braces, which he had discarded some time previously. But Roosevelt had lost so much weight since beginning his diet that the braces were loose and ill-fitting. Since his long illness that spring, moreover, he had not stood to deliver an address; he was not used to it.

In the middle of his speech Roosevelt suddenly felt a sharp pain in his torso. Radiating upwards and outwards through both shoulders, it qualified as severe discomfort, but Roosevelt finished his speech anyway, then turned to his two doctors. Within the hour they had taken an EKG and performed various laboratory and clinical tests. To their relief they found "no unusual pathology."[56] Bruenn speculates the pain might have come from Roosevelt's upper-body exertion to maintain his stance in the loose fitting, now unfamiliar leg braces. In any case, subsequent tests also were negative, and as far as we know today, the pain never recurred.

From our distance it would be difficult to assert the exact cause of Roosevelt's acute pain at Bremerton, but the medical evidence now available offers some informed speculation: first, the pain could have been caused by a small tear in the aorta (an aortic aneurysm) that bled very little and sealed itself, or, secondly, Roosevelt easily might have suffered an episode of angina pectoris. Either possibility fits his known medical history; the symptomatology in any case amounted to early warning of serious trouble ahead.

Contrarily, when Roosevelt returned to the White House on August 17, McIntire was feeling cautiously optimistic about the president's recuperation from the difficult spring of 1944 and considered the incident at the Bremerton shipyards to be a simple muscle spasm. Other than that, to McIntire's knowledge, there had been no acute symptoms for almost three months. Roosevelt's blood pressure, while not normal, at least had remained fairly stable, and Roosevelt seemed less fatigued than before. McIntire continued his sanguine reports to a news-hungry but increasingly skeptical press—skeptical because Roosevelt's gaunt appearance after such long absence again had stirred uneasy rumors.[57]

The press in fact had seen very little of Mr. Roosevelt since his illness in March. He hadn't really *appeared* at the Democratic convention that renominated him, and for security reasons no one from the media had accompanied Roosevelt on his Pacific tour. When he then returned to more consistent public exposure in late August, the change in his physical appearance was quite dramatic. He actually had continued to lose weight long after Bruenn allowed the gallbladder diet to lapse, with Roosevelt by now saying he had lost his appetite. "Can't eat," he would complain. "Can't taste any food."[58]

As Roosevelt's running mate in 1944, Harry Truman did not really see much of the president, but what he did see—and hear—may have given him more forewarning than he ever let on. Truman had lunch with Roosevelt at the White House on August 18, just after Roosevelt returned from his Pacific trip following the Democratic National Convention. Reporters were waiting for Truman as he left the White House after the appointment. "He's still the leader he's always been and don't let anybody kid you about it," Truman told them. "He's keen as a briar."

But in her biography of her father, Truman's daughter Margaret says that wasn't the "whole truth," for privately Truman "was appalled by Mr. Roosevelt's physical condition." Roosevelt's hands had shaken so badly during their luncheon that he spilled most of the cream from a small pitcher into his saucer instead of pouring it into his coffee. Also, "he talked with difficulty." Truman concluded that while Roosevelt showed no signs of mental lapse, physically "he's just going to pieces." And Truman was "very much concerned." Then, too, when Truman said he was thinking of using an airplane to campaign that fall, Roosevelt "vetoed the idea." His revealing comment was: "One of us has to stay alive."

Concerned, Bruenn eliminated the digitalis treatment for a few days, aware that loss of appetite is an early sign of digitalis toxicity. When an EKG tracing showed no indication of too much digitalis, however, Bruenn resumed the heart stimulant and looked for other ways to enhance Roosevelt's nourishment.[59] Looking back now, we fairly safely can speculate that Roosevelt's anorexia was symptomatic of congestive heart failure. For that matter, his appearance was typical of patients with severe heart failure, a look known as cardiac cachexia. With his sudden weight loss, combined with the body's natural dissipation after long illness, the president looked wasted, his normally rounded features sharpened and emaciated. His gauntness was only accentuated by his refusal to buy new clothing or to have his old wardrobe tailored—Roosevelt's suits literally hung off him, and his short collar fell away from his neck.

The president of course was a public figure, albeit one with long periods spent out of the public eye. Moreover, he was a politician engaged once more in a campaign for reelection. His changed appearance did not go unnoticed. Among the first to capitalize on how he looked were Republican-leaning newspapers that now, in the heat of another losing campaign, began to cite Roosevelt's "haggard" appearance. Once again, Steve Early and his White House press aides began to counter with charges of underhanded journalism.

This time, Early's counterattacks took on a sharper tone. The charges and rumors appearing in the more antagonistic press were striking too close to the truth. For his own part Republican contender Tom Dewey never explicitly said anything about Roosevelt's state of health, but the challenger's campaign pointedly was built upon the theme of youthful, energetic leadership, and Dewey once did make reference to "tired old men" in the White House, a crack that hit close also to

Roosevelt's odd tendency to surround himself in these critical wartime years with surprisingly moribund leadership. By this time the
faithful Louis Howe had succumbed to long, terminal illness; his
replacement as right-hand man, Harry Hopkins, also was patheti-
cally sick, while several in Roosevelt's wartime cabinet were frail and
sickly men. Secretary of State Cordell Hull, for instance, had been
advised by his doctors to give up croquet, probably the most seden-
tary of all sports. Had he really researched and gone public with the
facts on the health of American leadership in those years, up to and
including Roosevelt, Dewey would have had a field day.

Steven Early, meanwhile, tried some subtle, indirect tactics to temper the doubts that *were* coming to light on occasion, but the strategy
didn't always work. The *Washington Post*, for one, resented Early's
countercampaign, not so subtle after all. "It is impossible," said the
Post editorially, "to plan a precise course which will prevent a courageous president in failing health from daring fate once more, or discourage politicians dependent on the prestige of a popular leader
from pushing an ailing man into a campaign. But at least we can
make it plain that those who ask questions shall receive answers, and
not be brushed off as malicious obstructionists."[60]

Implicit in the *Post*'s language of course (*failing health, daring
fate, ailing man*) was the widespread recognition, a public awareness, that Roosevelt was not a well man, that he at the moment was
an actuarial risk of some kind. The obvious conclusion that he might
become incapacitated or even die in a fourth term as president may
or may not have been uppermost in the American public's mind
—there is no doubt, though, that the same public had only impressions to consider and no facts.

The effort at the White House, understandably but also unfortunately, was to dispel any negative impressions abroad in the country.
As the tepid pace of the campaign began to quicken, Roosevelt himself was roused enough to shake off his previous lethargy. Seeing that
the president, angered by Republican jibes, was ready to do battle,

Steve Early and other campaign aides decided upon a frontal attack to counter the health rumors. They quickly sketched out a series of rallies giving Roosevelt heightened public exposure, and as election day drew near, their public events became more bold, more reckless. Disregarding the limits set by Roosevelt's doctors, the White House staff began arranging parades, the most daring of them to come in early November, only days before the election, in the form of an open-air cavalcade along the streets of New York City.[61]

On the morning of the great day the skies over Manhattan were dark and overcast; by noon a cold drizzle, mixed with sleet and driven by gusting winds, pelted the city streets. Amazingly, no change in plans was ordered. Roosevelt rode the length of the designated route in an open car, waving and smiling to the crowds all the way, and of course was thoroughly drenched. Roosevelt simply returned to his hotel suite, bathed, changed clothing, and in the evening delivered a major foreign policy address, apparently none the worse for the wear. As one chronicler has noted, that one performance succeeded in defusing Republican claims and innuendo meant to depict Roosevelt as an ailing president.[62]

But Early and other advisors to the president were not content to rely solely on such staged appearances in the campaign of 1944. They were also concerned with the source of the rumors about Roosevelt's health, because the reports that Early was reading in the press contained too many specifics, too much clinical detail, to be simple guesswork. Neither McIntire nor Bruenn had leaked any such information, but it was a troublesome problem, for now even Roosevelt's congressional allies were stirring uneasily in response to the health question. Early continued to release glowing reports to the press, but he also tried to investigate and pin down the source of the leaks. When the effort proved fruitless, however, he was unable to staunch the flow.[63]

Late in October Early received a substantive lead. It came in the form of a troubling letter from Breckinridge Long, assistant secretary of state, who had stumbled across some rather accurate hearsay. Just "yesterday," Long wrote, an army colonel had told him that someone at the Bethesda naval health facility had passed the word that Roosevelt "definitely has a serious heart disease." The unnamed colonel had heard the tale in just the past few days, it seems. Long added that it was none of his business to know the truth of the rumor, but he did think any military physician leaking such information should be court-martialed.[64]

Alarmed but also given an excuse to investigate more vigorously, even officially, Early now turned to the FBI, but instead of reaching the agency's director, J. Edgar Hoover, in person, Early was shunted to E. A. Tamm, Hoover's second-in-command, who seemed reluctant to cooperate. The request sounded a bit politically tinged, said Tamm, and on matters of security within army or navy ranks it was up to those branches to do their own investigating. Reluctant to try that course, Early then said the Secret Service might be the logical agency, but he left Tamm with the impression that he "had little confidence in them when it comes to investigation."[65] In any case, Tamm obviously had doubts that any federal statute had been violated, and Early had found no satisfaction with the FBI chieftain.

Whether at Early's instigation or not, State Department official Long now carried his complaint, in memo form, straight to the FBI director himself. Hoover's response was quick. Later to be noted for a fascination with White House affairs, Hoover did not in 1944 balk at the legal question raised by Tamm. Instead, he immediately made arrangements with Early to begin an investigation and composed a note for subordinate Tamm: "I have talked to Early and told him we would go ahead. Just what facts did he give you?" Clearly, Hoover thought the matter important enough, or politically expedient enough, to take on the active role of reporting developments personally to Early.[66]

Internal documents from FBI files reveal that a frenzy of activity now took place. The morning after Hoover's agreement to undertake the investigation, three FBI agents already had interviewed the mysterious Army colonel who had spoken to Long. They had to visit him at the Mayo Clinic in Rochester, Minnesota, where he was on leave. The FBI has censored specifics of that interview with the Mayo physician, but a personal summary composed by Hoover for Steve Early's benefit named Dr. Bruenn as at least one unwitting source of the Roosevelt rumors. The case that emerges is one of idle gossip among informed personnel who simply put two and two together, then indulged in speculation that was both astute and inappropriate.[67]

It happened that someone at the Bethesda facility had seen a photograph of Bruenn standing beside Roosevelt early in the summer. The navy doctor then later appeared in photos of the presidential entourage. That Bruenn was a respected cardiologist and that he had also been relieved rather suddenly of his normal duties at Bethesda were enough to give force to the rumors.[68]

In the absence of anything more specific, meanwhile, there was little Hoover or Early could do. Apparently at the press secretary's insistence, however, Hoover continued to send his agents to interrogate suspects in the medical community. The resulting reports characterized the doctors interviewed as "nervous" or "ill at ease." Several were interviewed a number of times, and Hoover's agents found what they termed "contradictory" testimony. As in most cases of gossip, though, the investigation found everybody pointing a general finger at everybody else and no one willing to swear by his own story. One particularly frustrated agent reported there was no doubt the Roosevelt story originated at Bethesda, to be "distributed as scuttlebutt gossip" by, most likely, *various* doctors. The medical center's commanding officer, said the same investigator, "should point out to members of his staff that as a matter of medical ethics, the doctors should not be engaged in discussions of this kind, and that as a matter of military discipline, they should not be engaged in backroom gossip about their Commander-in-Chief."[69] Whether because of subsequent disciplinary actions at Bethesda or because of those repeated and unsettling interviews, the overall effect of Hoover's investigation was indeed to silence the physicians' gossip.

Still, Early's public relations ploys and the FBI probe he encouraged seem in retrospect to have been excessive. Certainly the ethics and legality of using the FBI in the matter were questionable. Those issues aside, however, the intensity of the White House reaction betrayed its concern with rumors or leaks of confidential information that had political (but also, it could be argued, security) implications.

As an incumbent president during time of war, Roosevelt held considerable advantage over his challenger. But fear that Dewey might be elected, not because he was more competent but because he was healthier, seemed, by the record, all too real to Roosevelt's New Dealers. The rumor, the talk, no doubt their own asides one to the other, about the precarious state of Roosevelt's health was to them unnerving, self-perpetuating—more and more a predominant theme. Like many such things, even today, the "inside" talk *was* inside, confined largely to Washington, to political and medical circles. By the time any details filtered through the media to the general public, the gist was so muted and sketchy as to be highly doubtful.

How much did the general public really know as they went to the polls that November? In one onlooker's view, a columnist for the *Saturday Evening Post*:

> Actually, the state of Mr. Roosevelt's health was a secret from millions of Americans who voted for the President on the theory that he could reasonably be expected to live out his term in office, where he was indispensable if America was to achieve a strong and lasting peace. To be sure, some voters thought they detected signs of unfamiliar weakness in Mr. Roosevelt's radio voice. Others thought the pictures revealed signs of serious illness, but doubters were continually assured by Admiral Ross McIntire, the President's medical adviser, that his patient was "in better physical condition than the average man of his age," that his health was "good, very good," that he was in "splendid shape."[70]

Roosevelt won the election of 1944 handily, but despite the cele-
brations and brave promises of a new future, he continued to deteriorate. If, as this writer suggests, Roosevelt were "indispensable" to a
lasting peace, then hopes for that peace were being carried by a dying
man.

———

Hiding the Illness: Roosevelt, the Press, and the FBI

After the election of 1944, a worried Dr. Bruenn arranged an extended
stay for Roosevelt at his beloved Warm Springs in Georgia. The national
vote of confidence had been a brief tonic for Roosevelt, but now, just
days after the election, he was exhausted, by some accounts even
depressed.[71]

Unpredictable mood swings were a Roosevelt characteristic, as others have noted. Psychoanalytic biographer Hugh L'Etang, for instance,
has attributed Roosevelt's "buoyant self-confidence and arrogant cock-
sureness" to "euphoria resulting from cerebral degeneration."[72] The
same analyst blames a possible "cyclothymic temperament which
led to swings of mood at monthly intervals" and adds that Roosevelt
"had a distinct tendency towards depression, which was discernible
to very few people because of his ingrained ability to hide it through
his words or actions."[73]

Like any good politician, it seems, Roosevelt had the self-discipline
and the acting ability to assume a role appropriate to the occasion
before him, mood or no mood. When he was arranging a truce with a
political enemy, for example, he became the glad-handing politician
projecting an emotional appeal to his opponent, while still appearing calm and self-assured. Even with his closest advisers, Roosevelt
rarely indulged in open self-pity or like hints of melancholy. He did
present different faces, says still another historian, but more as the
function of an ebullient personality than for reasons of pathology or
political gamesmanship. "FDR's condition varied sharply from day
to day," says this source; "he always picked up and bounced back

quickly. . . . his inner vitality, even though weakened, was so radiant that, after a few moments' talk, he could make almost any visitor completely forget that he seemed ill."[74]

But now, after the 1944 election, that "inner vitality" seemed to be waning, his mood becoming more grave, more lethargic, at times grim. His anorexia was back; he now *avoided* food and rarely ate more than a bare minimum of what was set before him. Bruenn had to coax him to drink eggnogs between meals to maintain his strength. The loss of appetite was a mystery to his physicians, and Roosevelt again was losing weight.[75] He did agree to Bruenn's proposed postelection vacation at Warm Springs, however. Roosevelt arrived there on November 27 for a planned two weeks of rest and relaxation, and the change in scenery did appear to regenerate his appetite, somewhat. Still, both Bruenn and McIntire were worried about Roosevelt's persistently pale color (Bruenn called it "fair"). To increase Roosevelt's appetite, Bruenn therefore again reduced the digitalis dosage, even though tests still failed to indicate any toxicity.[76]

Another problem that Bruenn could not solve was that Roosevelt's high blood pressure did not respond to the rest therapy; at one point, following mild exercise in the pool, the reading climbed suddenly to an alarming 260/150. Thereafter, Roosevelt was prohibited from any exercise for fear it would trigger another acute episode. The vacation was not entirely a restorative success.[77]

Now, simultaneously, there came a fresh spate of rumor and speculation, fueled by Roosevelt's even more wasted appearance and by his fresh absenteeism from Washington. For unexplained reasons J. Edgar Hoover had not abandoned investigating the "leaks" about the president's health, either. Even after the election was over, FBI field agents continued to submit reports to their headquarters. While Roosevelt was resting at Warm Springs, Hoover and his men, in fact, had pieced together the newest story making the Washington rounds. The memo from Hoover to Steve Early on this subject is worth quoting here at length:

Recurrent rumors concerning the President's health are surging and echoing through Washington. The present "inside" story currently being discussed by most people, but mostly newspapermen, is alleged to emanate from "informed White House circles." The story is as follows:

Dr. William Calhoun "Pete" Sterling has established a good reputation for his surgery specializing in prostate, kidney, and similar ailments. The story states that "Pete" Sterling was recently called for an extensive examination of the President and although an operation was necessary, Dr. Sterling refused to operate because of the very bad condition of the President's health. "Pete" Sterling is alleged to have declined to operate on the grounds that the President's condition was so bad that he would probably die from the operation and Dr. Sterling did not want to jeopardize his entire future in the medical practice by being known as the man who had killed the President. Accordingly, the "White House" called into the case Dr. Frank Lahey of Boston. Dr. Lahey allegedly concluded that an operation was absolutely necessary and "the White House" decided that the operation would be performed after the Presidential election.

The story continues that the President is suffering from "Proxysmal tochycordia" [phonetic spelling—most probably Hoover meant paroxysmal tachycardia] which is described as a sudden increase in heart action which causes trembling, shaking, etc. This affliction, it is stated, frequently follows polio attacks. The rumor then outlines that Dr. Lahey was insistent that the President build up his physical condition, as a result of which the President went to Warm Springs, Georgia, for a stay of ten days, which has been lengthened to 20 days, in order to build up all possible resistance. Dr. Lahey allegedly has demanded that the operation be performed at the Lahey Clinic in Boston because it is alleged that the advertising value of his operating upon the President in Boston will be worth "millions of dollars to the Lahey Clinic." Dr. Lahey is supposed to reason that even though the operation is unsuccessful and the President dies, most people would concede that Dr. Lahey and his clinic must be pre-eminent if the President went there for an operation.[78]

For their part, neither McIntire nor Bruenn mentions any consultation with Dr. Sterling; Lahey's name does not reappear in their own accounts after his initial visit in March 1944. But the health rumors, now of morbid and sensational quality, plagued the president's front men. J. Edgar Hoover's latest summary was only confirmation of their worst fears. The situation might have been more manageable for the White House if details of Roosevelt's shaky condition really had been confined to his two official physicians. In the light of the Sterling story one instead may wonder if Bruenn and McIntire were more alarmed than their matter-of-fact memoirs suggest, if perhaps they did seek further consultation in their effort to pinpoint the etiology of Roosevelt's ailments.

Here, too, we see the conflict in priorities for Drs. McIntire and Bruenn. As conscientious doctors, they of course would have felt compelled to seek the best possible care for their patient—especially, human nature would dictate, this particular patient. At the same time, Roosevelt was not simply a patient, but president of the United States and commander-in-chief of its military forces in time of war. The loyalties tugging at his two physicians were often at odds and were never resolved. The laymen staffers of the White House, on the other hand, were not altogether wrong in fearing that the image of an ailing leader would impair major policy initiatives on both the domestic and foreign front. And so the conflicting military and political demands of the day were sometimes set against the doctors' best professional impulses.

Occasionally, the White House managed to merge the competing interests of policy and leadership versus the hidden presidential illness. At the National Naval Medical Center in Bethesda, for example, Roosevelt visited the place incognito at least twenty-nine times from 1941 to 1945. The subterfuge in Roosevelt's visits involved the use of an alias for the president on each of those occasions, yet any personnel he encountered must have realized the familiar looking, crippled man before them wasn't a "James D. Elliott" or an "F. D. Rolphe." Then, too, the disappearance of Roosevelt's medical records from that Navy facility remains unexplained even today. Recent correspondence with the chief legal officer at the National Naval Medical Center produced no trace of the records. Further, the Federal Office of Personnel Management says there are none extant for a "Mr. Roosevelt"; even invocation of the Freedom of Information Act unearthed nothing from the government under Roosevelt's own name.

What does turn up, though, is the fact that Roosevelt appeared at Bethesda as a patient twenty-nine times under as many false names. Thus, at various times, doctors at Bethesda had treated or seen a Mr. Delano, a Mr. James D. Elliott, a Ralph Frank, a Rolphe Frank, various people named Rhodes by different spellings, even a George Adams and a John Cash—all of them false names for the president of the United States. This information was obtained by use of the Freedom of Information Act; a summary of that research appears in a letter from the chief legal officer at the Naval Medical Center, Bethesda, Maryland, dated November 17, 1981. The data, however, fails to specify the dates upon which the false names were used to disguise Roosevelt's visits to the naval facility so handy to the White House.[79]

Such permutations, of course, would have made it difficult for a stray lab report or medical chart to betray Roosevelt's presence and true identity. It might even have allowed Bruenn and McIntire the flexibility to seek consultations with others of their profession. That same presidential identity, however, would have been impossible to hide altogether. Despite best efforts at secrecy, at least part of the truth would have emerged, as someone, whether a consulting physician, a nurse, an orderly, or anyone else, accidentally saw the president or took note of the unusual activity attending him under any guise. Even before Steve Early instigated the FBI operation, Dr. Lahey had been harassed by a persistent reporter from the St. Louis Post Dispatch who kept insisting that Lahey knew something.[80] The reporter of course was quite correct, but the case went unproven at the time. Given the proportions of that case, the surprise is not so much the spate of rumors, but rather the fact that the White House managed to squelch them so effectively.[81]

Neither Roosevelt nor his doctors seemed aware of the speculation on the president's health. McIntire, it appears, merely assumed such rumor-mongering was typical of what the White House insisted were the underhanded tactics of its opponents. By the end of 1944, in any case, the issue of rumor had become a minor consideration after all—the real worry now for the White House staff, doctor or layman, was whether Roosevelt would have the strength to carry out his plans for the coming term. Many of his intimates, in fact, believed the next four years would prove even more trying than the last. At that very moment, for instance, the Allied advance on Berlin had run aground in Belgium, stymied by an awesome, suicidal German counterattack costing thousands of American lives—the Battle of the Bulge. And in the Pacific, where the Japanese were being dislodged from the Philippines and most of their major southern island holdings, they still were inflicting heavy losses among the American soldiers pushing them back. Even as U.S. forces began the slow encirclement of the Japanese homeland, there remained the truly horrific question of somehow ending the war with the retreating but still implacable enemy.

At home Congress also had become a problem. The war was costing approximately $300 million a day, a staggering sum being financed by a conservative Congress that most reluctantly had been led into deficit spending.[82] As if to underscore their opposition on economic matters, the House and Senate recently had overridden Mr. Roosevelt's veto of a massive tax bill. Politically, Roosevelt's fellow Democrats knew that part of the national loyalty they commanded was a result of their successful conduct of the war, but there was no political guarantee for the postwar period. They would face an economy in inflated disarray, the great American war machine then to be shut down, the economy to be burdened at the same moment by millions of war veterans seeking civilian jobs.

With such hard facts in mind, it was the task of Bruenn, McIntire, and others to pull Roosevelt out of the depressive malaise that followed the 1944 election and help him to marshall the strength to confront the problems his recent reelection only guaranteed would be his as president.

4

Diplomacy and Failing Health

Roosevelt and the Final Decline

■■■■■ In the weeks before his fourth inauguration on January 21, 1945, Mr. Roosevelt attended a series of meetings with his cabinet and various other administration officials to map out a proposed course for his latest term in office. Thus, he met with a number of persons who hadn't seen him for a month, or longer. And their reactions now ranged from fear to outright grief.

As far back as September, journalist and future playwright Robert Sherwood had made note of being "unprepared for the almost ravaged appearance of his face."[1] Lord Moran, Winston Churchill's physician, also saw Roosevelt in September when the two world leaders conferred in Quebec, Canada. Moran at that time noted "you could have put your fist between his neck and his collar."[2]

Now, in January 1945, the reactions were more than simple apprehension for Roosevelt; they were panic over the certainty that his condition must be terminal. John Gunther, who saw the president in private just before the inauguration, wrote: "[I was] terrified when I saw his face. I felt certain that he was going to die."[3] At a subsequent cabinet meeting, Labor Secretary Frances Perkins for the first time thought he looked bad. She saw the oversized clothes, the thin face, the gray color, dull eyes. "As I sat beside him," she added, "I had a sense of his enormous fatigue. He had the pallor, the deep gray color of a man who had been long ill. He supported his head with his hand as though it were too much to hold it up. His lips were blue. His hand shook."[4]

Yet neither McIntire nor Bruenn offer such comment in their notes on that period. Perhaps their daily contact with Roosevelt somehow had inured them to his progressively wasted appearance; perhaps in their clinical observations they had lost their sense of perspective. Whatever the case, it now was Roosevelt's closest associates, previously suppressing any such worry, who suddenly came to the realization that his condition quite possibly was beyond hope. Roosevelt himself apparently sensed what was coming. On the day of his inauguration he met privately with his son James. He took the occasion to explain the terms of his will and ask his son for help in getting his papers and like affairs in order. At the end of their talk Roosevelt slipped off a family ring from his own hand and told his son to take it.[5]

The import of the ritualistic passing on of the generations was of course unsettling to the younger Roosevelt. But he tried, he later said, to believe Roosevelt simply was being prudent or overly maudlin, rather than conclude his father gently was preparing both family and self for the worst. In retrospect James felt the fourth-term campaign of 1944 "was Father's death warrant." He had seen the president only twice in recent months, once before the campaign and again on Inauguration Day. "Each time, I realized with awful irrevocable certainty that we were going to lose him."[6]

Eleanor Roosevelt, too, suddenly became very solicitous and asked those of Roosevelt's inner circle "not to push the President too hard." Previously, she had been the cause of bitter complaints by Bruenn for her insistent and inappropriate demands upon the president during his months of illness. Anna Boettinger, the president's daughter, meanwhile urged Roosevelt's doctors to make him rest more.[7]

Even as these and others saw Roosevelt failing before their eyes, it should also be noted that he was girding himself for the most demand-

ing and important war conference yet—several days of difficult negotiation with Stalin and Churchill at a small resort town in the recently
recaptured Crimea, Yalta by name. Given what we now know of Roosevelt's precarious condition, the timing and location for the conference could not have been worse. The meeting of course appeared
inescapable at the time, for both Stalin and Churchill had insisted
upon some sort of negotiations after the successful Allied landing at
Normandy the previous June; heavy on each participant's mind was
the shape of the postwar world soon to come. Churchill in particular
was concerned that an agreement with Stalin be worked out before
Berlin fell, for the prime minister had few illusions about the nature
of the Anglo-American alliance with the Soviets. Willing as he was
to permit the Russians to absorb horrendous casualties on their grim
march to Berlin, he did not want that same stoic determination to
allow Stalin too big a piece of a defeated Europe.

For his part, Stalin sought an agreement that would sanction what
his armies were about to realize: effective control over Eastern Europe.
Roosevelt, increasingly forced to play the role of peacemaker between
his British and Soviet counterparts as the war dragged on, had
begged off from a summer conference of the Big Three by claiming
his domestic duties and the 1944 election as a double excuse. Since
he and Churchill had met quietly at Quebec in September, however,
Stalin would not be content as distant spectator to any further bilat-
eral meetings.

Perhaps in deference to the Soviet ruler's sensitivities over the
Quebec session, Roosevelt allowed Stalin and his camp to chose the
site of the pending conference and to do the initial planning. Roosevelt repeatedly had invited Stalin to the United States for conference,
but the Soviet premier always had declined for reasons, ironically, of
"delicate" health. He asserted that his doctors expressly prohibited
any prolonged travel, and he in fact had suffered a heart attack a few
months earlier. But in addition, Stalin was terrified of flying and
always traveled whenever possible by car or by train.[8]

From his point of view, then, the Crimean coastal locale was ideal. Not only was the rail line from Moscow to the resort town still intact, but, further, having recently run the occupying Germans out of that Black Sea area, he would have the psychological advantage of entertaining his Allied guests on his own, freshly recaptured territory. Perhaps, too, Stalin wished to impress the leaders of two more affluent nations. The Livadia Palace, built in the opulent style of the late Romanovs, would serve as the meeting place for the plenary sessions of the Yalta Conference.

By the time the Americans realized how painfully inconvenient a location the Soviets had chosen, it appeared too late to protest, Roosevelt's own delicate condition notwithstanding—nor desirable to admit. Churchill only added to White House worries by passing along increasingly pessimistic reports from his advance men. "If we had spent ten years on research," he warned, "we could not have found a worse place in the world than Yalta . . . it is good for typhus and deadly lice which thrive in those parts."[9] The road conditions, he added, were so poor that their schedules were bound to be delayed once he and Roosevelt landed. Worse yet, the Germans had purposely infested the area with vermin prior to their departure; the town would have to be disinfected before *he* would set foot in it. Roosevelt subsequently ordered the USS *Catoctin*, a medical ship, to send delousing crews ashore to improve things somewhat.

Despite such discouragements, Roosevelt proceeded according to plan. He held a very abbreviated inaugural celebration January 21 and left two days later from Norfolk, Virginia, aboard the USS *Quincy*. The trip to Yalta took a total of twelve days: eight spent on shipboard, to the island of Malta; then a 1,200-mile flight to Saki, an isolated airfield in the Crimea; and finally the six hours it took to drive a mere eighty miles along the lone road leading to Yalta. Bruenn reports that Roosevelt managed the arduous journey well, experiencing only minor discomfort during the plane trip—again at a low ceiling (only six thousand feet this time), despite the proximity to Nazi-held territory.

Once Roosevelt arrived, though, there was again shock and consternation among those who hadn't seen him for even a short period of time. Averell Harriman, U.S. ambassador to Moscow and an advance man for the American delegation, had conferred in Washington with Roosevelt after the November elections. Now, Harriman was "terribly shocked at the change since." To him "the signs of deterioration seemed . . . unmistakable."[10] And Churchill, alarmed enough at their meeting in Quebec the previous September, now saw his old friend and compatriot in somber, elegiac light. Roosevelt of course was "ailing," and more: "His captivating smile, his gay and charming manner, had not deserted him, but his face had a transparency, an air of purification, and often there was a far-away look in his eyes."[11]

The decline in Roosevelt's health continued unabated during his stay at Yalta, an ominous venture that now seems ill-conceived. As Eleanor Roosevelt later would say, however, he saw no honorable way out of the meeting, "and when he made his mind up that he wanted to do something, he rarely gave up the idea."[12]

Bruenn continued to monitor his patient carefully, but the journey itself had left Roosevelt understandably exhausted. Then, too, upon his arrival at Yalta, he developed a racking cough that kept him awake at night. Putting aside all weariness, though, Roosevelt convened the conference as scheduled on February 4 and asked that its formal negotiations be scheduled late in the day (about 4 P.M.) and that they be limited to three hours or less. Stalin and Churchill readily agreed, yet even that abbreviated routine sapped Roosevelt's strength.[13]

Equally draining must have been the tough substance of the meeting with two powerful personalities, antagonists both abstractly and concretely. The Yalta Conference had more or less flowed into place as a rather natural progression of the worldwide war, as an attempt to tie up the loose ends in the tripartite alliance. Having nearly defeated their common enemies, the Allies no longer stood on common ground; like most political marriages, the alliance among the Soviets, the

British, and the Americans had been one of mutual convenience. Apart from the initial danger of Nazi victory, there was little that could have brought about such a coalition of disparate ideologies —one a Marxist state, one a constitutional monarchy, one a democratic republic. The ending of the Nazi menace simply unleashed old enmities that for a time had been restrained. As others have commented, differences over the conduct of the war itself—the timing of the Soviet-sought "Second Front," horrendous Russian losses, Russian designs on Poland—had sown further seeds of discontent among the Big Three.

As always, behind such abstracts were the very real and fallible men who affected events in their time. And in their own, most fallible twilight of times, when they were ailing and feeble, the problems became intractable. As the record shows, Cold War warriors in this country have long asserted that America's reputation and best interests were "sold out" at Yalta. The charge here is that Roosevelt conceded to a despot as evil as Hitler all the fruits of victory in Europe for which so many Americans had given their lives. In the test of wills at Yalta, these critics say, Roosevelt was found wanting. Others, wishing to be kinder, temper that criticism with the reminder that Roosevelt was a sick man who should not have been negotiating with Stalin in the first place. There were, however, other factors too.

When Roosevelt opened the Yalta negotiations, circumstances in the American camp could not have been worse. Roosevelt himself was now a dying man. He had been suffering from unrelieved hypertensive heart disease since at least 1941, when his symptoms of diastolic hypertension first appeared, as far as we know today. Further, his illness had been in an acute phase for at least a year. His blood pressure remained fatally high, despite Dr. Bruenn's alleviation of the most painful symptoms. The president's illness was complicated by an assortment of other problems: chronic respiratory infections, gastric disturbances, congestive heart failure, and, as a fault of the very office he held, lack of opportunity to take the prolonged rest he needed to ease the stresses and anxieties exacerbating his condition. Add, too, the remote location of the Yalta summit—the trip itself would have been overly taxing and ill-advised for anyone as fragile as Roosevelt.

The presidential entourage included another extremely sick man, Harry Hopkins, right-hand man to the president. A victim for a startling number of years of what had been diagnosed as stomach cancer, Hopkins by all rights should have been dead. His own gaunt appearance by the final months of 1944 left any observer pained to see him. His doctors at the Mayo Clinic in Rochester, Minnesota, had long been predicting his death and had urged him to rest and make himself as comfortable as possible. But the peripatetic man's devotion to Roosevelt, and Roosevelt's own well-timed requests for his help, had kept Harry Hopkins in service. For the trip to Yalta, Hopkins literally was carried from his bed and spent the entire travel time in prone position.[14]

As an added aggravation, Roosevelt arrived at Yalta with a brand new secretary of state. Edward Stettinius, formerly lend-lease administrator and undersecretary of state, had succeeded the moribund Cordell Hull and had held the nation's top foreign policy post for only a few weeks before the important Yalta meeting.

The Americans were handicapped also by their own misperception of both the Soviets and the British. Unbelievable as it may seem today, pollster George Gallup in 1945 conducted and gave the White House a secret sampling of popular opinion that purported to show that Americans held the Soviets in greater esteem than they did the British. In the American mind the Soviets had shown greater valor, had lost more lives, than the British, and it seemed to them only fair that the Russians should be more highly rewarded. So the opinion poll went, providing evidence of a sort for Roosevelt's long-held view that the British historically were incorrigible land-grabbers, a people who could not repress the imperialistic instinct. Roosevelt expressed the very same sentiment to Churchill as early as 1941 in their secret "Atlantic Charter" meeting in the Bay of Argentia. The

old days of European empire-building, Roosevelt had told the star-
tled prime minister, must come to an end. Now, in 1945, it seemed to
Roosevelt that the American people agreed with him.[15]

Still, Roosevelt did not enter the halls of the Livadia Palace entirely
bereft of suspicion about Soviet intentions. He knew full well the
totalitarian nature of their society. But Roosevelt felt that reason, dialogue, and negotiation would make the Soviets see that their security
was best achieved by cooperation with the other two world powers
sitting at the Yalta table. His attitude, naive or not, was indicated in a
private letter sent to Harold Laski, the noted London School of Economics professor, just before the Crimean conference began. "I am
inclined to think," wrote Roosevelt, "that at the meeting with Marshall Stalin and the Prime Minister I can put things on a somewhat
higher level than they have been for the past two or three months."[16]

In addition to his own optimism Roosevelt also had the invariably
enthusiastic reports on the Soviets from Harry Hopkins, who early in
the war had visited and negotiated with Stalin in Moscow as an
emissary for Roosevelt. By Hopkins's inordinately rosy view, expressed
as assurances to Roosevelt, the Soviets would cooperate if the American side simply demonstrated goodwill.

While the agenda for Yalta was open-ended and conceivably would
encompass the entire globe, Roosevelt went to the meeting intent on
three goals: an agreement on a postwar international security organization (the United Nations), a settlement on the boundaries and governmental structure of Poland, and an assurance from the Soviets
that they would enter the war against Japan after the Nazis had been
defeated. Of those three goals it was the nascent United Nations that
held top priority for Roosevelt. Despite failure in the Wilson era to
construct just such a peacekeeping organization, and despite Roosevelt's own misgivings about the real intentions of both Allies at Yalta,
he still felt, as he had told Laski, that he could persuade Stalin and
Churchill to overcome their self-interest and seek the common good.

In any case, the Big Three now haggled over details of their postwar visions for seven days. Roosevelt at the outset won Stalin's concession on creation of the United Nations. Of course, the Soviet leader had said, how could anybody oppose such a well-meaning plan? But almost as quickly he said that each of the USSR's "autonomous" republics should be given a vote of its own. Understandably aghast, Churchill countered that if the Soviets were granted one vote per republic, then the United Kingdom should get a vote each for her many dominions. An aide to Roosevelt wryly remarked that similar logic would give the United States forty-eight votes—one for each state. Roosevelt finally negotiated Stalin down to three votes: one for the Soviet Union proper, and one each for the republics of Byelorussia and the Ukraine. After all, maintained Stalin, they had "bled so much" during the war.

On the second question, the war against Japan, Roosevelt had even less trouble convincing Joseph Stalin. As early as 1943, when the Soviets were pressing for an Allied second front, Stalin had casually remarked to a visiting Cordell Hull that the USSR naturally would want to participate in the struggle against the Japanese enemy to the east—and thus reclaim territory lost at the time of Japan's surprise attack at Port Arthur in 1905. In order to consolidate Stalin's agreement now, though, Roosevelt felt constrained to concede a Soviet "interest" in the Kuril Islands in the Pacific, a concession that left the smarting Churchill wondering who indeed was the real imperialist. As events later played out, of course, the Soviet Union indulged in a last minute declaration of war against Japan, contributed practically nothing to that war effort, and yet claimed its spoils of war.

It was the final issue, the sovereignty of Poland, over which the Big Three argued most vehemently at Yalta. For the British the Polish issue was not only one of national security but, as Churchill put it, a matter of honor. It had been the German invasion of Poland that brought England into the war in the first place. Moreover, while awaiting the day of victory, a Polish government-in-exile operated from London under British protection and also bravely shared in the

Allied war effort in Europe. Churchill had come to know and respect the ousted government's leaders, who were widely considered true Polish patriots. For Stalin, however, the question was both more simple and more complex. In the early days of the war, for instance, his own Soviet Union had joined Adolf Hitler in the rape of Poland, a partnership dissolved only when the führer then turned on Russia. Now, in the closing days of the same war, Stalin had no interest in honor or ties to Poland, but rather in his own country's security. For years the contiguous Polish landmass had been a corridor through which Russia's enemies had crossed to attack from the west. Now Stalin would have a friendly and docile government ruling a subservient Poland that would serve as a buffer zone for the USSR. To this end he had his own select government of exiles waiting in the wings at Lublin. The moment the Nazis were driven from Poland, Stalin fully intended to install his well-trained cadre as a puppet regime.

He of course did not use quite the same terminology, but Stalin obviously had come to Yalta determined to have his way on Poland. For three grueling days of negotiation, Churchill and Roosevelt debated the issue with the Soviet premier; what they got for their pains was only a paper concession: the London government-in-waiting was out, and the Lublin group was in. But, the signed papers said, the latter would be reorganized "on a broader democratic basis." Just what that basis would be was left unstated, as many in attendance naturally noted. For one, Admiral William Leahy, Roosevelt's attaché, remarked, "Mr. President, this is so elastic that the Russians can stretch it all the way from Yalta to Washington without even technically breaking [it]." Roosevelt acknowledged the point but wearily added, "it's the best I can do for Poland at this time."[17]

Home to Rest and Recuperate

Four days after the initial negotiating session at Yalta, Roosevelt returned to his quarters in the Crimean resort town "obviously greatly fatigued," according to Bruenn.[18] That was the day the Big Three had begun their difficult bargaining over a distantly supine Poland, a debate that soon degenerated into acrid argument between Churchill and Stalin. Roosevelt vainly tried to maintain a semblance of Allied goodwill, but the powerful personalities of his two companions refused to be placated.[19]

After the day's "arduous . . . and emotionally disturbing conference," says Bruenn, Roosevelt's color had faded, and for the first time he exhibited *pulsus alternans*, or irregular pulse.[20] On that alarming note Bruenn restricted Roosevelt to bed all the next morning, a development that curtailed Roosevelt's already trimmed-back planning sessions with his aides. The White House doctor also insisted that his ward should take an hour's nap in the afternoon, thus limiting the time available for preparation or strategy meetings before Roosevelt rejoined Stalin and Churchill for their daily plenary sessions.

The question still lingering is how greatly did Roosevelt's weakening condition affect his part in the negotiations and, ergo, their ultimate outcome? Was his illness associative or causative? No one can ever be sure, but even if Roosevelt indeed had "reached the limit of his negotiating powers," as historian James McGregor Burns suggests, Stalin held all the cards. His armies occupied the whole of eastern Europe, and more than either Churchill or Roosevelt, the Russian ruler was willing to absorb drastically high casualties to purchase land. This ruthless tactic may have wiped out a generation of Soviet youth, but it did have its benefits, the most obvious of which Stalin was reaping at Yalta, whether his partner Allies liked it or not.[21]

According to U.S. diplomat William Bullitt, Roosevelt did not operate from naïveté, ignorance, perfidy, or illness at Yalta, but rather "from acceptance of the facts." In Bullitt's view, "Russia occupied Poland. Russia distrusted its Western Allies. Russia had a million men who could fight Japan. Russia could sabotage the new peace organization [the United Nations]. And Russia was absolutely determined about Poland and always had been."[22] Yet the testimony by principals of the day tends, in sum, to be ambivalent, even conflicting. If Stalin indeed were in the stronger bargaining position, Roosevelt still seemed strangely reluctant to challenge points that remained contestable.

Again, there was a litany of shocked reaction among those thrown into Roosevelt's company. Anthony Eden, who met Roosevelt at Malta as the latter was en route to the Crimea, was among those stunned by the president's appearance. "The President gives the impression of failing powers," Eden later recalled with characteristic reserve. Lord Moran, Winston Churchill's own physician, saw Roosevelt at the same time and made the out-of-hand diagnosis of hardening of the arteries. Churchill himself of course had noted Roosevelt's vacant, faraway gaze.[23] Bruenn, however, contended that his patient was fully in command of his faculties, though tired—tired enough for prescribed rest periods during the day.[24] Eden, for his part, later conceded that Roosevelt was alert and in control during the afternoon sessions at Yalta. Moreover, the four American negotiators to whom Roosevelt most often turned for advice—Byrnes, Stettinius, Leahy, and Harriman—all assert that Roosevelt was his usual skillful self during the meetings, although Byrnes does mention alarm over Roosevelt's quivering hands and white face.

As for the ailing Hopkins, who was present for all the Yalta sessions, little is known of his interaction with his almost equally ailing chief. Perhaps due to his own fatigue, he never intervened formally, but there nonetheless are clues to his continuing and well-documented influence on Roosevelt. At one point, for instance, the Soviets were talking about forced reparations to be paid by the soon-to-be-defeated Germany, and the British were objecting to Stalin's astronomical demands. The implications turned ugly when Stalin then suggested repayment by labor—that is, by conscripting thousands of German citizens to work in the Soviet Union after the war. Churchill intimated that Stalin thus would revive slavery, and in moments it would be Roosevelt's turn to react to still another fight among the Allies. Before Roosevelt could intervene, however, Hopkins slipped him a note warning, "The Russians have given in so much at this conference that I don't think we should let them down." Hopkins also advised: "Let the British disagree if they want to—and continue their disagreement at Moscow. Simply say it is all referred to the Reparations Commission." And so it was that Stalin's outrageous demand went uncontested by the American delegation, although the Soviet position sent Churchill into a livid rage, euphemistically recorded in the minutes of Yalta as a British "objection."[25]

At another point, when Roosevelt expressed doubts as to Stalin's willingness to cooperate, Hopkins assured: "We can do business with Stalin. He will cooperate." Arguably enough, given the superior Soviet military position, perhaps there really was little Roosevelt could exact from Stalin, but he often cited Hopkins in justification of a belief that Stalin could be trusted. To Bullitt, practical in his summary of the facts but also a viscerally anti-Soviet diplomat, Roosevelt once submitted that he would not dispute Bullitt's facts or his logic. Beyond those, however, Roosevelt said it was his "hunch" that Stalin was not "that kind of man." Said Roosevelt, too: "Harry [Hopkins] says he's not and that he doesn't want anything but security for his country, and I think that if I give him everything I possibly can and ask nothing from him in return, 'noblesse oblige,' he won't try to annex anything and will work with me for a world of democracy and peace."[26]

While Bullitt surely must have blanched at such a blissful view, it may be that Roosevelt was playing the consummate politician, assuring a constituent that the agreements were drawn up by gentlemen and thus should be honored. It may be, too, that Roosevelt could not quite admit that American military strategy had left the Soviets in a position to dictate the terms of peace in Europe. Yet it could be maintained that because of Roosevelt's failure to coordinate military and foreign policy throughout the war, events indeed had led to the unhappy imbalance so evident at Yalta.

President Wilson and Mrs. Wilson, 1921. Note Mr. Wilson's clenched left fist, as well as the slight droop in the left side of his face. *(Courtesy of Firestone Library, Princeton University)*

Jim Farley, Harry Hopkins, and President Roosevelt, circa 1940. (*Courtesy of Franklin D. Roosevelt Library*)

Franklin D. Roosevelt returns to the White House with Mrs. Roosevelt after the third inaugural, January 20, 1941. *(Courtesy of Franklin D. Roosevelt Library)*

Roosevelt in joint press conference with Winston Churchill, Washington, D.C., December 23, 1941. *(By permission of United Press International)*

Roosevelt after addressing the Foreign Policy Association, with William
Lancaster, association chairman; Secretary of War Henry L. Stimson;
Secretary of the Navy James V. Forrestal; UNRRA Director General Herbert
H. Lehman, New York City, October 21, 1944. *(Courtesy of Franklin
D. Roosevelt Library)*

Roosevelt makes a point to Churchill at Yalta. (*Courtesy of Franklin D. Roosevelt Library*)

JAMES E. PAULLIN, M. D.
WILLIAM R. MINNICH, M. D.
CHRISTOPHER J. McLOUGHLIN, M. D.
WILLIAM L. PAULLIN, JR., M. D.
1010 MEDICAL ARTS BUILDING
ATLANTA 3, GEORGIA

May 25, 1951

Dr. Albert S. McCown, Director
Communicable Disease Control
Department of Health
Richmond 19, Virginia

Dear Dr. McCown:

In reply to your letter of May 23 I wish to say that the facts concerning
the illness and death of President Franklin D. Roosevelt are already published and well documented.

He was first seen by me April 2, 1944 in consultation with Dr. Ross
McIntire. The diagnoses on him at that time were: Essential hypertension
with arteriosclerosis. The hypertension was variable. He had some EKG
evidence of coronary artery disease, and some evidence of cardiac enlargement. There was some evidence of sinus infection and bronchial irritation
which caused most of his symptoms at that time.

As you probably know, the demands on Mr. Roosevelt at this time, together
with the tremendous load and burden which he was carrying as a result of
World War II and his efforts to get the United Nations going, demanded
more of him than most any human being could possibly stand, irrespective
of his disposition or his desires.

I saw The President two or three times after this. The last time I saw
him was April 12, 1945, when Admiral McIntire called and asked me to go
at once to see him at Warm Springs, Georgia. As soon as the message came
through from Admiral McIntire I left my office in the Medical Arts Building at 2:00 o'clock, and at exactly 3:28 P.M. drove up in front of the
Little White House at Warm Springs. I went immediately to the room where
The President was seriously ill. In the room at the time, and working
with him, were Dr. Howard G. Bruenn, Lt. Commander Fox, and The President's
valet. He was in extremis when I arrived. His pulse was barely perceptible.
Heart sounds could be heard. About three and one-half minutes after my arrival his heart stopped beating. Within five minutes after my arrival in
the room all evidence of life had passed. At 3:35 P.M., EST, Dr. Bruenn
and I announced his death to his cousins.

From the history, the observations of Dr. Bruenn during this attack, and
the physical findings, it was our considered opinion that Mr. Roosevelt
undoubtedly died of massive cerebral hemorrhage. There were no available
facilities at Warm Springs Foundation for performing an autopsy, and since
The President had expressed a wish to Miss Delano, his cousin, that he
did not wish to be embalmed, I felt there was nothing that we could do
until the arrival of Mrs. Roosevelt.

Letter from Dr. James E. Paullin to Dr. Albert S. McCown concerning
Roosevelt's death

In reviewing my connection with the case, the surprising thing to me is that the man could absorb as much punishment as he did during the years he was President of the United States without having had some accident related to his arterial system long before he did. The tension under which he lived, the great responsibility which he assumed, and of which he was constantly conscious, would have been enough within itself to raise the blood pressure of any normal human being tremendously.

These are the facts concerning the death of Mr. Roosevelt. I was present at the time of his death. I personally examined him, and I know that rumors which have been circulated concerning him are absolutely false in every respect.

I do not feel in giving you this information that I have violated any of the relationships which existed between doctor and patient. As a matter of fact, on December 12, 1949, Mrs. Eleanor Roosevelt gave me permission to discuss the last illness of President Roosevelt with Mr. John Gunther, and I see no reason why this should not apply to you.

With my kindest regards and best wishes, I beg to remain

Very cordially yours,

James E. Paullin, M. D.

JEP:iss

In June 1944, at the Chelsea Naval Hospital prior to back operation, Jack Kennedy receives Navy and Marine Corps Medal from Captain F. L. Conklin. *(Courtesy of John F. Kennedy Library)*

September 1946: the VFW encampment, Boston. *Left to right*: Mayor James
M. Curley, Governor Maurice Tobin, Jack Kennedy. *(Courtesy of Boston
Public Library, Print Department)*
This political pose, February 10, 1948, shows a sickly looking Jack Kennedy
five months after the onset of Addison's disease. *(Courtesy of John F.
Kennedy Library)*

Marching in the parade. Note that Jack is carrying, not wearing, his hat. After the parade, he collapses. *(Courtesy of John F. Kennedy Library)*

President John F. Kennedy addresses the nation on the Cuban missile crisis, October 1962. *(Courtesy of John F. Kennedy Library)*

How much Roosevelt's precarious health added to that imbalance is a matter, again, of conflicting testimony and conjecture. Bullitt himself would claim in 1948 that a doddering, moribund Roosevelt had capitulated to a strong, healthy Stalin at Yalta. Bullitt and many others, rising in shocked complaint in the early Cold War years of Soviet intransigence, would depict an ailing leader in such physical and mental decline that he weakly condoned the transfer of a portion of Europe from one totalitarian regime to another.[27]

At the conclusion of the Yalta Conference on February 11, 1945, Roosevelt boarded his navy ship but, surprisingly enough in the light of his frail health, did not proceed directly back to the United States. Instead, he detoured to Great Bitter Lake near Ismailia, Egypt, for a series of meetings with King Farouk of Egypt, Emperor Haile Selassie of Ethiopia, and Ibn Saud, monarch of Saudi Arabia. Roosevelt then went to nearby Alexandria, where he again met briefly with Churchill, without Joseph Stalin's brooding presence, then moved on to Algiers, where he hoped to confer with the exiled French General Charles de Gaulle, who pointedly declined to make his appearance in response to Roosevelt's invitation.

When the president at last returned to Washington from his exhausting trip, he still had to address a joint session of Congress to announce the agreements reached at Yalta. And now, for the first time in his long presidency, Roosevelt spoke to Congress while seated, his wan joke being that he was tired from carrying "so much metal" on his crippled legs.[28]

That uncharacteristic reference to his polio was by itself disquieting to any inveterate Roosevelt-watcher. Coupled with his seated delivery and the feeble, hesitant tone of his voice, though, it contributed to a picture that left many in the chamber dismayed. A few days later the Canadian prime minister, Mackenzie King, met with Roosevelt in Washington, later to comment: "My old friend looked so badly, so haggard and worn, that I almost sobbed."[29]

Harry Truman was another who noticed how badly Roosevelt looked as he reported to Congress on his negotiations at Yalta. Just a few days before, in fact, Truman had been badly shaken by a rumor in Washington that Roosevelt had died aboard the USS *Quincy* en route home from Yalta. Actually, Roosevelt's appointments secretary, Major General Edwin M. Watson, died at sea while traveling with the presidential party.

Margaret Truman noted that Roosevelt looked "terribly weary" in his appearance before Congress; his speech was "lifeless and rambling." The report did not add much to what already had been carried in the press, and not even Truman "could bring himself to comment favorably" upon the Yalta speech, she says. "He had to resort to sarcasm, when some friendly reporters caught him in the hall just after the joint session of Congress adjourned." When the reporters asked Truman what he thought of the speech, he said: "One of the greatest ever given." He then "joined the reporters in hearty laughter."

Clearly any astute reporter had more than a fair impression of Roosevelt's condition by this time, if not long before. Just a few weeks later, Truman and Roosevelt sat in full view at the head table for the annual dinner of the White House Correspondents Association. "Like everyone else," writes Margaret, "he [Truman] was appalled by how bad Mr. Roosevelt looked and even more alarmed by his dazed, vacant manner."

And so resumed the pattern of Roosevelt's final years in the White House. Robert Murphy, a State Department specialist on Middle Eastern affairs, was called into Roosevelt's presence on March 12 for consultation, and Roosevelt apparently sensed Murphy's shock. According to Murphy, the president said he was "aware of how badly he looked and mentioned he had lost 36 pounds."[30] By the end of the same month Bruenn was ready to concede the worst. Roosevelt's dramatic recoveries were becoming sporadic by now and in fact were markedly feeble. On some evenings he would rally briefly, regain his color, work as if driven, then slump into a state of enervation, listless-ness and inattentiveness. Bruenn determined upon one last attempt to help the president recuperate: since the San Francisco conference that would give birth to the United Nations was pending, Roosevelt could work on his keynote address while he rested at his beloved Warm Springs. Roosevelt agreed and accordingly left Washington on March 29, 1945.

Warm Springs and President Roosevelt's Final Days

Few people actually *plan* to die, and in the spring of 1945 Franklin Delano Roosevelt was no exception. Roosevelt went to Warm Springs for two weeks of rest; he also went to work at a somewhat leisurely pace upon his keynote address. And his heartfelt vision surely was a comprehensive, lasting global peace plan, with a legislative world body in place to settle or smooth over friction among its member states. It was a vision Wilsonian in origin, but Roosevelt was determined to see *his* generation's "league of nations" actually take hold. By all accounts of those around him, he was determined to pursue the goal of lasting peace, to make *this* league work.

In short, Roosevelt acted the part of a man with a future. And the public could be excused for sharing that view; not only did the public at large lack direct exposure to the terribly gaunt president, but his own doctor, Admiral McIntire, invariably tended to describe the president's health in positive terms. Looking back on Roosevelt's last twenty-eight months of life, unbelievably, McIntire later would write: "For a man of 62-plus, we had very little to complain about."[31]

On the other hand, a fact of course unknown at the time, Roosevelt had held his disturbing private session with son James on January 21, 1945, in which he explained the terms of his will and gave his son a family ring from his own hand. Another incident was also widely unknown: a detail of Secret Service agents mysteriously appeared on Vice President Harry S. Truman's trail shortly before

Roosevelt left Washington for Warm Springs on March 29. Truman, in typically direct and earthy fashion, asked, "What in the hell are they doing here?"[32]

It was a fair question because no other vice president in the nation's history had been accorded round-the-clock protection. It remains a question today because Secret Service records are embargoed by a seventy-five-year seal against public disclosure. On file at the Truman Library in Kansas, however, is an interview with Harry Vaughn, one of Truman's closest aides, and in it Vaughn insists the agents simply appeared one day and gave no explanation for their presence.

Margaret Truman tells the story a bit differently in her biography of her father, although the point remains the same. By her version Vice President Truman noticed that a young man had been sitting outside his small office in the Capitol for most of one day. "Who is that young fellow?" Truman finally asked his aide, General Vaughn. "Does he want to see me?" Vaugh replied no, that the young man was from the Secret Service. "Well, what the hell is this?" said Truman. "When did this happen?' Vaughn then told him, without elaboration, that he had been there a day or two.

According to Truman's daughter, though, the idea was Vaughn's own and not that of the White House. "Looking over Dad's security arrangements and knowing President Roosevelt's precarious health," she writes, "General Vaughn was appalled." He arranged a small Secret Service detail for the vice president by broaching the subject to Treasury Secretary Henry Morgenthau, who agreed that it was incongruous to have seventy-five to a hundred agents guarding the president and none protecting his next-in-line. Three men then were detailed as Truman's own entourage.

At Warm Springs, meanwhile, the two-week rest period began in a funereal atmosphere, although the entourage with Roosevelt tried to maintain an air of routine. In fact, there was a routine—the president underwent examination by Bruenn in the mornings, worked briefly, then had lunch and spent the afternoon sunning himself or floating passively in the swimming pool. Those around Roosevelt went about their normal business, the topic of the president himself discussed only in hushed, hesitant conversation. One who broke that unspoken rule was presidential aide William Hassett, who on the evening of March 30 directly confronted Howard Bruenn on the health issue. "He is slipping away from us and no earthly power can keep him here," said Hassett.[33] "Why do you think so?" replied Bruenn, apparently choosing his words with care. Hassett, according to his own diary entry of that night, then told the Navy doctor he understood his obligation to save life and not to admit defeat. "Then I reminded him that I gave him the same warning when we were here last December. He remembered."

Hassett now pressed further. "I know you don't want to make the admission, and I have talked this way with no one else save one. To all the staff, to the family, and with the Boss himself I have maintained the bluff, but I am convinced that there is no help for him."[34] By this point Bruenn had become "very serious," and Hassett noted that "we were both on the verge of emotional upset."

Bruenn, in fact, finally admitted to Hassett that there was "cause for alarm," an uncharacteristic display of pessimism for the Navy doctor. But he also said the situation was not hopeless, if "measures were adapted to rescue him [Roosevelt] from emotional influences, which he mentioned." Hassett does not reveal what those emotional strains might have been, but he does cite his own warning that those conditions "could not be met and [I] added that this talk confirmed my conviction that the Boss is leaving us."[35]

Thus besieged, Bruenn would spend the next ten days or so gingerly treating Roosevelt, screening guests and visitors, making certain that his patient was given time to relax and rest. In spite of Hassett's dire predictions, Roosevelt again began dramatic improvement. Within a week of their arrival at Warm Springs, noted Bruenn, "there was a decided and obvious improvement in his appearance and sense of well-being."[36] He even took hope from these signs:

having weathered the worst strains of the past year, perhaps Roosevelt indeed was making a belated recovery.

By April 10, Bruenn wrote in his notes, the improvement only continued. His patient's color was "much better"; Roosevelt's appetite was "very good," and the president was asking for double helpings of his food. He had not been weighed for a time, but he appeared to have gained "a little weight." He rested well, and he increased his activities somewhat. Perhaps most heartening: "He was in excellent spirits and began to plan a weekend, involving a barbecue and attendance at a minstrel show."[37]

The world outside Warm Springs refused to hold still for Roosevelt's benefit, however. With the Crimean dust of Yalta still on his traveling shoes, he already was receiving disturbing reports on Soviet conduct in Poland. The "elections" the Russians and their Lublin cohorts were staging amounted to an unmitigated sham, and protests by official American observers seemed to have no effect on the communists. Churchill repeatedly cabled his objections to Roosevelt, hoping to rouse him to action. And those entreaties in fact did have some effect: Roosevelt went so far as to compose a sharp letter to Stalin. It was ready to go out from the "Little White House," the six-room clapboard cottage FDR occupied two miles from the Warm Springs Foundation.

As another chore, Roosevelt was scheduled to deliver a Jefferson Day address to the nation by radio on April 13, now looming. Harry Truman, taking time off from his duties as presiding officer of the Senate, would say a few words of his own, then introduce Roosevelt.

On April 12 Roosevelt awoke in Warm Springs to an easy morning —the morning mail would not be in until about noon because bad weather had grounded the courier plane from Washington. Upon awakening, he complained of a slight headache, which was relieved when Bruenn gave him a light massage. He stayed in bed and browsed lazily through the *Atlanta Constitution*. But, historian John Toland later wrote, Roosevelt told an elderly maid entering his bedroom, "I don't feel any too good this morning." By late morning he was fully dressed in a dark suit, vest, and red Harvard tie, despite his preference for a bow tie and no vest. The reason was his appointment at midday to sit for a portrait by Elizabeth Shoumatoff.

As the morning proceeded, Bruenn called McIntire in Washington and told him that Roosevelt continued to do well. The subject of their conversation, meanwhile, was ensconced in a leather armchair while having amiable conversation with a pair of cousins, Margaret Suckley and Laura Delano. Hassett broke in with outgoing mail needing the presidential signature, and Roosevelt made a small joke about two of his chores. "Here's where I make law," he said at one point. A missive prepared by the State Department also caught his attention. "A typical State Department letter," he said. "It says nothing at all."[38]

Just before lunch, Roosevelt began sitting for his portrait while still perusing his paperwork. The artist set up her easel near the windows; the plan was to present the painting to Mrs. Rutherford's daughter. Miss Shoumatoff settled a cape of navy blue about Roosevelt's shoulders, then began her work.

At 1 P.M. Roosevelt warned that they had only fifteen minutes left for the sitting. As a few more minutes passed, his cousin Miss Suckley crocheted. Miss Delano filled vases with flowers, and Roosevelt lighted a cigarette. He suddenly looked up and began to vigorously rub his forehead. The hand fell. Miss Suckley asked if he had dropped something. He groaned and slumped over, his head on his desk. He managed to say, "I've got a terrific headache." He then fell unconscious.[39] Prettyman and another aide carried FDR to his bed while an urgent call went out to Dr. Bruenn, who was swimming in the nearby pool. It was just about 1:15 P.M.[40]

When Bruenn arrived minutes later, Roosevelt was unconscious, "pale, cold, and sweating profusely." Within minutes, too, the pupils of his eyes became unequal, the right one widely dilated. Roosevelt's blood pressure had shot up to 300/190, and Bruenn was unable to stimulate any reflex reactions. His breathing was heavy and his pulse rate was 104.[41]

Bruenn quickly injected Roosevelt with papavarine and amyl nitrate to "relieve the apparent intense vasoconstriction." But cursory examination confirmed the obvious—Roosevelt had suffered a massive cerebral hemorrhage; the long-awaited catastrophe had struck.[42]

Minutes later, at 2:05 P.M., Bruenn telephoned McIntire in Washington with the dreaded news. McIntire gave no medical orders but told Bruenn that he would tell Dr. Paullin at Emory University in Atlanta to proceed quickly to Warm Springs. Meanwhile, Laura Delano called Eleanor Roosevelt at the White House to report that Roosevelt had fainted; moments later, McIntire also called Eleanor to suggest they both go to Warm Springs that evening but to stick to her standing schedule in the meantime to avoid comment. He also told her he was not alarmed. Harry Truman, an afternoon session of the Senate still ahead of him, had no idea of the developments in Warm Springs. He would while away his time during one boring speech by jotting a note at his desk to his mother and sister.

In Georgia Dr. Paullin set off at best possible speed for Warm Springs over back roads he knew well, while Bruenn continued to tend his patient as best he could. Bruenn later chronicled his bedside watch with clinical thoroughness:

2:45 P.M.:   Color was much improved. Breathing was a little irregular and stertorous, but deep. Blood pressure had fallen to 240/120 mm Hg. Heart sounds were good—rate, 90/min.

3:15 P.M.:   Blood pressure was 210/110 mm Hg; heart rate, 96/min; right pupil, still widely dilated, but the left pupil, from moderate constriction, had become moderately dilated. Occasional spasms of rigidity with marked slowing of respiration was noted. During latter phases, he had become cyanotic.

3:30 P.M.:   Pupils were approximately equal. Breathing had become irregular but of good amplitude.

3:31 P.M.:   Breathing suddenly stopped and was replaced by occasional gasps. Heart sounds were not audible. Artificial respiration was begun and caffeine sodium benzoate given intramuscularly. At this moment Dr. Paullin arrived from Atlanta. Adrenalin was administered into the heart muscle.

3:35 P.M.:   I pronounce him dead.[43]

―――

Roosevelt's Death: The Political and Medical Postmortem

The time of Roosevelt's death was measured by Central time; in Washington the moment was 4:35 P.M. Eleanor Roosevelt, his widow now, was dutifully attending a thrift shop benefit at the Sulgrave Club, her public schedule still safely intact. She was at the head table, a piano recital in progress.

At 4:50 she was called to the telephone. It was Steve Early, clearly agitated as he said, "Come home at once." Eleanor did not ask why or for details; she knew "something dreadful had happened." Still, she went through the motions of returning to her group, applauding the pianist, and then making her excuses in order to leave.

In her sitting room at the White House, Early and McIntire together told her of Roosevelt's death. She sent immediately for Harry Truman. Upon his arrival at the White House at 5:25 P.M., Eleanor Roosevelt informed the vice president that the president was dead.[44]

In Warm Springs Roosevelt's staff quietly collected themselves and tried to make order of chaos in the Little White House; the atmosphere of course was one of numbing grief. In the evening both Eleanor Roosevelt and Dr. McIntire arrived; she then spent a few minutes alone with her husband's body. Minutes later, she spoke to Bruenn about the next steps—a train would carry Roosevelt to Washington one last time for funeral services at the White House. Eleanor insisted that Bruenn should not perform an autopsy. He apparently did not challenge her wishes but did arrange to have the body embalmed. The irregularity of that omission troubled Bruenn (and, incidentally, Joseph Stalin, who from afar insisted on autopsy to rule out the possibility of foul play). By the time the issue was settled Harry S. Truman already had been sworn in as president of the United States. That event took place a few minutes after 7 P.M., Eastern time, in the White House; Chief Justice Harlan Stone conducted Truman's swearing-in.

In London, meanwhile, the news of Roosevelt's death struck Churchill "a physical blow" and left him feeling "overpowered by a sense of deep and irreparable loss." In the enemy capital of Berlin, Goebbels excitedly called Hitler about midnight, local time. "I congratulate you!" he exclaimed. "Roosevelt is dead." In Japan, oddly, Prime Minister (Admiral) Kantaro Suzuki spoke of "profound sympathy" for the American people in their loss of a leader who could take credit for "the Americans' advantageous position today."[45]

Expressions of grief from all quarters were, in large part, the result of the unexpectedness of the event—and they were extraordinary. In the Soviet Union the hammer-and-sickle flag was bordered in black and lowered to half-mast. The English Royal Court went into an uncharacteristic seven days of mourning. The Vatican sent the Sistine Choir to the American Church of Santa Susanna in Rome to chant the Requiem Mass. Churchill roused himself to go before Parliament; in a shaky voice he declared Roosevelt's death "an unparalleled tragedy." Roosevelt's planned sharp rebuke to Stalin, however, was never sent after its composition during the last days at Warm Springs.

It may seem ironic, but in the same edition of the *New York Times* that carried the voices of grief and shock over Roosevelt's "sudden" demise, an interesting article lay buried under the headline: "Roosevelt Health Long in Doubt." The story itself reported various, apparently long-standing "rumors" about Roosevelt's health. The sources of those rumors turned out to be none other than veteran White House correspondents, who now were willing to say things like, "Others have seen Mr. Roosevelt appear to decline more in the last year and a half than might be attributable to his advancing age."[46] But *facts* about Roosevelt's health, the same newspaper story said, came only from Admiral Ross T. McIntire, the president's personal physician. And he, until virtually the very end, had insisted Roosevelt was in relatively good health. For most of his entire career as Roosevelt's doctor, McIntire had spoken only in glowing terms of a leader who, despite his physical paralysis from polio, dispatched his duties during the war with vigor and zeal.[47]

As might be guessed, the case of Roosevelt's ill health is a difficult one to make. For one thing, Roosevelt himself confounds the medical skeptic by the breathtaking scope of his accomplishments, amazing even for the healthiest of men. After all, he did overcome major physical handicaps to become president of the United States. He then won election to an unprecedented four terms. His response to the Great Depression was an entirely new vision of government's role in democratic America's free enterprise system, and it is not too much to say that his New Deal leadership forever changed the country's political, social, and economic structures. He then began to pull his country out of its stubbornly isolationist, prewar mood, led it and the free world through the most devastating war in history, and, finally, left his country and people the ranking power of the entire world. While some—many, in fact—would argue the wisdom of each step along the way, the fact that any one man could run such a course is indelibly impressive; the fact that a progressively sick man could do so is amazing testament to Roosevelt's personal will and inner strength.

Although his own actions thus would belie the notion of an ill man at the helm, the medical detective attempting to assemble the full picture finds many of its pieces missing or unavailable. To begin with there are few medical records extant today; most of the pertinent laboratory tests, clinical charts, x-rays, or reports thereof are missing. No autopsy was performed after Roosevelt's death—thus even the postmortem diagnosis of a massive cerebral hemorrhage remains tentative.

The most valid clinical impressions come from just one man, Howard Bruenn, who was with Roosevelt for exactly the last year of his life, from March 1944 to April 12, 1945, to the very moment that he himself pronounced Roosevelt dead. Although McIntire soon came forward with a book, *White House Physician*, Bruenn maintained a long silence, broken only in 1970 when he wrote an article about Roosevelt for the professional journal *Annals of Internal Medicine*. Bruenn explained that he finally wrote his detailed medical account "in the interest of accuracy and to answer some unfounded rumors."[48] The rumors springing up even before Roosevelt's death had been that he was dying of syphilis, stomach cancer, lung cancer, or unnamed cardiovascular diseases. Then, shortly after his death, some outsiders claimed to have evidence that Roosevelt suffered a series of strokes leading up to his final hemorrhage at Warm Springs. Both Bruenn and McIntire pointedly denied such allegations, and, indeed, there is no way to ascertain their validity. With that sort of speculation apparently in mind, though, Bruenn also noted in 1970, "Many people rightfully attach such importance to the health records of the men whom they have considered and elected to the office of President of the United States."[49]

Quite true, but Bruenn's own detailed report raised many questions because it was at odds with the glowing reports issued at the time by McIntire, to whom he reported. Bruenn's clinical analyses of at least *some* cardiovascular pathology in his patient, for instance, noticeably conflict with McIntire's optimistic appraisals of Roosevelt's condition. In his own book, written shortly after Roosevelt's death, McIntire expressed shock and dismay at Roosevelt's "sudden" death. He continued to maintain that Roosevelt was fit and healthy during most of his tenure as president of the United States, to ignore any disquieting signs. For instance, unknown to most historians, early in 1941 Roosevelt exhibited symptoms of anemia, a serious complication for patients with heart failure and a weakening condition in any case. He had complained of bleeding hemorrhoids, which McIntire treated only for pain at first. It was not until Roosevelt's red blood cell count dropped to 25 percent of its normal reading, and he became noticeably run down, that McIntire thought to treat the etiology of Roosevelt's condition. Even so, the records now available suggest that Roosevelt did not receive iron pills until Bruenn prescribed them in 1944, three years later. It was about 1941, too, the year the Japanese attacked Pearl Harbor, that Roosevelt apparently began to visit the naval hospital in Bethesda under a phony name, a practice that continued until 1945, the year of his death.

By all such circumstantial but cumulative evidence, it would be difficult to conclude that the true status of Roosevelt's health was *not* deliberately hidden, for any number of years. Both McIntire and Bruenn were "politicized" or became part of the political process to hide illness during Roosevelt's dying years. It was twenty-five years after Roosevelt's death before the public would know the true medical facts as recorded so accurately by Bruenn.

If great leaders are mortal, then they are also subject to the same frailties and fallibilities as the rest of humanity. But this aura of greatness often blinds them, and those around them, to this fact. Few people during the war years ever wondered what effect the frailties of these luminaries had on their capacity to make decisions. Even fewer wondered what effect the strains and burdens of office had on their leaders.

We quote from a letter by Dr. James Paullin, one of the consultants on President Roosevelt's case, to suggest how difficult it must have been to manage a serious illness under the circumstances imposed by politics. Writing to a curious colleague, Dr. Paullin notes that "the demands on Mr. Roosevelt at this time, together with the tremendous load and burden he was requiring as a result of World War II and his efforts to get the United Nations going, demanded more of him than most any human being could stand, irrespective of his disposition or his desires." He continues later on in this same vein:

> In reviewing my connection with this case, the surprising thing to me is that the man could absorb as much punishment as he did during the years he was President of the United States without having some accident related to his arterial system long before he did. The tension under which he lived, the great responsibility which he assumed, and of which he was constantly conscious, would have been enough within itself to raise the blood pressure of any normal human being tremendously.[50]

Dr. Paullin's letter indirectly provides a neat transition to our next case history. The demands of office are sometimes more than any mortal can adequately bear, even those fortunate enough to enjoy superb health. More importantly, none are immune to the ravages that a sudden unforeseen illness can inflict on a previously healthy person, irrespective, as Dr. Paullin notes, "of his disposition or his desires." But if people with responsible positions will not voluntarily step down when they are too ill to function effectively, who should make that decision for them? It is a question we raised in our study of Woodrow Wilson, and it is one we raise again in a slightly different fashion. In a democracy should the voters have access to this information before a candidate takes office? Equally important, what are the appropriate roles for the medical profession and the media to take when a candidate does have a serious medical malady? The case of John F. Kennedy, which we discuss in the following chapter, throws these questions into relief.

5

John F. Kennedy

"I'm the Healthiest Candidate"

■■■■■ The illness and death of President Roosevelt should have formed the plot of a cautionary tale in American history. The country had lost a powerful leader in one of its most critical hours. Despite reports to the contrary, this "sudden" death had been slow, painful, and lingering and had its effect on the conduct of the country's public affairs. Should it not have made the voters more wary, the media more skeptical? Yet we in this country have a remarkable tendency toward historic amnesia. Before and after the Roosevelt episode are two similar eras in the history of the American presidency in which the press, the public, and the president himself behaved much as they did during the Roosevelt years. Nearly twenty years before Roosevelt's death another president, Woodrow Wilson, had entered office as an ailing man and had finished out his second term as a paralyzed, semicomatose invalid. Less than twenty years after Roosevelt's death, another ailing man, John F. Kennedy, sought and won the presidency.

The particular cases of these two presidents, Wilson and Kennedy, have in recent years been thoroughly researched and described. We have summarized the evidence that Weinstein and others have collected about Wilson, which suggests that Wilson had suffered a series of strokes long before he assumed the presidency and that his bizarre and futile political maneuverings during his second term were, in part, a function of his cerebral degeneration. In *The Search for JFK*, journalists Joan and Clay Blair piece together the years between Kennedy's birth and his entry into politics. As they develop the story, it becomes increasingly obvious that the youthful, "vigorous" John F Kennedy had actually spent most of his life suffering from a variety of maladies, the two most important of which were a congenitally weak back and Addison's disease.[1]

In July 1960 Senator John F Kennedy of Massachusetts sat in a Los Angeles hotel room pondering his political future. He had come to the West Coast as the clear front-runner in the race for the Democratic presidential nomination. The previous six months had seen him wage an aggressive series of primary battles against older, more seasoned politicians, dispelling many misgivings about his youth and inexperience. His dazzling string of victories in the primaries notwithstanding, the last few votes needed to secure the nomination still eluded him. Democratic party elders, whom the Kennedy blitz seemed to have caught unawares, were not yet willing to concede the fight to this young upstart.

As the primaries wound down, only Texas Senator Lyndon B. Johnson remained in any position to topple Kennedy. But Johnson's strength was primarily regional. The Senate majority leader could command a sizable block of votes from Texas and the southeastern states, but his support softened quickly as he moved outside those regions. Johnson's delegate votes, however, were making life difficult for Kennedy. Kennedy knew that under the best of circumstances all the conservative Johnson could do would be to force changes in the Kennedy platform. What Kennedy really feared, however, was that Johnson would block his nomination on the first ballot, then wait to see if Kennedy's delegates would defect during the subsequent rounds. If Kennedy could keep some major bombshell from erupting during the convention, he felt certain of winning the nomination.

The week just previous to the convention, however, saw Kennedy's worst fears realized. A last-minute attack by the anti-Kennedy forces set in motion a series of events which nearly cost Kennedy the nomination. Two days before the convention opened former President Harry S. Truman had gone on national television, questioning whether Kennedy had the "maturity and experience" to discharge presidential duties.[2] Kennedy, sensing a Johnson ploy behind the attack, responded quickly, saying that the president needed "the strength and health and vigor of . . . young men." The Johnson camp took Kennedy's statement as a slur on their man, who was older than Kennedy and whose health was suspect.[3] John B. Connally, director of Citizens for Johnson, and India Edwards, former vice chairman of the Democratic National Committee, held a press conference in which they stated that Kennedy had covered up the fact that he had been suffering from Addison's disease for several years. According to conference transcripts, Mrs. Edwards said that she had been told by "several doctors" that Kennedy had been taking treatment for the disease and that "he would not be alive today if it were not for cortisone." She added that she was making this revelation because Kennedy was "muscle-flexing" and disparaging their own candidate's health. John Connally proposed a health test for all the candidates and said that he would be happy to make Johnson's medical records available to the press.[4]

It was precisely this sort of eleventh-hour attack which Kennedy had most feared. Throughout the early primary races Kennedy had turned a potential disadvantage, his relative youth and inexperience, into a strong campaign theme. His slogan, "It's time to get the country moving again," was a thinly disguised attack on the graying Eisenhower administration. Kennedy had played on Dwight Eisenhower's age, his cautious approach to policy, and, subliminally, on his heart attack while in office. What Kennedy claimed to offer, in contrast, was an energetic administration, run by healthy young men brimming with "vigor." Now, Johnson's people had turned Kennedy's own argument against him: one of the myriad symptoms manifested by

Addisonians is their almost palpable lethargy.[5] It was a charge that the "vigorous" Kennedy camp could no longer afford to ignore.[6]

Even before Kennedy spokesmen could respond, suspicions planted by the health charge disrupted Kennedy's well-laid plans. The morning after the Johnson press conference, Kennedy invited California Governor Pat Brown, who led the delegation from his state, to breakfast. Kennedy's support in California was suspect; the West Coast Democrats were wary of this New Englander and had come to the convention uncommitted to any particular candidate. Kennedy had hoped to persuade Brown to commit his delegates to him before the actual voting started, thereby securing enough votes to sail through the rest of the convention.[7] Kennedy wanted to strike a political bargain, but the California governor had another question on his mind. As Kennedy himself recounted to Kenny O'Donnell, a longtime aide, the meeting was a disaster: "Do you know the first thing he said to me when we were alone? Here's a fellow I never met before in my whole life, and I am sitting down to breakfast with him, just the two of us in the room, and he looks at me and the first thing that comes out of his mouth is, 'I understand you've got Addison's disease.'"[8] Clearly, the charges about Kennedy's health would not rest; Kennedy would need to refute them directly.

Robert Kennedy and Pierre Salinger, John Kennedy's press secretary, labored feverishly to piece together a statement that would quell suspicions without attracting too much attention to the charges.[9] Almost three weeks previously, on June 11, in anticipation of this troubling problem, Kennedy workers had prepared an outline of a medical statement quoting from Drs. Janet Travell and Eugene Cohen, who were familiar with Kennedy's case.[10] The statement was reworked and issued by Robert Kennedy:

> John F. Kennedy does not now nor has he ever had an ailment described classically as Addison's disease, which is a tuberculose destruction of the adrenal gland. Any statement to the con-

trary is malicious and false . . . in the postwar period [he had] some mild adrenal insufficiency. This is not in any way a dangerous condition and it is possible that even this might have been corrected over the years since an ACTH [adrenocorticotropic] stimulation test for adrenal function was considered normal in December 1958. Doctors have stated that this condition he has had might well have arisen out of his wartime experiences of shock and continued malaria.[11]

That statement is a remarkable piece of political double talk. The assertion categorically denies that Kennedy had Addison's disease, yet it mentions the very tests and symptoms associated with the disease. Moreover, the statement had the approval of two doctors who, it was implied, were well acquainted with details of the case. The press dutifully reported the story the following day, but, surprisingly, the matter was pursued no further. Newsweek and U.S. News & World Report also carried the story in their weekly editions, their articles being basically paraphrases of the press statement.[12] The issue died as quickly as it had come up. Only toward the end of the fall campaign, when it became obvious that Nixon and Kennedy would go down to the wire together, did anyone bring the matter up again. Republican Congressman Walter H. Judd, a physician who had been in private practice before entering politics, made a feeble attempt to charge that Kennedy was physically unfit for the presidency, but by this time no one gave his remarks the slightest credence. The day after Robert Kennedy issued this medical statement, Lyndon Johnson, sensing that his strategy had backfired, disavowed any connection with the Connally-Edwards press conference. Johnson felt that he had misplayed his hand. The charges made during the conference did not get the coverage in the press which they deserved, in part because, as Pierre Salinger claims, "the press shared my view that the accusation went far beyond the latitude of fair play, even in the rough and tumble of convention politics."[13]

The end of this particular episode does have one final twist. After John Kennedy won the nomination, he quickly turned to the task of choosing a running mate who would aid the ticket. With an eye on both ideological and geographic balance the logical choice at that point would have been Lyndon Johnson. But the Kennedy operatives were still seething about Johnson's last-gasp tactics which had come close to scuttling their plans. Whenever John Kennedy raised the issue of Johnson's availability, he found himself under a barrage of criticism. As the deadline for announcing the vice presidential candidate drew near, Kennedy sequestered himself in his hotel room and made one crucial phone call: to Lyndon Johnson. The Texas senator accepted immediately. When Kennedy announced his decision to his aides, there was furious outcry. Kennedy admitted that he shared their distaste for Johnson, but felt that it was the most politically expedient move. Perhaps the most implacable of Johnson's foes was Kenny O'Donnell, who had vainly tried to get Kennedy to promise that he would not pick Johnson. Kennedy tried to soothe O'Donnell; his aide would have none of it and in a burst of anger asked Kennedy if he realized that should he die, Johnson would assume the presidency? Kennedy's reply is most telling, if self-deceptive: "Get one thing clear, Kenny, I'm forty-three years old, and I'm the healthiest candidate for President in the country, and I'm not going to die in office. So the Vice Presidency doesn't mean a thing."[14]

O'Donnell would later recall these words with pain after Kennedy's assassination, but the full ironic quality of Kennedy's statement eluded him. Kennedy convinced O'Donnell, and himself, that at forty-three years of age he could reasonably expect to live out his term in good health. Moreover, Kennedy had begun to believe the "youth and vigor" line which his campaign managers had concocted: "I'm the healthiest candidate for president in the country." Nothing could have been farther from the truth as John Kennedy's painful trail into politics demonstrates.

———

A Painful Apprenticeship

> At least one half of the days that he [Jack] spent on this earth
> were days of intense physical pain. He had scarlet fever when he
> was very young and serious back trouble when he was older. In
> between he had almost every other conceivable ailment. When
> we were growing up together, we used to laugh about the great
> risk a mosquito took in biting Jack Kennedy—with some of his
> blood the mosquito was almost sure to die.[15]

This statement by Robert F. Kennedy, which formed part of the
preface to the memorial book *John F. Kennedy: As We Remember
Him*, is difficult to reconcile with his brother's own "healthiest candidate" line. It is even more difficult to reconcile with the youthful,
outgoing, athletic image that the Kennedys consciously promoted
during the 1960 campaign and continued to promote throughout
John Kennedy's administration. In retrospect, this myth, which per-
meated and dominated the popular imagination during the early
1960s, turns out to have been just that: a myth. The record of John
Kennedy's early years has not been so much blurred by time as it has
been consciously distorted and reshaped by various hands. Beginning with his childhood and continuing through his school days, his
adolescence, his military service, and his first entry into politics, it is
at times impossible to distinguish fact from legend.

When Joan and Clay Blair set out to write a sympathetic but scru-
pulous biography of John F. Kennedy, they found their patience—and
sympathies—quickly dissipated. Indeed, what started out to be a
full, in-depth treatment of Kennedy's entire life ends abruptly with
Kennedy's election to the House of Representatives in 1946. They
found, to their chagrin, that what they call a "cover-up" of Kennedy's
war records, his academic records, and, most importantly for our
purposes, his medical records was "simply too vast, too overwhelming. Our time and our resources—and our patience and sympathy

—ran out."[16] Yet the results of their prodigious and painstaking research have done a great deal to explode many of the myths, as well as to uncover little-known facts about Kennedy.

Young John Kennedy was subject to the same maladies as afflict most children. But while other children suffer acute illnesses and tend to recover quickly, Kennedy's bouts of poor health seemed to linger and recur.[17] In spite of his frail constitution, he tried to carry on a normal, outgoing childhood, with varying degrees of success. Rose Kennedy, who kept index cards cataloging each of her children's illnesses and treatments, writes of John: "He went along for many years thinking to himself—or at least trying to make others think —that he was a strong, robust, quite healthy person who just happened to be sick a good deal of the time."[18] In addition to the normal run of childhood diseases which she catalogs—measles, chicken pox, german measles—John Kennedy also had a serious bout with scarlet fever, from which he nearly died; suffered a chronically weak stomach, which forced him to forgo alcohol and tobacco, as well as forcing him to take a bland diet most of his life; and was born with a congenitally weak back, which worsened considerably as he grew older.[19]

This childhood of sickbeds followed him into adolescence. Despite Kennedy's delicate health, his father insisted that he attend Choate School in preparation for college. Unlike his older brother, Joseph, Jr., who had preceded him at Choate and who had excelled at practically all of his academic and extracurricular endeavors, John was a lackluster student with little success on the playing fields. Jack's poor performance was a source of concern to his father, who had ambitious plans for his eldest sons, leading the elder Kennedy to write a series of letters to his son, reprimanding him for his dismal record and encouraging him to apply himself with more diligence. While the letters indicate that Joseph Kennedy was generally solicitous of his son's well-being, they tend to ignore the fact that John was intermittently ill throughout his entire career at Choate. His precarious health took a rather severe turn during his junior year in 1933, for example, when he came down with what has been variously described by observers as jaundice, hepatitis, and "a blood disease." Whatever the correct diagnosis, it kept Kennedy in bed at Choate throughout most of the fall term and left him debilitated and lethargic after the illness had run its acute phase. A few years later, when John Kennedy asked his old headmaster for a letter explaining his mediocre performance, George St. John wrote: "Part of Jack's lack of intellectual drive is doubtless due to a severe illness suffered in the winter of his fifth form [junior] year. Though he has recovered, his vitality has been below par, he has not been allowed to enter into any very vigorous athletics, and has not, probably, been able to work under full pressure."[20]

To improve John's academic records, and to expose him to a different academic environment, Joseph Kennedy arranged for his son to study for a year with Harold Laski in England. The noted socialist economist was then at the London School of Economics and agreed to tutor Kennedy's second boy (as he had done earlier with Joseph, Jr.) for a year. In the fall of 1935 John set sail for London with his father and dutifully enrolled at the school. One month later he withdrew unexpectedly and sailed back to the United States. There was no explanation for the withdrawal. In a letter written a year later to the Harvard Admissions Office, however, Joseph Kennedy explained that his son's sudden departure was precipitated by medical problems: "I took him abroad last year, but he had a recurrence of a blood condition and I brought him home to be near his doctors." As the Blairs point out in their research, although the exact nature of the illness is unspecified, a "blood condition" was a common way for laymen in those times to describe either jaundice or hepatitis. Furthermore, Joseph Kennedy's use of the word "recurrence" in the letter suggests that Jack had not fully recovered from his previous illness of 1933.

Despite his obvious poor health, John Kennedy insisted that he be allowed to enroll at Princeton that fall. His father, who preferred that his son attend Harvard, initially refused, citing Jack's health as the reason, as well as the fact that the semester was four weeks old. Jack persisted, however, and finally persuaded his father to pull some strings with Princeton friends. Kennedy was enrolled at Princeton in October 1935, but the year at Princeton was merely intended as an experiment, as a letter from Joe Kennedy to his son shows:

> Dear Jack,
>
> I had a nice talk with Doctor Raycourt . . . and we have decided to go along with your proposition as outlined by Dr. Murphy and see how you get along until Thanksgiving. Then, if no real improvement has been made, you and I will discuss whether or not it is best for you to lay off a year and try to put yourself in condition.
>
> After all, the only consideration I have in the whole matter is your happiness, and I don't want you to lose a year of your college life . . . by wrestling with a bad physical condition and a jam in your studies. A year is important, but it isn't so important if it's going to leave a mark for the rest of your life.[21]

Clearly, Joseph Kennedy saw Jack's enrollment at Princeton as provisional and had few illusions as to how his ailing son would fare. Jack tried vainly to succeed at Princeton, but circumstances were too much against him. He had already lost a month by virtue of his late enrollment, and as gamely as he tried to make up the work, he soon found himself floundering. To make matters even more difficult for him, he apparently suffered a relapse in his health within a month of his enrollment. At the beginning of December he decided to quit and, instead of going home, checked into Peter Bent Brigham Hospital in Boston, where the Dr. Murphy mentioned above in Joseph Kennedy's letter attended him. There are no extant letters or medical records from this period which reveal the nature of Kennedy's malady, other than the persistent complaints one finds of "general malaise" and fatigue. His stay at the hospital was extended to two months, at the end of which time the family sent him to a ranch in Arizona in the hope that the warm climate and relaxed atmosphere would improve his health.[22]

The summer of 1936 saw Jack Kennedy well enough to try once again to continue his studies, this time at Harvard. Again, he was required to explain his academic record and his abbreviated stay at Princeton. Jack Kennedy admitted for the first time in his letter that health had been a factor, stating that he attended Princeton in order to "be closer to my doctors in New York." Harvard accepted his explanation, and Jack began as a freshman in the fall of 1936.[23] His health during his four years at Harvard was, by comparison, relatively good; that is to say, he suffered no illnesses acute enough to force him to discontinue his work or severely restrict his activities. Yet failing health did continue to plague him. His attempts at sports, for example, were inevitably frustrated by some illness or another. In his first year he tried out for and made the freshman football team but subsequently had to withdraw from the sport because of his bad back. Similarly, an unspecified illness during his sophomore year, which forced him to take a month's bed rest, quashed his hopes of making the swimming team. There is also evidence that in addition to his weak back and various "blood diseases," Kennedy may have had some sort of severe gastrointestinal problem during his years at Harvard. Rose Kennedy mentions Jack's "delicate" stomach in her memoirs, but the only indication we have that he was treated for this condition is a prescription the Blairs discovered at the Kennedy Library from Jack's doctor at the Lahey Clinic, Sara Jordan: "Continue care in diet. Take Trasentin[?] tablet before each meal & in early morning. Take a Trasentin[?] tablet on first awakening. Apply heat to abdomen on first awakening for fifteen minutes before arising. Take no Ampliozel[?] except for distress. Continue using Ceritraine acid tablets and vitamin B complex faithfully."[24] This prescription could have been ordered for several varieties of stomach disorders, including ulcers, but there are no further records allowing a more specific diagnosis.

There is one further incident worth mentioning in connection with John Kennedy's Harvard days. In the summer of 1938 he and room-mate Lem Billings took an automobile tour of Europe. The trip proceeded apace throughout the continent, but apparently after a month or so it had to be cut short. Billings recounts that Jack became fatigued and nauseated and by the time they returned to London, whatever illness Kennedy now had flared dramatically: "Jack got desperately sick in London. His face was all puffed up and he got a rash and we didn't know anybody to even get a doctor."[25] Billings suggests that Kennedy may have suffered an allergic reaction to a stray dog that they picked up during their travels but does not elaborate further on the subject. Again, in the absence of further information and medical records it is impossible to assess the nature of this illness. However, it is important to note that Kennedy's Harvard years were plagued with the same sorts of medical setbacks he had always suffered. Despite his various illnesses, Kennedy was graduated on time from Harvard in the spring of 1940. It is a testament to his tenacity and courage not only that he finished his college career on schedule, but that he had worked hard enough during his final two years to so improve his grades and write a thesis that he took his degree cum laude.

John Kennedy's activities and the state of his health in the years immediately following his graduation are difficult to document. His early biographies state that he spent a semester at Stanford University, ostensibly auditing courses in preparation for a career in law. Stanford, however, has no record that Kennedy completed a semester there, although several faculty members recall Kennedy sitting in on their classes from time to time. Other researchers have speculated (in our opinion correctly) that Kennedy probably was forced to leave Stanford early, again because of health. There are two letters in the Kennedy library suggesting that Kennedy was hospitalized during the winter of 1940–1941. In one letter dated December 31, 1940, for example, columnist Arthur Krock wrote to young Kennedy wishing him a Happy New Year, and adding, "When I say, in return, Happy New Year, I mean every good wish that your expedition to New York will prove a turning point in the record of your health." Joan and Clay Blair traced Kennedy's travels that winter not to New York, however, but to the New England Baptist Hospital in Boston, where he was hospitalized for undisclosed reasons. In another letter William Bullitt, ambassador to France and a friend of the Kennedys, wrote to Jack in February 1941, hoping that Jack's trip to Rochester, Minnesota, had been "successful." As far as anyone knows, Kennedy had no close friends in Rochester. It seems possible to assume that he may have gone to the Mayo Clinic in Rochester for treatment.

Kennedy, now twenty-three years old and nearly a year out of college, had no defined ambitions and was in precarious health. Though he entertained vague notions of a career in law, he never went beyond requesting Harvard University to send his transcript to Yale Law School. His ambivalence was no doubt due in part to his health problems and in part to the world political climate. For many young men in 1941 the gathering war in Europe loomed large and might have colored whatever decisions they made. Kennedy had registered for the draft during his brief stay at Stanford, but his action was a patriotic formality. Roosevelt had yet to declare a state of emergency, and in any case Kennedy's medical record would have precluded his enlisting during the first draft. In this somewhat confused, dissipated mood Kennedy spent the better part of the spring and summer of 1941 traveling with his mother and sister in Latin America, trying to regain some of his vitality while deciding on his future.

When Kennedy returned to the United States in July, the threat of war was real. His older brother, Joseph, Jr., was making plans to enlist, and many of Jack's college friends had already joined the armed services. Caught up in the frenzy of military fervor which had arisen during his absence, young Kennedy decided to follow his brother's lead. It was a choice of which their father wholeheartedly approved, despite his avowedly isolationist sympathies, for the elder Kennedy saw the military as a suitable stepping stone for the advancement of his sons. Knowing what we now know of Jack's health, the push to get him into the war seems reckless, and indeed it was. Joseph Kennedy, Sr., though fully aware of his son's various maladies, encouraged and aided Jack's efforts to pass the navy physical. A simple medical history would have been enough to disqualify John Kennedy from entering the war at that early date. His records would have shown a young man of twenty-four years of age, with a chronically weak back, whose recurring illnesses since childhood had forced him at various times to interrupt his life with prolonged hospitalizations.[26]

Yet the Kennedy boys were adamant not only about joining the armed services, but about securing "interesting" jobs within the Navy. Mr. Kennedy, as was his custom, found a way of satisfying both desires by exercising his considerable influence. In July 1941 Captain Alan Kirk had recently been appointed head of the Office of Naval Intelligence in Washington. Kirk's previous tour of duty had taken him to London, where he had served on Ambassador Kennedy's staff as the naval attaché. Joseph Kennedy apparently persuaded Kirk to circumvent naval regulations, for there is no record that any objections were raised to Jack's enlistment. In a letter dated August 4, 1941, Kennedy expressed his appreciation to Kirk:

> Dear Alan,
>   To write to tell you what a swell guy I think you are would be nothing new for you to hear because long before you were going out of your way [to help the Kennedys] I knew what a real person you were.

Kirk's reply was equally solicitous:

> Dear Mr. Kennedy,
>   Thanks very much for your pleasant letter of the 4th. . . . It was no trouble to me to be helpful with such fine young men as

yours. We are delighted Joe is getting along so well and I think it is fine he is in the Navy air game. About Jack, I shall hope to hear that his plans are progressing favorably and I will see that he gets an interesting job.

Whatever blandishments were offered, or pressures applied, Joseph Kennedy's machinations worked. Joseph, Jr., was sent to naval flight school, and Jack was sworn in, without a physical examination, on September 25, 1941. True to his word, Captain Kirk (now Rear Admiral Kirk) found "interesting" work for Jack: as a Far Eastern intelligence specialist in the Office of Naval Intelligence in Washington, D.C.

Jack's war record is subject to at least as much distortion as is his medical record. We know, for example, that he worked in the naval intelligence until just after the attack on Pearl Harbor and then was suddenly transferred. In later interviews with reporters Kennedy would claim that the desk job bored him and that he asked to be transferred. There are, however, no records of a transfer request. The Japanese attack in December had caught many people unawares, including various branches of armed services intelligence, most notably, naval intelligence. One of the many people who were swept under in the wave of recriminations that followed was Ensign John Kennedy. For some time he had been dating Inga Arvad, a Swedish journalist with strong ties to the Nazis who had been under FBI surveillance. Some of their conversations had apparently been taped by FBI agents.[27] There was fear that Kennedy had breached security, and his superiors immediately wanted to cashier him. Instead, Kirk had Kennedy transferred to a menial public relations job, away from classified materials, in Charleston, South Carolina. Kennedy spent the better part of winter in this purgatorial job in Charleston before filing a transfer request to go to officer candidate school. His request was finally approved, and he was sent to the school at Northwestern University in July 1942.

While Kennedy was in Chicago, a recruiter for the recently established patrol-boat units came to the Northwestern campus. Kennedy
was enthralled with the recruiter's stories of PT boats' exploits in the
South Pacific and immediately filed for another transfer to one of the
PT training schools. Kennedy's ambitions to skipper one of these
boats was probably ill-advised. Built out of cheap, light-weight materials, the PT boats were armed with torpedoes and were designed to
carry out quick, destructive sorties against larger, more cumbersome
Japanese vessels. As they skipped rapidly over the surface of the
water, the flimsily constructed boats delivered bone-rattling jars to
the crew aboard. It was not only dangerous work, but exhausting and
enervating as well. It was not the sort of assignment for one with a
history of severe back pains and susceptibility to fatigue, among
other things. Because of the paucity of volunteers for these boats,
however, the Navy failed to scrutinize candidates very carefully. In
fact, this was one of the few training programs which did not require
a physical examination. An ensign could, after two short months, be
given command of his own PT boat without undergoing the regular
fitness program. John Kennedy was one of those ensigns who, after
training from October 1942 until the end of the year, was graduated
from the program and given command of a PT boat.

Almost immediately, Kennedy had an apparent relapse. On the
cruise from his training center near Boston to Jacksonville, Florida,
Kennedy had to put ashore to be treated for what some of his crew
remember as back pain, others as "fatigue." He was, at any rate, out of
commission for several weeks. Then, finally, he was given command
of a PT unit in the South Pacific and given orders to report to the
Solomon Islands on February 19, 1943.

The next year of Kennedy's life becomes even more difficult to
substantiate for a number of reasons. First, many of the dispatches
from the South Pacific were heavily censored or classified as state
secrets because of the war. Even the log books, for example, fail to
pinpoint Kennedy's exact whereabouts during this time. Second, we

have seen that a number of official documents—Kennedy's navy physical, fitness report, etc.—were either dispensed with or suppressed. Finally, and perhaps most importantly, Kennedy's service records in the Pacific quickly evolved from fact to legend; the exploits of the PT 109 passed from the annals of obscure naval history into American folklore. Kennedy, in turn, was transformed from a junior grade ensign commanding any one of several hundred small ships in the Pacific into an instant war hero. The details of how this metamorphosis occurred is another story, but we mention it in passing only to note that because of this myth-making, we can only surmise how Kennedy's health fared during the year he was in active service.

During the summer of 1943 Kennedy was in command of a number of different PT boat outfits, some of which were actively engaged in the Pacific war. To our best knowledge he was never relieved of command because of fatigue, back pain, or any other illness; considering Kennedy's previous health history, this fact is rather surprising. One would have suspected that the strains of constant excursions on the rickety PT boats, combined with battle stress and the inadequate and haphazard diets the men were served, would have wreaked havoc with Kennedy's delicate system. An interview with the widow of Lennie Thom, one of Kennedy's fellow commanders, provides a partial answer to this riddle: "The main thrust of Lennie's letters was that he was worried about Jack's health. He wrote me that Jack was ill—he didn't say what was the matter but that a team of horses couldn't get him to report to sick bay. Lennie said Jack feigned being well, but he knew he was working under duress."[28] Thom's letter suggests that Kennedy was in fact ill, but refused to succumb to his maladies. The chronic shortage of fighting men in the Pacific, especially officers, would also have made Kennedy's superiors reluctant to relieve him of command even had they noticed that he was less than fit. That Kennedy survived his tour of duty in the Pacific, including the famous PT 109 wreck that left him and his crew stranded on an island for six days, is remarkable. He had served for nearly a complete year on board a type of ship which the Navy had, from the outset, classified as "expendable."

The PT 109 incident, however, did spell the end of Kennedy's active military career. Together with his crew, he was taken to a nearby medical evacuation hospital to be treated for lacerations, malnutrition, and exposure. While some of his men, many of whom had been seriously injured in the incident, were immediately shipped to larger base hospitals, Kennedy inexplicably languished for several months in the South Pacific. Toward the end of his tour of duty Kennedy was suddenly relieved of the vessel to which he had been assigned, the PT 59. The ship's logs indicate that on November 18, "Lt. J. Kennedy left the boat as directed by the Dr. at Lambu [an island base]." One of Jack's colleagues claims that Kennedy suddenly began to suffer a variety of maladies, "a bad back, malaria, severe undernourishment, mental and physical 'exhaustion.'" Another friend recalls Kennedy complaining of a "splitting headache" and terrible back pains. One of the doctors who eventually examined Kennedy at the base hospital would later recall only that "X-ray machines picked up a problem with Jack's back. He had an injured intervertebral disk in the lumbar region, not a fracture. It was what we call a chronic disk disease of the lower back." Two points in this physician's report are noteworthy. One, he makes no mention of malaria or any other type of tropical fever. Second, he notes that Kennedy's back problems were "chronic" and not the result of a fracture stemming from the wreck of the PT 109. When queried about his use of the word "chronic," the physician replied: "He [Jack] told us that he had had a problem with the back before he came to the Pacific. It was not a disabling disease, but something that, at times, could be quite painful." The back pain, however, was disabling enough for Kennedy to request transfer stateside for medical reasons. In January 1944 his request was honored.

On his arrival in Los Angeles Kennedy decided to make another journey to the Mayo Clinic in Rochester before going home to see his family. Again, there are no official records of this visit; it is, however, substantiated by a portion of a letter which Joseph Kennedy wrote to some friends that same month: "We found him [Jack] in reasonably good shape when he returned, but the doctors at Mayo don't entirely agree with me on this diagnosis."[29] Despite Joseph Kennedy's optimism, his son's medical problems persisted and soon worsened. Jack spent the spring of 1944 in a variety of stateside administrative posts before being granted sick leave in May 1944. During subsequent campaigns, Kennedy's biographers would contend that Kennedy spent the time recuperating from his experiences in the Pacific, alluding, for example, to some vague symptoms suggesting malaria. What actually happened, however, was that Kennedy's back pain became unbearable. Several doctors, including those who had seen him in the South Pacific after his PT incident, had been recommending surgery for some time. For one reason or another Kennedy failed to accept this advice. When he was attached to Chelsea Naval Hospital in Boston, he finally decided to undergo this surgery. The operation, however, was performed by a surgical team from the Lahey Clinic at the New England Baptist Hospital.

Torby MacDonald, a friend and fellow PT boat commander who visited Kennedy in the hospital, recounts the painful scene: "He was lying in bed all strapped up as a part of the treatment to mend his back. He was suffering from a recurrence of malaria, and his skin turned yellow. His weight had dropped from 160 to 125 pounds." MacDonald's account is the only extant report of this incident in Kennedy's life. It is curious to note that he claims that Jack had a "recurrence" of malaria; there was no suggestion of Kennedy's having this disease in the doctor's reports from the South Pacific. The skin pigmentation to which MacDonald refers, however, will figure as a clue in a future medical puzzle in Kennedy's life.[30]

––––––

The Debut of Politics and Addison's Disease

The remainder of 1944 was a dismal time for Kennedy. The back operation was only a partial success; Kennedy would once allude to the operation by mysteriously saying that his physicians in 1944 needed to have "read one more book" before they treated him. The operation apparently did relieve Kennedy's acute pain, but his general discomfort and general run-down condition persisted. He spent most of the fall of that year in and out of Chelsea Naval Hospital as an outpatient, most probably doing rehabilitative exercises. August 1944 also brought the family the news of the death of Joe, Jr. The eldest of the Kennedy children had volunteered for a hazardous, experimental flight over the English channel, and his plane, carrying several tons of charges in its hold, had exploded shortly after takeoff. Later that year, Kathleen Kennedy's new husband, Billy Hartington, was also killed in action. The year 1944 also brought to an end Jack Kennedy's military career. On December 27 he went before the retirement board and was discharged at his full rank (lieutenant) because the board determined that his illness "is permanent, is a result of an incident in the service, and was suffered in the line of duty." Although Kennedy's combat service certainly exacerbated his condition, we have seen that it is not altogether correct to state that his injuries were a direct result of the PT 109 incident. Following his discharge, Kennedy returned to the same ranch in Arizona to which he had gone just before he entered Harvard. He spent several months there, hoping that this visit would have the same salubrious effect that it had had before.

During this time, and for the rest of 1945, Kennedy turned his energies to journalism. A book based on his senior thesis at Harvard, *Why England Slept*, had done exceedingly well and had eventually become a best-seller, giving Kennedy the confidence to try his hand at writing. His father, a close friend of William Randolph Hearst, landed him a job with the giant newspaper chain, and Kennedy spent the summer of 1945 traveling throughout Europe filing dispatches for Hearst. One such trip took him to Potsdam, Germany, to cover the first postwar meeting between the Allies. Strangely enough, Kennedy wrote no stories of the conference. Researchers who traced his travels during this time lost his trail when he arrived in Potsdam, then picked it up again two weeks later in London. One of Jack's traveling companions provides an explanation for this sudden disappearance.

> He [Jack] came back to Grosvenor House [in London]. Then he got very sick. I've never seen anyone so sick in my life. He had a hell of a high temperature. It scared the hell out of me. I thought he was going to die. He told me it was a recurrence of malaria. I'd never seen anyone go through the throes of fever before. . . .
>
> I got hold of a naval officer who was attached to [Secretary of Defense] Forrestal's party. Then some Navy Doctors came and they confirmed it was malarial fever. Then, late one night, Forrestal came by to see Jack. He was really worried about him.
>
> This went on for several days, then Jack got better. I went over to Paris for a few days by myself. I'm pretty sure Jack went back to the States on Forrestal's plane. I didn't see him again until I got back to the States—a week or two later.[31]

Whether or not Kennedy actually had malaria is difficult to assess. Though malaria is not mentioned in the Navy doctor's report from the South Pacific, several of his friends' accounts of the various illnesses Kennedy had during 1944 and 1945 mention "yellow skin," "malarial fever," etc. The account above states that navy doctors in Forrestal's party "confirmed" that Kennedy had malaria, but these documents are missing. Similarly, we wonder if Kennedy's unaccounted-for visits to Mayo and his recurring bouts of lethargy, fatigue, and nausea, which date back at least as far as his days at Choate, are connected.

We raise these questions to put into perspective the most confusing, complex, and obscured facet of Kennedy's medical history, namely, the claim that John Kennedy suffered from Addison's disease. Most recent biographies mention, almost as an afterthought, that Kennedy had some "adrenal insufficiency"[32] or that he took cortisone. Some omit this aspect of Kennedy's life altogether. For their part Kennedy and his later political associates either denied the assertion or so twisted the facts of the case that they become meaningless. In their book on Kennedy the Blairs categorically claim that Kennedy had been diagnosed as an Addisonian in 1946, shortly after his congressional race. Before beginning that segment of Kennedy's life, however, it might be helpful to summarize some aspects of Addison's disease.[33]

This disease of the adrenal glands was first described in 1855 by Thomas Addison. In published accounts of his discovery he writes:

> The patient, in most cases I have seen, has been observed gradually to fall off in general health; he becomes languid and weak, indisposed to either bodily or mental exertion; the appetite is impaired or entirely lost . . . slight pain is from time to time referred to in the region of the stomach. . . .
>
> We discover a most remarkable, and so far as I know, characteristic discoloration taking place in the skin . . . to present a dingy or smoky appearance, or various shades of deep amber or chestnut brown. . . . The body wastes . . . the pulse becomes smaller and weaker, and . . . the patient at length gradually sinks and expires.[34]

The disease is caused by either tubercular destruction or gradual atrophy of the adrenals. As one modern text points out, the development of the disease tends to be slow:

> In most cases Addison's disease is insidious in its evolution, [and] adrenal destruction is a gradual process. . . .
>
> When more than 90 percent of the adrenal cortex has been destroyed . . . the patient develops the clinical disease as it was seen by Addison. "Addisonian crisis" is the term applied to the patient whose hypotension [low blood pressure] progresses to shock and, if untreated, to death. Addisonian crisis is characterized by anorexia, vomiting, abdominal pain, apathy, confusion, and extreme weakness.[35]

Because of the decrease or nonexistent activity of the adrenals, an Addisonian's natural resistance weakens and he thus becomes much more susceptible to infections. Moreover, any kind of shock, whether from an operation, excessive stress, or vigorous exercise, can precipitate a crisis.

Since the hormones secreted by the adrenal cortex are vital to life, the mortality rate was extremely high before adequate treatment was discovered. In the 1920s, for example, one researcher found that nine out of every ten Addisonians died within five years of the onset of the disease. A few years later it was reported that the mortality rate of Addisonians who were kept on a high-salt, low-potassium diet and were managed carefully dropped to about 78 percent. Endocrinologists then began to try replacement therapy for Addisonians by using adrenal extracts taken from animals. A major breakthrough occurred in 1939 when scientists developed desoxycorticosterone acetate (DOCA), a synthetic compound, which has properties similar to those found in adrenal hormones. Initially, DOCA was injected in affected patients and was used in conjunction with the high-salt diet. Later, DOCA pellets were developed which were implanted in the back or thigh of the patient, effectively eliminating the need for constant injections. The new DOCA treatments, along with well-regulated diets and schedules, dramatically improved the lot of Addisonians. If they survived the dangerous initial phase of an Addisonian crisis—and avoided future stresses and exertions—people with this disease had a brighter future.

When John Kennedy decided to run for Congress in 1946, this is as far as treatment for Addisonians had progressed. Until this time, one could strongly suspect that many of Kennedy's illnesses were symptomatic of an Addisonian in the early stages of the disease: his recurring bouts of fatigue and malaise, his "delicate" stomach and lack of appetite, his chronic infections and high fevers, and, finally, the several instances of a "jaundiced" complexion. Also to be taken into account are the known trips to the Mayo Clinic, where experimental work on adrenal disorders was being done. These symptoms and events, although they are highly suggestive, remain speculative, and there is no documentation, either in letters or medical records, to verify that Kennedy was being treated for Addison's disease at this time.

However, if Kennedy in fact had Addison's disease during the 1946 campaign, he showed no traces of it until the end of the race. Kennedy had been running a ferocious campaign to secure the Democratic party's nomination in the eleventh congressional district in Massachusetts. Despite his tremendous financial and organizational resources, Kennedy was a political neophyte trying to break in to a district that was run by seasoned "pols" who managed the primaries through their ward machinery. He could claim no previous political experience, his youthful appearance (he was then twenty-nine) was a handicap, and he had less name recognition than did the veterans of previous primaries.[36] Kennedy's response was to organize a hectic campaign schedule of speaking tours, hand-shaking sessions, and political parties, necessitating eighteen-hour-long days. The campaign culminated in a huge Bunker Hill Day Parade through the downtown district of Charlestown, Massachusetts. Kennedy led the five-mile trek, waving at enthusiastic crowds that lined the street.[37] By the end of the march Dave Powers, his campaign manager, says that Kennedy was "exhausted." However, another Kennedy aide, Bobby Lee, at whose home Kennedy stopped after the parade, remembers a more dramatic scene: "Jack was ill. He turned yellow and blue and collapsed. He looked like he had had a heart attack. We took him up to the second floor, took off his underwear, and sponged him over. I called his father and I was instructed to wait until a doctor came. His father asked me if he had his pills. He did, and he took some pills. Then, after several hours, they took him from my residence."[38] Lee's recollections are important for several reasons. First, they are the only indication we have that Kennedy had had any major medical crisis since his back operation in 1944. Second, Lee mentions that Kennedy was "ill," not just "exhausted" as Powers says. Third, there is the description of Jack's turning "yellow and blue"—again, another indication that there was something peculiar about Kennedy's pigmentation that is suggestive of Addison's disease. Finally, there is the question of the pills which Joseph Kennedy instructed them to administer to Jack. This is the first time that any mention is made of Kennedy's being on any kind of medication. Unfortunately, Lee does not mention what the medicine was, but the casual way in which reference is made to "his pills" suggests that John Kennedy took them on a regular basis.

Kennedy disappeared from view the day after this incident, then made a final speech to his campaign workers on the day of the primary voting. There is no record that he checked into a hospital, nor is the name of the doctor whom Bobby Lee mentions known. The primary race turned into a Kennedy landslide, and in this heavily Democratic district it was a foregone conclusion that Kennedy would easily defeat his Republican opponent in November. Given the expected ease of his race later that year, Kennedy took the rest of the summer and most of the fall to recuperate and, as one aide remembers, "to play." He made various trips to New York and one to Rochester, Minnesota, but it is impossible to tell whether or not these trips were related to his health. Photographs of Kennedy from this period show him to be extremely underweight, and although his complexion looks wan, we cannot tell if the skin was discolored.

As expected, he won the November election handily and was sworn into office in January 1947. As a freshman congressman, Kennedy's duties were light, and he spent much of his first year in Washington trying to establish his own network of contacts and his reputation. Mary Davis, who was Kennedy's personal secretary and administrative assistant, remembers Jack's haphazard working habits and, more importantly, his haggard appearance:

> He had just come back from the war, and wasn't in topnotch physical condition. He was such a skinny kid! He had malaria, or yellow jaundice or whatever, and his back problem, and he

was rather lackadaisical. He wore the most godawful suits. Horrible-looking, hanging from his frame. He was not that actively involved then and was just getting used to being a member of Congress. He didn't know the first thing about what he was doing. . . .

When he first came, he'd never been in the business world, and his health wasn't that good. Joe had been killed and it fell to Jack to pick up the cloak and go into politics. He was sort of lost for a while.[39]

Shortly after Kennedy arrived in Washington, he tried to arrange a trip to Europe in June of that year, ostensibly to survey the economic rubble left over from the war. The Pentagon refused his visa application, claiming that Kennedy had no business to conduct there since he sat on no related congressional committees. Undeterred, Kennedy applied again and was finally given permission to visit occupied Germany in late August. None of his biographers is quite certain what Kennedy expected to do in Germany, and there is a great deal of confusion as to his travel itinerary. In fact, Kennedy never made it to Germany, and the trip abroad apparently triggered his first documented Addisonian crisis.

The chronology of events in this particular medical crisis is difficult to reconstruct. The first evidence we have that Kennedy was ill is a cable he sent from London to Ted Reardon, an aide back in his Washington office, dated September 13, 1947, which read:

> Get two prescriptions of Doctor Sullivan of Baltimore for here. Have them filled and get to Patricia [JFK's sister] Sailing Wednesday from New York. Important.
> /s/John Kennedy[40]

The next message Kennedy sent to Reardon, five days later, is even more confusing:

> If you did not get Doctor Sullivans two hair prescriptions to Pat on time give them to J. Patrick Lannan Hotel Pierre New York sailing Saturday.
>   /s/Jack[41]

There is no record of Kennedy's ever having been treated by a Dr. Sullivan, and the reference to "two hair prescriptions" was more likely a code: all congressional cables were a matter of public record. What had actually happened was that Kennedy had entered an Addisonian crisis and most probably was trying to get some sort of medication without anyone finding out. Unfortunately, Kennedy became ill so suddenly that his plan to return to New York to take "Dr. Sullivan's" medicine never materialized.

Seeing that Reardon had not been able to get him the medicine in time, Kennedy, who was by then quite ill, called Pamela Churchill, a friend from his father's days at the Court of St. James. According to her, "On the day we arrived in London, Jack called me up from Claridge's and asked if I had a doctor. He wasn't feeling well. So I called my doctor, who was Lord Beaverbrook's doctor, Sir Daniel Davis. He's dead now. I asked him to go around and see Jack at Claridge's. He did—and put him straight in a hospital, the London Clinic."[42] Alone and desperately ill, Kennedy spoke with another friend, Kay Stammers Menzies: "He [Jack] called me and said he was ill. I asked what was the matter. He said he didn't know—but when he got out of bed he couldn't stand up. . . . He was darned ill, terribly thin, and not a good color."[43] The British doctor who first saw Kennedy was shocked at his appearance and his symptoms. After he took Kennedy to the London Clinic, he called Pamela Churchill up again and gave her his diagnosis: "That young American friend of yours, he hasn't got a year to live."[44] According to Churchill, Dr. Davis said that Kennedy had Addison's disease.[45]

When the Kennedy family received word that Jack was ill in London, their first action was to send a private duty nurse to London to care for Jack. She arrived in early October, by which time Kennedy's condition had stabilized sufficiently enough for him to sail home. He arrived in Boston on October 16. The newspapers reported that Kennedy was suffering from "war-related" injuries. Frank Waldrop, who was then a reporter for the *Washington-Times Herald*, recalled the scenario: "He [Jack] went to England on a trip. He got sick. The word was given out that he'd had some kind of attack from swallowing sea water and oil in the P.T. 109 thing. I guess the truth was it was the onset of the Addison's. I know he was given extreme unction and brought off the ship on a stretcher and it was touch and go."[46] When Kennedy arrived in Boston, he was taken to the Lahey Clinic, where he was treated by Dr. Elmer C. Bartels, a thyroid specialist. In an interview with Joan and Clay Blair, Dr. Bartels confirmed that Kennedy actually had Addison's disease and not a "partial adrenal insufficiency" as would later be claimed. Bartels remembers when Kennedy came into the clinic:

> He was not in the crisis stage when he returned to Boston, as he'd been on active treatment. I don't know what his condition was in England—just that they made the diagnosis over there. He had an episode of weakness, nausea, and vomiting, and low blood pressure, which led to the diagnosis. The reason you collapse in Addisonian crisis results from low blood pressure.
>
> When you develop Addison's, there is loss of appetite, loss of weight, great fatigue. Pigmentation of the exposed areas of the body and hands. And the hair stays brown. That's the only *nice* thing about Addison's, your hair remains brown and doesn't turn gray. You always stay young-looking.
>
> Without a functioning adrenal gland one is very sensitive to infection. It used to be fatal in the old days before we had adrenal replacement—hormones. The patient invariably died of infection—even getting a tooth extracted was serious.
>
> I'm sure that's the first time Jack knew he had Addison's disease. There are certain tests one does to confirm the diagnosis, although the clinical history is quite definite. So on the clinical

grounds and laboratory studies it was confirmed that that was the problem. Addison's disease.[47]

When the Blairs interviewed Bartels, they asked him if earlier descriptions of Kennedy's bouts of fatigue, his frequent infections, and references to his "jaundiced" complexion were the result of Addison's disease. Bartels refused to speculate: "Addison's disease isn't a chronic disease in the sense you have it for five years and then discover you have it. When you develop Addison's disease it's usually known within the year."[48] Kennedy was given the standard treatment of the day, that is, daily DOCA injections for several weeks, followed by DOCA pellets implanted in his thigh, which were replaced every three months. Throughout this entire ordeal Kennedy continued to maintain publicly that he had simply had another febrile relapse; his aides fed stories to the press that Jack had not completely recovered from malaria or, more ambiguously, that Kennedy's maladies were war-related. We have seen, for example, that Frank Waldrop was told that Jack's illness in London in 1947 was the result of swallowing "sea water and oil" from the PT 109 accident.

Although Bartels's treatment successfully saw Kennedy past his Addisonian crisis, Jack's performance in the House of Representatives suffered. After the onset of Addison's in late 1947 Kennedy had one of the highest rates of absenteeism in Congress, and he sponsored no legislation, nor did he conduct any major congressional investigations. Later commentators, even the most sympathetic of them, would admit that Kennedy's performance in the House was "unspectacular," "lackluster," or "undistinguished." One has to suspect that Kennedy's mediocrity in the House of Representatives was related to his illness. Despite his poor record and his still delicate health, Kennedy was reelected to the House in 1948 and 1950.

By this time Kennedy was taking cortisone in addition to his DOCA implants. Dr. Phillip Hench, an endocrinologist at the Mayo Clinic, had discovered in 1949 that cortisone worked wonders with arthritic patients. Subsequent research showed that it was equally beneficial to Addisonians. Although the drug was initially extremely expensive and difficult to secure, there are documents showing that Kennedy was one of the first Addisonians to receive cortisone and that he kept a ready supply of both cortisone and DOCA in safety deposit boxes around the country. Though there is little indication of how his health fared during those two terms, one incident is particularly revelatory. After surviving the dangerous initial phase of his disease, Kennedy was told by Bartels that he needed to temper his hectic schedule and take care in his diet. Kennedy apparently followed this advice until late in 1951, when he took a round-the-world trip with Bobby Kennedy. In *As We Remember Him*, the memorial book published after John Kennedy's assassination, Bobby says that when they reached Okinawa, Jack came down with a sudden, high-grade infection and that his temperature "reached 106 degrees and that medical authorities at the military hospital to which he was taken didn't think he would live." The Blairs tried vainly to get the medical records from the army hospital in Okinawa. When that effort failed, they tried to find someone besides Bobby who remembered the incident. Again they failed. The only documentation of that particular episode comes from Dr. Bartels, who was still treating Kennedy at the time. According to Bartels, "Jack just wasn't taking care of himself." Bartels spoke with Bobby over the phone, diagnosed the illness, and prescribed extra doses of cortisone and antibiotics.[49]

Matters relating to the remaining eight years which led up to Kennedy's nomination and successful campaign for the presidency become progressively more obscured. The Blairs had given up trying to document Kennedy's illnesses and whereabouts after 1947. According to them, everyone had a different story to tell, documents were missing, and key aides and colleagues refused to talk. For one reason or another, Kennedy found his illnesses a source of great embarrassment, as well as a potential political liability. He apparently gave specific instructions to his aides to piece together a cover story which would relate his myriad hospitalizations to his war service. For example, in 1947, when Kennedy was in the London Clinic recovering from his Addisonian crisis, the following statement was made in the *Boston Herald*:

> Congressman John F. Kennedy announced today that he was "much better" after a month's bout with malaria and planned to sail for home this week.
>
> Kennedy, who has suffered malaria since 1943, said the attack began while he was visiting Ireland, forcing him to abandon plans for a tour of France and Italy.[50]

Subsequent newspaper and magazine reports would echo this line. It became the standard explanation issued whenever Kennedy was confined, hospitalized, or feeling slightly fatigued. For example, when Kennedy was forced to cancel his speaking engagements for the rest of 1947 and early 1948, his office issued the following press release: "As you perhaps know, Congressman Kennedy suffered an attack of malaria while studying labor conditions in England. At present he is confined to the hospital and has been advised to give up all speaking engagements for the next few weeks."[51] The malaria story was an excellent cover. It explained Kennedy's complexion, excused his fatigue, and subtly played for sympathy by relating his present condition to his war record. Despite recurring medical troubles and his poor record in Congress, Kennedy ran successfully for the Senate in 1950, defeating a formidable opponent, Henry Cabot Lodge. In the campaign biography handed out to reporters, Kennedy's hospitalizations were not mentioned. The health question never arose during the campaign.

Although Bartels seems to have been able to stabilize and manage the Addison's disease, Kennedy's back continued to plague him. The 1944 operation had provided some respite from the pain, but as time wore on, his condition began to deteriorate. By early 1954 the pain became so intense that Kennedy could barely walk. No safe amount of pain killers alleviated his condition, and his only temporary respite from the agony was to soak himself for hours in a tub full of hot water. In desperation he asked his physicians at the Lahey Clinic if the new "double-fusion" back operation would help him. Because of the danger of infection and of shock in an Addisonian patient, Lahey doctors strongly opposed the idea. Bartels argued that the operation was unnecessarily risky:

> We didn't want him to be operated on. That's one of the problems of Addison's disease: the increased risk in an operation, even with hormones. The patient doesn't tolerate surgery well. We simply wouldn't do the operation in Boston. Ned Haggart [the back specialist at the Lahey Clinic] recommended conservative treatment. Physiotherapy, exercise, etcetera. We didn't want him to have any stress other than what was positively necessary. We were not sold on the *need* for an operation.[52]

Dissatisfied with the recommendations from the Lahey Clinic, Kennedy sought a second opinion from two other doctors: Ephraim Shorr, director of the Endocrinology Service at the Cornell Medical Center, and Philip Wilson, an orthopedic surgeon then at the New York Hospital for Special Surgery. After discussing the dangers inherent in such an operation, Shorr and Wilson agreed to try the procedure on Kennedy. Bartels, distressed at this latest turn of events, still tried to persuade Kennedy to change his mind. "It was questioned whether it was absolutely certain that Jack had Addison's disease. I went to the hospital in New York to see him before he was operated on. I stressed the increased risk in doing surgery on a patient with Addison's disease."[53]

It is curious to note that even as late as 1954 some doctors wondered whether or not Kennedy actually had Addison's disease. Kennedy at this time had a DOCA implant and was taking a maintenance dosage of 25 milligrams of cortisone daily. Why, seven years after he was diagnosed and treated as an Addisonian, would there still be this confusion? Bartels's protestations notwithstanding, Kennedy went ahead with the operation on October 21. Kennedy survived the operation, but just barely. One of Bartels's greatest fears for Kennedy was realized: a few days into his postoperative recovery, Kennedy developed a severe infection. Once again, his life hung in the balance; once again, he was given the last rites of the Catholic church. The situation was so grim at one point that, according to Arthur Krock, Joseph Kennedy came to Krock's office and "told me he thought Jack was dying and he wept sitting in the chair opposite me in the office." Treated with larger doses of cortisone and antibiotics, Kennedy overcame the infection and was discharged four months later after a slow and painful rehabilitative period.[54]

As before, Kennedy's office tried to minimize the illness, saying simply that he had had a spinal fusion to repair back injuries suffered during the PT 109 accident. The *New York Times* ran three short articles on the operation, but none mentioned that Kennedy had suffered postoperative complications which almost cost him his life, and none certainly mentioned that he had Addison's disease.[55] In November 1955, however, Kennedy's carefully hidden medical history became a matter of public record. Philip Wilson, the surgeon who headed the team that had operated on Kennedy, was so pleased with the final success of this operation on an Addisonian that he wrote an article for *The Archives of Surgery* in which he outlined Kennedy's medical history as a case study. Following medical ethics, Kennedy's name was not used. From the description of the patient in the article, however, it is clear whom they are talking about:

> A man 37 years of age had Addison's disease for seven years. He had been managed fairly successfully for several years on a program of desoxycorticosterone acetate (DOCA) pellets of 150 mg. implanted every three months and cortisone in doses of 25 mg. daily orally. Owing to a back injury, he had a great deal of back

pain which interfered with his daily routine. Orthopedic consultation suggested that he might be helped by a lumbosacral fusion together with a sacroiliac fusion. Because of the severe degree of trauma involved in these operations and because of the patient's adrenocortical insufficiency due to Addison's disease, it seemed dangerous to proceed with these operations. However, since this young man would become incapacitated without surgical intervention, it was decided, reluctantly, to perform the operations by doing the two different procedures at different times if necessary and by having a team versed in endocrinology and surgical physiology help in the management of this patient before, during, and after the operation.[56]

The fact that Kennedy had Addison's disease was now a matter of public record. Even though his name was omitted from the article, it would have taken very little detective work to figure out that the "37-year-old man" hospitalized in October 1954 in New York Hospital and John Kennedy were one and the same: the ages were the same, the doctors were the same, the back operation was the same, the dates of the operation and recovery were the same, and so on. Remarkably enough, no one made the connection, at least not publicly. Yet the fear must have loomed large in Kennedy's mind that someone, somewhere, would unravel the medical puzzle he had created.

The Press, the Doctors, and the Keeping of a Secret

Had Kennedy not decided to run for the presidency, his medical history might well have gathered dust on the shelves of some library. Literally thousands of case histories appear annually in various medical publications. Even a case as medically significant as Kennedy's, particularly the fact that his was one of the first successful surgical procedures on an Addisonian patient, would have caused little comment in a profession accustomed to almost daily discoveries of new "miracles."[57]

Kennedy faced two problems with the publication of this article. One was, simply, the fact that its discovery would suggest that Kennedy had been deceitful regarding his health all these many years. The second problem was even trickier. Despite the recent advances made by medical scientists in treating Addisonians, of which Kennedy's successful operation was but one example, the disease was associated in the public's mind with the same grim prognosis as one associates with cancer. Given the tone of Kennedy's attacks on the Eisenhower administration, Addison's disease was probably the least convenient of maladies from which he could have suffered. Tagged as a "rich man's disease," it had an exotically tragic ring to it, conjuring up images of listless aristocrats who slowly dissipated, then died. The image of a robust, young war hero which Kennedy had cultivated and would continue to use to challenge the Republicans would be irreparably damaged.

As the 1960 campaign approached, the question of the candidate's health became, for the first time, front-page material. Eisenhower's heart attack and Nixon's near ascendancy to the presidency had given the question topical importance. Compounding the problem were rumors which circulated throughout Washington in the late 1950s that Kennedy "had more than back trouble: incurable cancer, tuberculosis, or 'some other malady.'" James McGregor Burns writes that Ambassador Kennedy, who knew full well the extent of Jack's medical problems, released a press statement refuting the "unfounded and disturbing rumors that are being circulated in Washington."[58] Despite Kennedy's case history being a matter of public record, however, no one made the connection publicly or raised the issue of Addison's disease. For their part Kennedy and his aides decided, in the words of one biographer, "to tough it out—bluff his way through the reportorial digging."[59] To the extent that any mention would be made of Kennedy's ill health, it would be tied to his war record, specifically, to the PT 109 incident.

The ploy succeeded brilliantly. The first step in this strategy was to have Dr. Janet Travell, a rheumatologist treating Kennedy for his chronic back pain, issue a confusing statement about Kennedy's health, which in part read:

> In 1943, when the PT boat which he (JFK) commanded was blown up, he was subjected to extraordinarily severe stress in a terrific ordeal of swimming to rescue his men. This, together perhaps with subsequent malaria, resulted in a depletion of adrenal function from which he is now rehabilitated.
>
> Concerning the question of Addison's disease, which has been raised [during the 1960 Democratic convention]. This disease was described by Thomas Addison in 1855 and is characterized by a bluish discoloration of the mucous membrane of the mouth and permanent deep pigmentation or tanning of the skin. Pigmentation appears early and it is the most striking physical sign of the disease. Senator Kennedy has never had any abnormal pigmentation of the skin or mucous membranes; it would be readily visible.
>
> Senator Kennedy has tremendous physical stamina. He has above-average resistance to infections, such as influenza.[60]

It has been pointed out that Travell's statement is a minor master-piece of misdirection. Though she does not actually deny that Kennedy had Addison's disease, she strongly implies that to call him an Addisonian would be a misdiagnosis. She says, for example, that Kennedy was "rehabilitated" from a "depletion of adrenal function," yet fails to note that he was taking a regular treatment of both DOCA implants and cortisone. She also notes that Kennedy currently had none of the discolorations of the skin or gums which characterize an Addisonian, although she fails to mention that the cortisone treatment would clear some of the abnormal pigmentation. Her statement that Kennedy never had any discoloration of either his skin or his gums is, at best, an exaggeration since there were frequent references to Kennedy's "jaundiced" or "Atabrine-yellow" complexion. Finally, Dr. Travell states that Kennedy had "above average" resistance to infections, which is precisely one of the characteristics of the cortisone therapy.

Travell's misstatement would become the basis for all subsequent press releases and newspaper stories about Kennedy's health during the 1960 campaign. For example, James McGregor Burns, who published a biography of Kennedy just before the presidential race, calls Kennedy's "partial adrenal insufficiency" a result of his heroics on board the PT 109. He then adds a new twist to the story.

> While Kennedy's adrenal insufficiency might well be diagnosed by some doctors as a mild case of Addison's disease, it was not diagnosed as the classic type of Addison's disease, which is due to tuberculosis. Other conditions, often not known, can cause inadequate functioning of the adrenal glands. As in Kennedy's case, this can be fully controlled by medication taken by mouth and requires a routine endocrinologic checkup as part of a regular physical examination once or twice a year.[61]

Burns's use of the phrase "classic type of Addison's disease" in relation to tubercular destruction of the adrenals is misleading. Although Thomas Addison himself was convinced that the etiology of the illness was tuberculous, subsequent research clearly showed that other diseases could cause adrenal atrophy and precipitate an Addisonian crisis. As early as the 1920s, for example, epidemiologists had found that at least 50 percent of Addisonians in the United States lost their adrenal function from some malady other than tuberculosis. The only thing "classic" about tubercular adrenal destruction was Addison's description of it. Burns's point, finally, is irrelevant. Whatever the origins of Kennedy's disease, he was still an

Addisonian requiring daily medication in order to survive.[62]

The tactics devised by Kennedy and his aides were remarkably successful. They admitted enough about his illness to square with the public's knowledge of his hospitalizations and to give him the air of complete candor, but they never came forward with the complete story. They also managed to relate his maladies to his war record, giving his ill health a ring of heroism. In a sense Kennedy and his doctors had created a fictional medical history, complete with documents and correlated with newspaper accounts of the events in his life. By the time John Connally made his charges about Kennedy's health during the Democratic presidential convention, Robert Kennedy and Pierre Salinger would refer reporters to the "full exposition" of the subject in Burns's book, which was in turn taken almost verbatim from Janet Travell's statement.

The story of Kennedy's illness had by now acquired the circular, redundant quality of an aphorism. Journalists, commentators, and political aides quoted each other's statements as "evidence" of Kennedy's good health. The most ironic episode of this circular documentation would occur in 1968, when Dr. Travell claimed in her memoirs that Kennedy had never had Addison's disease and then proceeded to quote from Burns's book to support her assertion.[63] Kennedy himself brilliantly executed an aggressive campaign against Richard Nixon belying any rumors about his maladies. He and his aides had created the image of a young, heroic politician, full of vital energy, an image which both the general public and the media accepted and which carried John F. Kennedy, with his back troubles, near deaths, and Addison's disease, into the White House.

The Lessons of History and a Partial Assessment

Assessing the life of an historical figure who lived within the last two decades presents its unique problems. Historians who write about recent current events tend to limit themselves to narrative exposition.

They tend to be gatherers of facts. In the case of John Kennedy, however, even the "facts" have a peculiar, elusive quality to them. The Kennedys of the twentieth century lived their lives with one eye on the realities of the day and another eye on the eyes watching them. Like Henry Adams, who wrote his letters fully expecting them to be collected and published after his death, the Kennedys created and lived events in the expectation that one day they would be of importance.

If the most insignificant details of Kennedy's life have this well-crafted quality to them, one can see why the more significant matter of his major illnesses would have been so reworked and contrived when it finally became public knowledge. We mentioned earlier the frustrations which Joan and Clay Blair experienced when they tried to piece together a complete biography in the early 1970s. They felt that they were writing a story twice over: once from the available Kennedy literature, then from the obscured documents and reluctantly given interviews which contradicted most of what they had been led to believe. They finally gave up in vain. A few years later, columnist Garry Wills attempted the same feat. His book, *The Kennedy Imprisonment: A Meditation on Power*, takes a different track; it assumes from the outset that most of what came to be known as "fact" in Kennedy's life was the product of careful editing, misdirection, and lies. Where previous biographers had been ingenuous and sympathetic, Wills is cynical, at times scathingly so.

When the question of Kennedy's illness arises, Wills attributes the denials to the Kennedys' need to manipulate and distort events to their advantage:

> The impulse to hide weakness led to the sequestration of John Kennedy's medical records. The Blairs, in their search for the doctors who had treated the young Kennedy, found it hard to document the precise time and place of various treatments. His bad back had been with him from childhood, but he told John Her-

sey (who wrote up Kennedy's PT 109 story in the *New Yorker*)
that it originated in the strain of rescuing his comrades after
his boat was sunk. (Those comrades do not remember his mentioning any back injury at the time.) The habit of covering up
his multiple health problems culminated in the series of lies
about his Addison's disease. When Lyndon Johnson revealed the
existence of the problem in the 1960 campaign (thereby incur-
ring Robert Kennedy's fiercest anger), the Kennedy campaign
issued outright denials. Its spokesmen later rationalized this
by saying he did not have Addison's disease because the public wrongly thought the disease invariably fatal; so it would
give a false impression to use the term, even though it was the
correct one. But they not only did not use the term. They
expressly denied it was applicable in any sense, and portrayed
Johnson as a candidate willing to invent any lie convenient to
his purposes.[64]

Wills's own assessment of John Kennedy (and of his brothers and his
father) is harsh, perhaps too harsh. Yet we share some of his antipa-
thy for what happened. It is a feeling born not out of some personal
animosity toward the Kennedys, but out of fear of the danger to
which public institutions—the press, the Congress, the military, and
the presidency—were subjected.

We know, for example, that John Kennedy should never have been
allowed to enlist in the armed forces during World War II, much less
be given a commission and command of a ship. Even a cursory
physical examination would have disqualified him from active service. Yet under pressure from Joseph Kennedy, the navy waived all
possible objections to John Kennedy's enlistment in the service,
despite the fact that he was a very sick young man. Heroism in a time
of crisis is to be commended, but America was awash with heroes
and near heroes during World War II. Giving John Kennedy a PT
boat command created a new hero, but it was an inexcusable act of

recklessness and disregard for the safety of the men who would serve under him. That John Kennedy's delicate health might have jeopardized the lives of his men was a possibility that neither the Kennedys nor the navy gave much consideration.

Again, when John Kennedy ran for Congress in 1946, his ambitions and those of his father superseded their concern for the public welfare. John Kennedy collapsed at the end of his campaign with what were probably the first signs of Addison's disease. In 1947 these symptoms erupted into a full-blown Addisonian crisis, which almost cost him his life and effectively kept him from attending to his congressional duties for the rest of the year. Despite his illness, he ran for Congress again in 1948 and won. He distinguished himself during this second congressional term by his absence and mediocre work on committees, and we are led to conclude that his illness played a major factor in this lackluster performance. Yet rather than learning from his recent history and taking a respite, Kennedy ran for the Senate in 1952 and again won. Within the year he had another Addisonian crisis while touring Okinawa, so severe that military physicians there gave him up for dead. Less than three years later, at the end of 1954, he underwent a series of back operations which, due to the precariousness of his condition, almost killed him and kept him from his work for the remainder of 1955.

Thus, by the time John Kennedy won his 1958 Senate race, effectively launching his national political career, he had served for twelve years in Congress, during which he had been chronically, at times dangerously, ill and had been given the last rites of the church on at least three occasions. When the health issue came up in 1960, it was little wonder that the Kennedy camp should have been so prickly. Yet we marvel not at their anger in response to Lyndon Johnson's charges, but at the manner in which they brazenly denied the charges and then turned them to John Kennedy's advantage. It is one thing to say that one's candidate is healthy and fit for a particular political office;

it is quite another to play that theme as a campaign issue (as Kennedy had done against Eisenhower and the Republicans), when in fact John Kennedy was lucky simply to be alive, much less running for the most powerful office in the world. Apart from whatever damage John Kennedy's political tactics inflict on one's sensibilities and conscience, there is the more important question of the damage inflicted on the presidency and the other public offices in this country. Whatever talents and qualities John Kennedy may have possessed during his service in Congress were effectively blunted by his myriad illnesses. One might feel admiration for Kennedy's demonstrable heroism in overcoming his illnesses were it not for the fact that he was gambling not only with his future, but with the future of his men in the South Pacific, the future of his constituents from Charlestown, Massachusetts, and later, the future of the people of the United States and conceivably of the entire world. That Kennedy felt compelled to mislead the public about his illness, then to brand his critics as liars when they correctly charged that he was an ill man, also detracts from the heroic qualities.

Having chronicled the manner in which Kennedy obscured his serious illness in his quest for the presidency, his defenders might well respond that nothing happened, that all of our worries and criticisms are for nought. Kennedy died not from Addison's disease, but from an assassin's bullet. Not only did he not lead us to the nuclear holocaust many people feared during the "bomb" hysteria of the 1960s, he successfully managed a nuclear confrontation with the Soviets. So what, one might ask, is the problem? The problem is not what actually happened, but what potentially could have happened. Kennedy's management of his Addison's disease has nothing to do with political savvy and a lot to do with the remarkable success of modern medicine. It matters that the public was not told, that John Kennedy felt wary enough about the public response that he had to hide his maladies. It matters that John Kennedy would say, in private and in confidence, to Arthur Schlesinger: "No one who has real Addison's disease should run for the presidency, but I do not have it." Finally, it matters that John Kennedy, an ardent student of history, should have forgotten the frightening lessons of the Wilson adminis- tration, when another president denied an illness and the country had a moribund leader.

6

The Twenty-fifth Amendment and the Decisions of History

■■■■■■ The well-publicized health problems of President Reagan stand in sharp contrast to the case studies we have presented thus far. Reagan's illnesses have made us more acutely aware of the significant role that health has played in the lives of many of our presidents. Generally, the American people and the press have treated questions about the health of our leaders as an area of personal privacy and have failed to give any real thought to the physical conditions of many presidential aspirants. As we have documented, some chief executives, with the aid of their physicians and their staffs, have successfully hidden major illnesses from the public.

Several excellent studies have been published regarding our presidents and their health.[1] History reveals that by no means have all of our past presidents been in robust health, mentally or physically. To what extent their ill health has been a factor in world history is, indeed, an intriguing question, but one difficult to document. In 1969 Hugh L'Etang noted that in the previous sixty years, six of America's ten presidents and eleven of Britain's thirteen prime ministers had suffered more or less incapacitating illness, some of them at crucial times in their nation's history.[2]

Michael P. Riccards, a political science scholar, in an excellent article has reviewed the illnesses of some of our earlier presidents. In the following paragraph he explores the relationship between presidential illness and particular decisions and events. He points out:

> Madison's Administration provides us with a good example of how physical illness can affect a President's ability to perform his duties. In 1813, Madison contracted a severe case of what was vaguely called "bilious fever," an ailment from which he nearly died. Unfortunately at the same time, Madison had submitted the name of his Secretary of Treasury, Albert Gallatin, to be a member of the diplomatic delegation for the proposed peace conference in Russia. Madison, who had been a superb party leader under the first three Presidents, now found himself unable to deal with many of his own partisans. Partly because of the severity of his illness, Madison neglected to contact the necessary recalcitrant Senators and Gallatin's nomination was defeated.[3]

The illness of Grover Cleveland is perhaps the best documented evidence of cover-up of presidential illness. During his second term in 1893 Cleveland discovered that he had cancer of the palate. In the midst of a serious monetary crisis Cleveland—a strong advocate of sound money and the gold standard—was hesitant about the consequences of any publicity over his illness. Finally, his doctors, under the tightest security, operated on him aboard a yacht anchored in the East River. Two weeks later they performed a second operation to remove the final traces of cancer. When the true story broke, Cleveland and his doctors simply denied it. In the meantime President Cleveland was successful in preventing the Sherman Silver Act from becoming law, and he continued to perform his duties without any noticeable effects from his operations. Only in 1917 was the full story of his condition confirmed.

The first time in history that the public immediately knew the full truth about a president's illness was during the Eisenhower administration. Riccards summarizes the events as follows:

Before his election, Eisenhower had suffered from some health problems. During his command in World War II, Eisenhower had hypertension and periodically from 1925 on he also had spasms of cramping pain in the mid-abdomen and mild fever. But generally, Eisenhower appeared rather healthy when he assumed the Presidency at the relatively advanced age of 62. However, in a twenty-six month period at the close of his first time in office, Eisenhower suffered from three major illnesses.

First, on September 27, 1955, the President had a coronary thrombosis. Then in June of the next year, physicians operated on his intestine after having diagnosed his abdominal pains as attacks of chronic terminal ileitis, known as regional enteritis or Crohn's disease. Then in November 1956, immediately after his reelection and the prolonged discussion of his health in the campaign, the President suffered a cerebral occlusion. On each occasion, Eisenhower's press secretary provided the media with extensive, detailed descriptions of the President's condition.

During Eisenhower's first illness, the Cabinet under the direction of Assistant to the President, Sherman Adams, was able to conduct the government's day to day business without any major problem. Eisenhower had previously delegated wide responsibilities to Adams, Secretary of State Dulles, and Secretary of the Treasury, George Humphrey. This collegial relationship may have been aimed in part at preventing then Vice President Nixon from assuming any major policy making powers, or it may have simply reflected the natural consequences of Eisenhower's managerial style. In any case, no important decisions had to be made during the President's recuperation.

However, during the June 1956 period after Eisenhower's intestinal operation, the President's absence may have confused American foreign policy in the Middle East. For some time, the United States had been drifting in and out of a financial relationship with Egypt over the proposed Aswan Dam. In the five weeks after his operation, the President was absent and the weight of his subordinates' judgement, especially Secretary Humphrey, was thrown heavily against the proposal. Whether Eisenhower would have decided differently, if he were well and present at his desk, is difficult to ascertain. American Middle East policy was highly ambiguous and Eisenhower's health was an added question during this period.

Indeed, during his last illness, even Eisenhower had some real concerns as to whether he could continue. Although his physicians were quick to pronounce him 95% recovered, Eisenhower in his memoirs is a bit more candid. He notes that after that attack, he frequently experienced difficulty in saying what he wanted to say. On occasion, he reversed syllables in a long word and he was compelled to speak slowly and cautiously if he were to enunciate correctly.

After his third major illness in as many years, Eisenhower was sensible enough to recognize that he had to create some arrangement should he suffer permanent disability. He issued a private letter to his Vice-President outlining procedures to be followed if such a disability should occur. It must be remembered that Congress had yet to recommend an amendment concerning Presidential disability and succession; Eisenhower's action was a cautious, but important step to fill the constitutional void.[4]

The authors of the Constitution attempted to deal with the problem of presidential disability or death by writing the following into their basic charter: "In case of the removal of the President from office, or of his death, resignation, *or inability to discharge the powers and duties of the said office* [emphasis added], the same shall devolve on the Vice President, and the Congress shall by law provide for the case of removal, death, resignation or inability, both of the President and the Vice President, declaring what officer shall act accordingly, until the disability be removed, or a President shall be elected."

Pursuant to this constitutional authorization, Congress attempted to clarify the matter by enacting the Presidential Succession Act of 1947. This law established the following order of succession to the powers and duties of the presidency: vice president, speaker of the house, president pro tempore of the senate, secretary of state, secretary of the treasury, secretary of defense, attorney general, secretary of labor, secretary of health, education, and welfare (now health and human services), secretary of housing and urban development, secretary of transportation. Such persons would have to fulfill certain requirements: natural-born U.S. citizenship, a minimum age of thirty-five years, and residency in the United States for at least fourteen years.

The ambiguities inherent in both the original Constitution and the Presidential Succession Act gave rise to uncertainties about who would determine that a president was unable to exercise the duties and powers of his office, as well as about when and how such inability should be considered terminated. There was also concern that once presidential powers were yielded, they would be permanently forfeited.

Following his heart attack, ileitis, and a stroke in the 1950s, President Eisenhower tried to avoid potential problems by executing an agreement with Vice President Nixon outlining the temporary devolution of presidential authority in the event of Eisenhower's incapacity to exercise the powers and duties of the office. The agreement provided that the president would declare his own inability if he were able to do so. Moreover, if the president were unable to do so, the vice president "after appropriate consultation" would make this determination. In either event the vice president was to serve as acting president until such time as the president resumed the powers and duties of office by declaring his inability to be at an end.

President Kennedy continued this practice, specifying the cabinet as the "appropriate" body for consultation. President Johnson, first with House Speaker McCormack, and later with Vice President Humphrey, reached similar agreements.[5]

The illness of President Eisenhower nonetheless stirred some constitutional experts to worry about the adequacy of the Constitution's mechanism for the transfer of executive power when the chief executive is "unable to discharge" his duties. Congress began a series of hearings, but little was accomplished until the assassination of President Kennedy in 1963. A subsequent set of hearings then resulted in the adoption of the Twenty-fifth Amendment in 1964 by Congress and final ratification by the states in 1967. In his book *The Twenty-fifth Amendment*, John D. Feerick, now dean at Fordham Law School, outlines in great detail the history of the congressional hearings which resulted in the preparation of the amendment and its final adoption by Congress.[6]

This amendment clarified and made legal some issues of presidential succession which had become custom but had not been put into law. Section 1 states: "In the case of the removal of the President from office, or of his death or resignation, the Vice President shall become President."

This section clarifies the situation. In the case of a vacancy in the presidency, the vice president automatically becomes president. That is, he assumes the office *as* president, not just the duties of the office as acting president.

The question of a vice presidential vacancy, which had never been addressed, is clarified in Section 2 of the amendment: "Whenever there is a vacancy in the Office of Vice President, the President shall nominate a Vice President who shall take office upon confirmation by a majority vote of both houses of Congress." The term "vacancy" in this section includes death, resignation, or removal of a vice president but does not satisfy his possible *inability* to serve. Nor does it speak to situations of presidential disability during which the vice president acts as president, leaving a vacancy of uncertain duration in the office of vice president. In addition, there is no provision for cases of simultaneous presidential and vice presidential incapacity nor for instances of vice presidential incapacity at a time when the presidency becomes vacant. It is likely that both Article 2 of the Constitution and the Presidential Succession Act of 1947 would become operative in such situations.

Section 2 of the Twenty-fifth Amendment was put to its first test during the Watergate crisis, which began with the resignation of Vice President Spiro Agnew. At this time Gerald Ford was appointed to fill the vacancy created by Agnew's resignation pursuant to Section 2 of the amendment. When President Nixon resigned and Mr. Ford became president, the amendment gave the country its first nonelected president. The subsequent appointment of Nelson Rockefeller provided the second use of the amendment, giving us both a president and vice president who were not elected by the people. One commentator, arguing for a repeal of the amendment, points out that if either of the known assassination attempts on President Ford had been successful, Nelson Rockefeller would have become our second nonelected president, and he then would have appointed yet another nonelected vice president.

Section 3 of the amendment addresses the question of a president *voluntarily* declaring his own inability to serve: "Whenever the President transmits to the President Pro Tempore of the Senate and the Speaker of the House of Representatives his written declaration that he is unable to discharge the powers and duties of his office, and until he transmits to them a written declaration to the contrary, such powers and duties shall be discharged by the Vice President as Acting President." This section gives to a president who voluntarily declares his own inability the unilateral power to declare both the beginning and end of such inability.

Legislative history indicates that any type of inability to perform the powers and duties of office is encompassed by this section. The use of the term "inability" or "unable" derives from a recognition that "disability" does not necessarily imply incapacity to make and communicate decision. Inability in the context of Section 3 includes not only physical and mental illness, but also travel from one nation to another or any imaginable circumstances under which the president is unable to perform the powers and duties of that office.

Under ideal conditions this section is workable. It resolves past concerns that power once given up is not permanently surrendered by specifying that the vice president acts as president until the president regains his ability. However, if there is no vice president to act as president, or if the vice president is ill or otherwise unable to exercise the powers and duties of office, a president acknowledging his inability to serve is not provided with an alternative solution. This is because under Section 3 only the vice president can act as president, and under Section 2 there is no provision for vice presidential inability. Section 2 does allow for the filling of a vice presidential vacancy, but until someone has been nominated by the president and confirmed by the Senate, there is no vice president. It is also possible that the vice president may become unfit while acting as president, another situation for which the amendment does not provide.

The most troublesome cases of presidential inability are those when a president cannot or will not declare his own inability. Section 4 of the Twenty-fifth Amendment addresses this problem:

> Section 4. Whenever the Vice President and a majority of either the principal officers of the executive departments or of such other body as Congress may by law provide, transmit to the President *pro tempore* of the Senate and the Speaker of the House of Representatives their written declaration that the President is unable to discharge the powers and duties of his office, the Vice President shall immediately assume the powers and duties of the office as Acting President. Thereafter, when the President transmits to the President Pro Tempore of the Senate and the Speaker of the House of Representatives his written declaration that no inability exists, he shall resume the powers and duties of his office unless the Vice President and a majority of either the principal officers of the executive departments or of such other

body as Congress may by law provide, transmit within four days to the President Pro Tempore of the Senate and the Speaker of the House of Representatives their written declaration that the President is unable to discharge the powers and duties of his office. Thereupon Congress shall decide the issue, assembling within forty-eight hours for that purpose if not in session. If the Congress, within twenty-one days after receipt of the latter written declaration, or, if Congress is required to assemble, determines by two-thirds vote of both Houses that the President is unable to discharge the powers and duties of his office, the Vice President shall continue to discharge the same as Acting President; otherwise, the President shall resume the powers and duties of his office.

Once again, the vice president is essential to the procedure set forth in Section 4. When a president is unable or unwilling to declare his own inability, the vice president and a majority of the cabinet are to inform Congress of that inability by a written declaration, whereupon the vice president immediately assumes the powers and duties of the office of president and continues acting as president until the inability ceases to exist. The president may inform Congress that the inability has ceased to exist. He must then wait four days (unless the waiting period is accelerated by the vice president), during which time the vice president continues acting as president and, along with the cabinet, has an opportunity to review the situation. If a challenge is not forthcoming within the four-day time limit, the president resumes his powers and duties. If the vice president, together with a majority of the cabinet concurring, objects to the president's declaration of termination of inability within the designated time frame, Congress is required to convene within forty-eight hours and to decide the matter within twenty-one days of convening. If the twenty-one day period expires and either Congress fails to act, or the challenge is not upheld by a two-thirds majority vote in both houses, the president resumes office.

Have the dangers to public safety and welfare from presidential disability been greatly lessened by the passage of the 25th Amendment to the U.S. Constitution and by more thorough news coverage of the presidency? That common belief is a comforting but false assumption. As in the past, the types of disabilities that are likely to endanger the public in the future are not ones such as President Eisenhower's ileitis, but, rather, those that may be hidden to all but the President's intimates and that are usually intermittent or chronic. There are ways to deal with this problem, but the 25th Amendment and more active reportage are not among them.

We would readily agree with this concise statement of the problem by Robert S. Robins and Henry Rothschild, M.D.[7] When the Twenty-fifth Amendment was first enacted, it appeared initially to provide for a methodical and legal transfer of power in case of the president's "inability to discharge his duties." Yet, it in fact is fraught with uncertainties. What, for instance, did the authors of the amendment mean by "unable to discharge the powers and duties of the office"? Does that refer specifically to illness? Are psychiatric as well as organic illnesses to be considered? Is the president's physician, who may have the keenest insight into the matter, required to break confidence with his patient and testify? How would laymen (who compose the majority of the cabinet and federal legislators) evaluate a medical opinion if one were tendered? Can we afford to tolerate a period of three weeks, which conceivably it might take, for Congress to declare a president unable to serve? Should there be no limitation on the number of times a president who has been relieved of his duties can challenge the decision? How do we define or judge inability to serve?

In an age of nuclear weapons, it is extremely critical that presidential power be in the hands of a person with sound mind and body. In case of an ambiguous or delayed transfer of power, who controls the U.S. armed forces? Until the end of World War II one might have supposed that even a delay of several weeks in the transference of command, while debilitating, could be tolerated. Events today, however, move at dizzying speed and could require instant response. It is unsettling to consider that, for example, letting loose the retaliatory might of America in response to a Soviet challenge may require that a decision be made in a matter of minutes. We must ascertain that whoever controls the nuclear code is sane and stable.

How does the Twenty-fifth Amendment provide for this new reality in world affairs? What has happened since the Twenty-fifth Amendment was enacted? The years of the Reagan presidency provide two examples: his intestinal surgery in 1985 and the attempted assassination in March 1981. In the latter incident there was no known formal transfer of command. The secretary of state, Alexander Haig, made an improper and ill-advised assertion that he was "in control" at the White House and proceeded to misquote the Constitution. Later that afternoon Secretary of Defense Caspar Weinberger informed Mr. Haig that the chain of military command passes from the president to the secretary of defense. At the same time Vice President Bush, who would have assumed the presidency had Mr. Reagan died, was a thousand miles away at a political rally and did not arrive in Washington until late that same evening. Yet after he was installed in the White House, there still was no formal, or at least no public, transfer of command.

In his book *Gambling with History*, Laurence Barrett describes a scenario that occurred within the first few hours after the shooting. Fred Fielding, legal counsel to the president, was in the White House with Haig, Defense Secretary Caspar Weinberger, and Treasury Secretary Donald Regan. Presidential aides James Baker and Edwin Meese were also present originally but soon left for the hospital to be near the president. Fielding, who had an intimate knowledge of the Twenty-fifth Amendment, had hastily prepared the necessary documents in case either Section 3 or Section 4 of the amendment was to be used by the president or the vice president.

While still at the White House, writes Barrett, Baker and Meese "briefly discussed the possibility that Reagan might relinquish his powers temporarily by invoking Section 3. *They quickly dismissed the idea* [emphasis added]. If a military emergency demanding an instant decision arose while he was under anesthesia, the National Command Authority system provided the means for coping." Barrett continued:

> Fielding also had on hand the documents that would have to be signed and sent to each house of Congress if Section Four came into play. Now, a few minutes after four-thirty, Fielding had those papers out. At one end of the oblong conference table he was going over the documents with two of the other participants, Haig and Daniel Murphy, a retired admiral who served as George Bush's Chief of Staff. Most of the others in the room were unaware of what Haig, Murphy and Fielding were doing. However, Richard Darman, a restless and inquisitive sort with a knack for troubleshooting, quickly realized what was happening.
>
> At that early stage of the Administration, Darman had only a middling place in the White House hierarchy along with the title of Deputy Assistant to the President. A number of others in the level just below the troika, such as Gergen, Brady, Friedersdorf, Allen and Fielding, nominally outranked him until later in the year. However, Darman was closely associated with Baker and one of his duties was central to White House operations: Darman personally controlled all papers going to and coming from the President.
>
> When he spotted the implementing documents related to the Twenty-fifth Amendment, Darman also recognized trouble. If the subject came up for general discussion in the Situation Room and word of that got out, it would create questions about Reagan's capacities. Worse, Darman sniffed the possibility, however remote, that the cabinet might actually seize the initiative. He made a

quick decision to head off both dangers. Darman quietly told Fielding, Haig and Murphy that neither the subject nor the documents belonged on the table. He suggested that he take possession of the papers. Darman supported that proposal with the half-truth that the Twenty-fifth Amendment was something for the President himself to consider. The others gave in. At that point Darman felt that he needed some backing. He got Baker by phone, told him what had happened, and suggested that Baker authorize him to retain physical possession of the implementing documents. Baker acquiesced, whereupon Darman went to his own office nearby in the basement and locked them in his safe. The issue did not come up again in the larger group and got no attention in the news coverage. That night [Attorney General William French] Smith and Fielding briefed Bush on the technicalities of the amendment.[8]

In an interview Mr. Fielding stated that the issue raised in Mr. Barrett's section about Darman's action was much too "dramatized" and not of major importance.[9]

All of those very important decisions affecting the safety of the United States, even the world, were carried out without consulting the president's physician about the seriousness of the president's condition, despite the fact that his physician, Dr. Daniel Ruge, was present at the shooting and accompanied the president to the George Washington Hospital emergency room. There it was determined that the president had been seriously wounded, and Dr. Ruge turned the minute-to-minute care of the president over to the surgical team of the hospital. However, he remained at the president's side during the diagnostic, surgical, and postoperative procedures.

Dr. Ruge has testified that he was not consulted by any member of the White House staff or the vice president until the morning following the shooting and resultant surgery. Early that following morning he was asked by Mr. Baker to meet with the staff. He was also asked to meet with Vice President Bush and the cabinet following his meeting with the staff. This he did, and the only questions asked pertained to the status of the president's health. Dr. Ruge replied that the president had recovered from the anesthesia and his condition was stable. He was not asked if the president was in a satisfactory condition to function as president. Dr. Ruge told us that if he had been asked he would have replied in the affirmative. However, he would have been concerned if the president had been forced to make a major decision involving the safety of the country.[10] Fortunately for all concerned, there was no known prevailing crisis situation at this time. To reassure the world of his ability to function the president was photographed signing a bill of no great significance some thirty-six hours after the shooting.

Was the decision of the White House staff against invoking Section 3 a sound one? Historians and constitutional experts undoubtedly can argue about the wisdom of the decision. Fortunately, the president survived the operation and was alert twelve hours after his surgery.

Four years later President Reagan cited, but did not actually invoke, the voluntary Section 3 when he transferred his authority to Vice President George Bush for the duration of his colon surgery in July 1985. Note the second paragraph of Mr. Reagan's letter, reprinted below:

Text of the President's Letter

[Bethesda, Md., July 13: Following is the text of President Reagan's letter to the President pro tempore of the Senate and the Speaker of the House notifying them that Vice President Bush would temporarily discharge the powers and duties of the President]

I am about to undergo surgery during which time I will be briefly and temporarily incapable of discharging the constitutional powers and duties of the office of the President of the United States.

After consultation with my counsel and the Attorney General,

I am mindful of the provisions of Section 3 of the 25th Amendment to the Constitution and of the uncertainties of its application to such brief and temporary periods of incapacity. I do not believe that the drafters of this amendment intended its application to situations such as the instant one.

Nevertheless, consistent with my longstanding arrangement with Vice President George Bush, and not intending to set a precedent binding anyone privileged to hold the office in the future, I have determined and it is my intention and direction, that Vice President George Bush shall discharge those powers and duties in my stead commencing with the administration of anesthesia to me in this instance.

I shall advise you and the Vice President when I determine that I am able to resume the discharge of the constitutional powers and duties of this office.

May God bless this nation and us all.

Sincerely, Ronald Reagan

In the first such delegation of power in U.S. history, Bush in effect was "acting president" for just under eight hours. Though Reagan did not invoke Section 3, he effectively followed the amendment's intent by transmitting his written declaration of pending disability to the Speaker of the House and the president pro tempore of the Senate, as well as to Senator Strom Thurmond, ranking officer of the Senate. Further, he would "advise" when he was able to resume the duties of his office. Surgery on President Reagan's colon began at 11:48 A.M., and at 7:22 the same evening Reagan reasserted his authority as president. Again, as had happened during the 1981 surgery, the White House staff played the major role in assessing the competence of Mr. Reagan to reassume office. The decision by Mr. Donald Regan and Mr. Fred Fielding to transfer the powers of the presidency back to Mr. Reagan was made less than eight hours after major abdominal surgery. Even though the president received spinal rather than general anesthesia, one wonders about the wisdom of such a hasty decision.

Mr. Fielding stated in an interview that the president's surgeon had stated that "everything was fine" and that the president "was alert."[11] Did the president's surgeon, in his eagerness to reassure himself and the White House staff that everything was fine, realize that his statements might or might not change world history?

Mr. Reagan's surgery on July 13, 1985, was not an emergency. The president and his executive staff had ample time to transfer the power of the presidency to the vice president as outlined in Section 3 of the Twenty-fifth Amendment to the Constitution. The eminent journalist William Safire commented as follows:

> What did this President do? In a moment calling for absolute clarity, he acted with deliberate fuzziness. He followed the law's procedures but challenged its premises. In the letter to Congress prepared for him by his uncertain legal trumpeters, he properly declared his anticipated inability to discharge his powers and duties, but then wrote of "the uncertainties of its application to such brief and temporary periods of incapacity" and concluded: "I do not believe that the drafters of this amendment intended its application to situations such as the instant one."

He further states:

> This section was tailor-made for the situation that confronted the President and his legal advisers last week. A president, in full possession of mental and physical faculties, decided to go ahead with a major operation. The whole world knew, as it should, the time of the operation and the approximate length of time the President would be unconscious. That was the time of danger to the nation that Section 3 was created to avert.

Safire believes: "The opportunity to strengthen one of the glories of the American constitutional system—that sense of stability that comes from strict adherence to the law in times of peril—was botched again."[12]

Attorney General Meese stated that the document which Reagan sent to the Speaker of the House and president pro tempore of the Senate was constitutional. But many have questioned the attorney general's interpretation of the constitutionality of this document as a means of transfer of the duties and power of the office of president.

The concept of a letter of agreement between the president and vice president outlining the transfer of power was initiated by Eisenhower after his first heart attack. The custom was apparently continued in the Kennedy-Johnson and the Johnson-Humphrey administrations. Since no such documents were used in those two instances, constitutionality did not become an issue. All of this, of course, came before the enactment of the Twenty-fifth Amendment in 1967.

Why did President Reagan and his executive staff choose precedent over a clearly defined constitutional method of declaring temporary disability and the transfer of power to the vice president? Mr. Fielding told us in an interview that after much discussion it was the president's personal choice not to invoke the Twenty-fifth Amendment.[13] Earlier, Mr. Safire had written:

> Underlying the President's fear of admitting his requirement to obey Section 3 in an emergency, I think, is the fear of having to deal with its pressure to declare inability for a longer period. Someday a President will be faced with a debilitating physical or mental ailment, and will find tempting an option that is short of resignation.
>
> Digging one layer below that, in seeking the motive for last week's curious refusal to admit precedent, we find the inherent threat to presidents of Section 4: the involuntary removal of an incapacitated executive by his Cabinet, possibly even over his objections, with the matter of authority left for Congress to decide.[14]

Although the vice president in most cases must initiate the proceeding to remove a president unable to "carry out the duties and powers of the office," there are two other groups which are inextricably involved in what is basically a political issue of tremendous magnitude.

First, the White House staff has a most intimate relationship with the president on a day-to-day basis. The Reagan scenarios and examples seen in the Wilson and Roosevelt years reveal the raw power of the White House staff in monitoring the executive branch of government. Those examples are classic demonstrations of the fact that unelected officials play a major role in the day-to-day management of our government. To our knowledge, Vice President Bush was not consulted about invoking or not invoking the Twenty-fifth Amendment during or before President Reagan's two surgical procedures.

Following the attempted assassination and the surgery which ensued, the White House staff made the decision not to invoke Section 3. For the colon surgery the president himself, but with the assistance of his staff, chose not to officially invoke Section 3. Clearly, the power and influence of the White House staff are well established in our political process. Should the question of presidential inability arise in the future, it will require a very powerful vice president to initiate the removal proceedings. From a political standpoint the vice president probably would be quite reluctant to initiate the proceedings on other than clear-cut, nearly disastrous medical grounds, lest he be charged with a political coup. The other officers of the executive branch may be even more reticent, as they serve at the request of the president.

Philip Buchen, who served as President Ford's legal counsel, summarizes the situation neatly:

> Top staffers are likely to worry that the Vice President, if he becomes acting President, cannot be depended upon, as they would be, to know and do just what the President himself would have wanted had he not been disabled. Worst fate of all, in the view of the White House staff, would be for the Acting President

to bring in assistants from the Vice Presidential staff.

When a President cannot perform his duties, the nation and this government, if it lacks an Acting President, may incur no serious difficulty for some time, especially if his incapacity escapes public attention. The staff can always appear to act for the President except to sign or veto bills passed by Congress, to submit nominations for Senate consideration or fill interim vacancies, to grant pardons, to make treaties, or to serve as Commander-in-Chief of the Armed Forces. However, a President in office should not want his assistants ever to believe they can function without a President in place who wittingly bears responsibility for everything said or done in his name. Otherwise, when the truth about a President's hidden incapacity becomes generally known, as inevitably happens, the decision and policies which had been attributed to the ailing President become suspect and the standing of the Presidency for that period in history becomes shaken. Also, just as happens whenever an administration practices deceit of any kind on the public, the Office of the President loses stature and respect.

Wherever he goes, a President is accompanied by sure signs of the unremitting responsibilities which the office puts upon its holder. In these times, a President is never away from means of instant communications between him and any department of the United States government and between him and the head of almost any foreign government, and always within his reach is the "football" containing secret codes that enable the President to signal an immediate response by this country if ever it should face a nuclear attack. Even while asleep, a President is subject to call at any time, and his aides will be rightfully criticized if, upon learning of a major calamity or an alarming threat to the nation, they do not inform the President until after he awakens.

Such well-known aspects of the office and the worldwide prestige which the American Presidency earns in advance for each new incumbent have given rise to extraordinary public expectations of what any person who holds in his hands the immense power of that office can and would do to cope with a sudden national emergency or world crisis. To keep and preserve the respect which the American public and people everywhere have for the capacity and dependability of the American Presidency is an important reason for not deliberately permitting an official hiatus, however brief. If the President becomes unconscious or otherwise disabled and the Vice President were not duly authorized to act, the circumstances that no person with the authority and power of a President is present and capable of acting does in itself debase the importance and value of the Presidency. Much more harmful, to be sure, would be the effect if a national emergency or world crisis were actually to erupt during an hiatus. Such considerations, among others, ought to convince every responsible aide to a President that whenever or however a situation arises for applying the 25th Amendment, he or she must not dissemble about the President's health or otherwise fend off use of the constitutional remedy for Presidential illness.[15]

Buchen's comments raise two vital issues. First, what constitutes inability to serve, and who would initiate the removal process if it might lead to political suicide? Secondly, is the presidential physician responsible solely to his patient or to the nation and conceivably the world? Admiral Grayson, for example, went to extreme lengths to hide President Wilson's illness from the cabinet, the Congress, and the public. Only Mrs. Wilson knew the seriousness of the president's illness, and even she was not given the full facts. Nor would she divulge any. Admiral McIntire was quite successful in keeping the seriousness of President Roosevelt's illness from the public, the Congress, and the cabinet. These examples point out the fact that the confidentiality of the doctor-patient relationship is a powerful force in maintaining silence about the physical condition of the

president. Both cases arose in the age before today's aggressive investigative reporting and the almost daily appearance of the president
on television, but the evidence was there and could have been
unearthed by enterprising reporters or officials.

A question arises as to whom the vice president and officers of the
executive department would consult in order to determine whether
or not a president might be capable of discharging his duties. The
president's physician? By the present ethical code of confidentiality
of the physician-patient relationship, however, it might be difficult
for the vice president to obtain accurate and complete information
about the president's health.

What is the present legal status of physician-patient privilege and
the president? Professor Paul Stephan of the University of Virginia
School of Law provided the following summary in September 1987:

> The President's physician is, among other things, a close aide
> and advisor of the President, and the Supreme Court has recog-
> nized a limited and as yet indeterminate privilege to protect
> communications with such advisers from casual Congressional
> inspection. In United States v. Nixon, 418 U.S. 683, 708 (1974),
> the Court declared:
>
> "The expectation of a President to the confidentiality of his
> conversations and correspondence, like the claim of confiden-
> tiality of judicial deliberations, for example, has all the values
> to which we accord deference for the privacy of all citizens
> and, added to those values, is the necessity for protection of
> the public interest in candid, objective, and even blunt or
> harsh opinions in Presidential decision-making. A President
> and those who assist him must be free to explore alternatives
> in the process of shaping policies and making decisions and
> to do so in a way many would be unwilling to express except
> privately. These are the considerations justifying a presump-
> tive privilege for Presidential communications. The privilege

is fundamental to the operation of Government and inextricably rooted in the separation of powers under the Constitution."

As is well known, the Court then ruled that this privilege, although constitutionally based, must give way to other constitutional interests such as a criminal accused's rights to confront witnesses, compulsory process, and due process of law, id. at 711. It implied a different result might be produced by a Presidential "claim of need to protect military, diplomatic, or sensitive national security secrets." Id. at 706.

Although predictions are difficult to make in this area, it seems unlikely that the Court would place communications between the President and his physician in the ultra-protected category of "sensitive national security secrets." Although a President might argue that broadcasting his physical frailities might aid our foreign adversaries, this claim at root seems no different from the assertion that the President's political and legal health is a matter of national security, a point that the Nixon case surely settled to the contrary.

What is less certain is the weight courts might attach to Congress' constitutionally-based interest in providing for cases of Presidential disability (Article II, 1,6) when it conflicts with the more general presumption of executive privilege. When called in to decide a dispute under Section 4 of the 25th Amendment, Congress undoubtedly can obtain anything it wants from the President's physician. But if it were to seek to impose more prophylactic measures such as full oversight and disclosure of the physician's contacts with the President, the claim of privilege might prevail. Cf. United States v. Nixon, 418 U.S. at 682 n.19 ("We are not here concerned with the balance between the President's generalized interest in confidentiality and . . . congressional demands for information"); Senate Select Comm. on Presidential Campaign Activities v. Nixon, 370 F. Supp. 521

(D.D.C. 1974) (congressional committee's need to know contents of Presidential tapes does not outweigh executive interest in confidentiality).

If Congress instead were to enact legislation to enable the Vice President and the Cabinet to have better access to information about the President's health, the authority of the 25th Amendment would seem sufficiently strong to overcome the presumption of executive privilege. Similarly, if Congress created some "other body" to substitute for the Cabinet under the 25th Amendment, that body also should be able to defeat any privilege claim. In either case the entity seeking to invade the President's confidences is in a position analogous to that of a grand jury seeking information about a matter within its direct competence.

In sum, the problem posed by a claim of executive privilege, used to shield the relationship between the President and his physician from external oversight, should differ depending on what body seeks to do the overseeing. The claim of privilege probably would be strongest were Congress simply to mandate that all dealings between the President and his doctor be exposed to public scrutiny. Although one might conceive of a First Amendment argument to buttress such a command, cf. Press-Enterprise Co. v. Superior Court, 464 U.S. 501 (1984) (First Amendment right of access to voir dire); Richmond Newspapers, Inc. v. Virginia, 448 U.S. 555 (1980) (First Amendment right of access to trials), on balance I suspect this argument would not be greeted with enthusiasm by the present Court. The claim of privilege would be weaker, but still colorable, were Congress to order periodic disclosure of these dealings to designated committees of Congress. The claim almost certainly would fail were Congress instead to provide for a system of oversight exercised by those bodies empowered by Section 4 of the 25th Amendment to make a determination of Presidential disability.

As a caveat, I might add that any accommodation reached by

one President and the Congress on this issue, were it to continue long enough to take on the coloration of an accepted practice, would be incorporated into the body of custom and tradition that informs our understanding of what the Constitution means. In particular a President who accepted the obligation to open up his relationship with his physician to some kind of outside scrutiny would tend to bind his successors.[16]

Although not stated specifically, the Twenty-fifth Amendment places the president's physician in an unexpectedly powerful political position. Though the president's physician cannot officially initiate the process of removing a disabled president, and though removal from office is primarily a political process, the decision by the vice president and the cabinet to initiate the proceedings must be based upon medical disability rather than political disability. This, then, places the president's physician in a very key position.

Dr. Daniel Ruge, physician to President Reagan, stated that "despite its glamourous name, the office of the White House physician is somewhat blue collar." It carries no job description and has only the powers implied from its entry as a line item in the budget. Ruge further states, "The job is so lacking in opportunities for creativity and medical skills that most physicians would shy away from it."[17] Dr. Ruge and Dr. William Lukash (who served under four presidents) both stated that the general requirements for the job would seem to call for a senior physician whose reputation has been made and who is willing to serve in the public interest.[18]

It appears that presidential physicians face the dilemma of either revealing the president's disability and unleashing the forces for medical removal of the chief executive or participating in a cover-up to keep an incapacitated president in office. The key observer in the health watch is the White House physician. Through a unique combination of access and professional training, he or she should be among the first to notice any deterioration in the president's capacity to serve. Although the physician has implied constitutional responsibilities in the event of presidential disability, he or she works from a cramped ground floor office in the executive mansion—primarily dispensing aspirin for headaches—and in the pecking order ranks with the curator and the usher of the White House.

Drs. Ruge and Lukash both felt that the time had come to formally recognize the responsibilities of the White House physician's post and to outline its powers. Though the position does not warrant the stature of a cabinet officer, the position should be strengthened. They both suggested that one solution might be to require Senate confirmation of the White House physician. The procedure would assure a minimum standard of competence and provide a formal congressional platform for discussion and consultation in case disability became an issue. Under the current format a recalcitrant president could invoke his right to executive privilege to muzzle the doctor. There is precedent for confirmation of White House officers in that the president's economic advisers and his budget directors are subject to congressional approval.

Former Attorney General Herbert Brownell, Jr., who served under President Eisenhower, says a written protocol involving the president, vice president, and White House physician would be useful in the event of gradual disability. The protocol would provide guidelines for both the vice president and the physician, either of whom might be hesitant to act without such authority. "Speed and certainty are the goals," says Brownell, who took charge of resolving the disability dilemma when Eisenhower suffered a heart attack in 1955.[19] Once there is a suspicion of disability, the matter could be turned over to Congress to resolve as the Constitution defines. The White House physician must be permitted to act without the fear of being accused of a plot to oust the president.

Without a protocol or some guidelines to help the doctor and the vice president trigger the disability machinery, it is likely that nothing would be done until the president's disability reached a dimension of national concern. If the disability were covered up, as it was in the Wilson and Roosevelt administrations, there would be no speedy and certain resolution and the disability issue would be shrouded in speculation.

In a personal interview former Senator Birch Bayh echoed Mr. Brownell's thoughts about presidential power and the political question of disability: "The thing that comes through is that there is nothing quite like presidential power. Historically—here again this becomes a larger problem, I think, when you get into the disability discussion—the question is not so much a medical question as a political one." Senator Bayh gave further insight into the method proposed by Mr. Brownell. "It is only natural I assume, that people around the President would think in terms of a President who was shot, killed, or almost killed. However, it is unwise if that is the only contingency that they plan for. It is a difficult thing to sit down and talk with the President of the United States and say, 'Mr. President, you know somebody might shoot you or you might have a heart attack.' That's a very difficult kind of thing to discuss, but I think it should be discussed. I had thought that starting with Eisenhower that had been a matter that had been discussed at the beginning of each administration, but apparently it was not the case."[20]

The question of how to determine the inability of the president to "carry out the power and duties of the office" has been discussed off and on since the constitutional convention. It received a great deal of discussion during and following President Eisenhower's illnesses. In 1957 President Truman proposed that when a president is stricken with an illness, there should come into being a Committee of Seven composed of representatives of the three branches of the government. This committee would select a board of leading medical authorities drawn from top medical schools of the nation. This medical board, thus chosen, would then make the necessary examinations, presenting their findings to the Committee of Seven. Should the findings of the medical board indicate that the president is unable to perform his duties and that he is, in fact, truly incapacitated and not merely stricken with a transitory illness, then the Committee of Seven would so inform the Congress. Congress would then have the right to act and by a two-thirds vote of the full membership could declare the vice president president. This proposal would hardly assure swift and decisive action.

Many articles since 1957 have pointed out the problem of the difficulty of a single physician, the president's physician, determining disability of the president. At the heart of the problem of invoking Section 4 is the design of a mechanism to resolve the dispute over the actual medical and mental condition of the ailing president. As was pointed out by William Curran, a noted law and medical expert, this was discussed in some detail during the congressional hearings. Curran states:

> The dispute over the President's condition would, in all likelihood, occur among such powerful figures in the government as the President, the Vice President, the President's personal staff, Cabinet officers, and members of Congress. Who could resolve such a conflict peaceably? An early suggestion was to create an "inability commission" of respected medical experts, either as a standing body or as an ad hoc group named during a specific crisis. It was also suggested that the commission could include, along with medical experts, officials such as the Chief Justice of the United States and selected Cabinet officers such as the Secretary of State. This proposal was weakened, but not abandoned, in 1958, when Chief Justice Earl Warren sent a letter to Congress in which he advised against involving any member of the Supreme Court in such a commission. Ironically, the Chief Justice did not follow his own good advice in the 1960s, when he allowed himself to be appointed chairman of the commission investigating President Kennedy's assassination. As pointed out earlier, assassinations and assassination attempts probably cre-

ate the most egregious crises involving the Chief Executive in this country.

The suggestion to create an inability commission was probably also weakened by the lack of experience at the federal level in the United States with centralized, nationally appointed medical or medicolegal standing commissions that have the authority to examine sensitive issues of mental or physical capacity, to deal with suspicious deaths, or to investigate sources of danger to human life.[21]

In 1981 Robins and Rothschild made the following suggestion:

Our proposal concerns the monitoring of the President's health while in office. We suggest that the position of the President's Official Physicians Panel be established, appointed by a special committee of Congress or a committee of high judicial officers. This panel of three physicians would have the right to meet with the President at least quarterly, be the medical officers in charge of a yearly medical evaluation, and have the right of access and full consultation whenever the President was ill. We further suggest that the tenure of the physicians be limited to one 4-year period and that only the body that appointed them could prematurely remove them from the position. The President would continue to employ whatever other physicians he desired and continue to use armed services physicians.

Records would be secret, and the relationship between the President and his Official Physicians Panel would be that of the strictest confidence, except in one set of circumstances. If in the opinion of the panel, a medical state of disability is present or if one is likely to take place without provision being made for it, they would be obligated to inform the Vice President, the principal executive officers, and the leaders of both houses of Congress. In such circumstances they would be permitted to reveal relevant medical facts.[22]

Dr. Milton Greenblatt in 1983 suggested the following:

> My personal view would be to consider establishing a Presiden-
> tial Health Commission of renowned specialists who would rep-
> resent expertise in various aspects of health, including mental
> health. This group would advise on (a) screening of candidates
> for medical and emotional fitness, (b) choice of the leader's per-
> sonal physician, (c) use of specialized consultants and other
> necessary resources, (d) use of hospitalization, (e) determination
> of which information will be released to the public, (f) education
> of the public on pertinent medical matters. The personal physi-
> cian of the leader would then be relieved of the responsibility of
> deciding by himself which health information to release. And,
> the public would be assured that the health of their leaders
> would be in the best professional hands. The most strategic and
> critical advice by this group would, of course, relate to advising
> when the office holder was unfit and when, after treatment, he
> was again fit to serve.
>
> How will such a commission be chosen, how long will mem-
> bers serve, how much authority will it be given beyond advisory
> functions, how would it be made as free as possible of political
> influence, and how would it renew itself over time—these are
> questions that require a great deal of thought. However, I believe
> there is urgency in these matters, and that important profes-
> sional organizations in medicine ought to begin to address the
> issues as soon as possible, and to make known the critical impor-
> tance of their work to the Executive and Legislative Branches
> and to the public.[23]

In 1987 William Safire again proposed the same concept: "Perhaps
the next President should ask a panel of doctors appointed by all
three branches of government to check him out once a year, the
results to be made public. In this case, the doctor-patient relationship might suffer; the patient-voter relationship would improve."[24]

In an attempt to respond to some of these suggestions, a group of distinguished physicians, including Dr. Ruge, convened to discuss in some detail the problems of the president's physician with particular emphasis on the confidentiality of the doctor-patient relationship versus the responsibility of the president's physician to society. No answers were provided, but it was pointed out that in 1957 the AMA council adopted the following statement: "A physician may not reveal the confidences entrusted to him in the course of medical attendance, or the deficiencies he may observe in the character of patients, unless he is required to do so by law or unless it becomes necessary in order to protect the individual *or the community* [emphasis added]."[25]

In an in-depth discussion of the Truman concept of a "Committee of Seven" or a similar advisory committee, it was suggested that this system would officially "protect" the president's physician but would probably prevent or hinder a real doctor-patient relationship between the president and the White House physician. None of the proposals would assure swift and decisive action, nor would the public place confidence in a medical decision which was by its very nature political.

Dr. Ruge, President Reagan's physician who was a member of the advisory group, stated that because of his or her position, it is possible for the president's physician to obtain consultants from any medical or surgical specialty to see the president at any time, including consultants for any type of illness or to help in judging presidential disability. Dr. Ruge felt that this system would be more workable than any of the proposed advisory committees.

At this writing the suggestion originally offered by Mr. Brownell appears to be one of the best possible solutions. To repeat, Mr. Brownell suggested a written protocol involving the president, vice president, and the White House physician. It might be important to include the president's chief of staff and legal counsel. The protocol would provide guidelines for both the vice president and the physician, either of whom might be hesitant to act without such authority. This protocol would be initiated at the beginning of each administration.

Could such a protocol be made mandatory by an act of Congress? How far can Congress go in spelling out the mechanisms or procedures that must be followed in order to write a decision about disability? In recent correspondence Feerick states that "inability was not defined in the text of the Amendment. This was not the result of oversight. Rather, it reflected a judgement that a rigid constitutional definition was undesirable, since cases of inability could take various forms not really fitting into such a definition."[26]

Senator Bayh responded to this question in an interview:

> I think they could pass an act that would provide for procedures. The question is whether you go beyond the procedure and the procedure becomes substance. But, I think they could establish a procedural format to be followed. I guess what we were trying to do with the 25th Amendment was find a way which would meet with public acceptance and then public officials, understanding that the public would accept it, would be willing to utilize it. In short, we wanted to find a way in which presidential disability would not become a matter of leprosy. Presidents get ill. That's particularly why we had that provision that was used by President Reagan. If a President recognizes he is ill and the people recognize that the President becomes ill and there is a ready way of disposing of this, it becomes less a major consequence when it happens. The stock market doesn't gyrate. The divisions aren't set and aborted. It's a matter of business as usual, which is the way I wished that President Reagan had approached this. I think that is a sure way of lessening any public reaction or concern.[27]

The use of Section 3 so that "it is business as usual" will depend primarily on the president and also the White House staff. It is a political decision with no or minimal input by the White House physician—with or without consultation with other physicians.

One suggestion would be to establish ground rules for the use of Section 3 in the previously proposed protocol for disability:

1. Section 3 would be invoked if the president were to receive a combination of anesthesia and narcotics which had a mood-altering effect for a minimum of twenty-four hours, or for a longer time in the case of major surgery.

2. After a suitable period of time had elapsed, the president could reassume power at his own request. This presents some serious problems, as exemplified by the following news release on December 20, 1986 (by Karen Tumulty and Michael Wines, *Los Angeles Times*):

> *Washington*—Despite earlier White House denials, President Reagan may have approved the first shipment of U.S. arms to Iran *while ill or under sedation, a condition that may have left him unable to recall his action later* [emphasis added], Attorney General Edwin Meese told the House Intelligence Committee yesterday, according to a committee member.
>
> That explanation lends additional credence to former national security adviser Robert McFarlane's contention that he received oral approval from Reagan for the deal.
>
> The U.S.-made arms were shipped to Iran by Israel, which would have been legally barred from selling them without presidential approval.
>
> "The explanation is that Reagan either was in the hospital or recovering," said Representative George Brown, Jr., D-Calif., the committee member. "He may have been under sedation. . . . [Meese] gave the impression that it was a difficult time for the president."
>
> Reagan underwent surgery for colon cancer on July 13, 1985; the first arms shipment occurred the next month. Brown quoted Meese, who testified behind closed doors, as saying that the

meeting between McFarlane and Reagan would have been private.

Meese's testimony, as related by Brown, would be the first time an administration official has edged away from the White House insistence that Israel made the August 1985 shipment on its own, without U.S. authorization. Israel has maintained that the shipment was approved.

The issue is crucial not only as a test of the veracity of McFarlane and administration officials, but also because an unauthorized shipment could be ground for suspending U.S. aid to Israel.

Mr. Fielding told us in his interview that he and Donald Regan had been assured by the surgeon that the president was "OK." They therefore advised the president, after very inadequate evaluation of cerebral function, to reassume office. Perhaps this was the best political decision, but it was very wrong from a medical standpoint. The immediate surgical results were "OK," but anesthesia, major surgery, and narcotics produce major metabolic changes, including brain abnormalities.[28]

Former White House Chief of Staff Donald Regan further corroborates this meeting. In his 1988 book, *For the Record*, Regan relates that a meeting between Reagan and McFarlane on the Iran hostages took place five days after the President's surgery for colon cancer. Regan notes that it was McFarlane who insisted on the meeting, citing a matter of "great importance," even though Reagan had requested that visitors be kept to a minimum while he was recuperating. According to Donald Regan's account of that meeting, "[the subject of] Iran took up to ten or twelve minutes." Regan then muses about the lasting implications of that exchange between the president and an aide: "It hardly seems likely that an entirely new policy, involving a brusque departure from past practices and established principles . . . could have been decided on in such a brief encounter."

The episode following President Reagan's cancer surgery highlights a very key question in any discussion of presidential illness. The question is whether or not the illness, acute or chronic, has affected the president's ability to make reasonable and competent decisions.

Dr. Norman Knorr, professor of behavioral medicine at the University of Virginia, summarizes the problem as follows:

A lot of people can function very well with different kinds of physical illness, such as heart disease, arthritis, or cancer. Once those diseases get very severe and the person with the illness feels overwhelmed by them or becomes very self-centered so that all of their energy is wrapped up in their illness, it becomes a problem in terms of their ability to make decisions.

The impact of the illness on the psyche is a very important factor in a person's ability to make decisions. So it becomes necessary to think in terms of the effect of an illness on the brain in order to evaluate someone's disability or potential disability in certain high-ranking positions or especially in an office such as the President of the United States.[29]

This "gray area" of mental aberrations presents the greatest difficulty in judging whether or not the president is disabled. At the present time we have no specific laboratory or radiological procedures to aid physicians in making a diagnosis of impaired judgment. Until such specific tests can be developed, reliance on the clinical judgment of experienced physicians must suffice.

Recently the health of candidates for president has surfaced as one of the issues to be publicized during a political campaign. President Reagan's staff went to great lengths to emphasize that despite his age the president was in excellent health. The staff of Democratic nominee Mr. Mondale, who was known to have high blood pressure, published an interview with Mr. Mondale's personal physician in leading newspapers. The essence of the report was that the high blood pressure was controlled with drugs. The drugs had no effect on brain function so in essence he was in "good health." It was probably the age issue that motivated President Reagan's campaign managers to bring up the matter of health. The public of today is quite health conscious. Because of this public attitude it is conceivable that the health of candidates might be an issue in future presidential elections.

One lesson which could probably be learned from history is that presidents are human beings and can suffer the same infirmities as all other citizens. In view of this the vice president should be selected, nominated, and elected on the basis of his qualifications to assume the presidency in case of disability or death of the president. As stated by Robert W. Kastenmeier, "We have learned through our first experience with the 25th Amendment that Vice President nominees must be judged as we would judge a prospective President."[30] It is extremely doubtful and unrealistic that this concept will ever be a factor in choosing a vice presidential candidate. Historically, the presidential candidate or the party chooses a person who will bring in a block of votes to elect a presidential candidate.

Throughout our history the office of vice president has not been formally endowed with much power. In this nuclear age, where major decisions may have to be made in seconds, it seems appropriate that the vice president be intimately acquainted with our foreign policy and security measures. It could be catastrophic if we had a repeat of the Roosevelt-Truman episode. Although we will not have all the facts until the release of President Truman's papers, it would appear from Mr. Vaughn's papers that Vice President Truman was left completely in the dark about our relations with our allies.[31]

In 1966, after Congress passed the Twenty-fifth Amendment and before it was ratified by all the states, Professor Richard Longaker, of the University of California, Los Angeles, made the following observations:

> Each case of presidential inability will impose its own set of imperatives and inhibitions on the President and the Vice President alike. Among the many variables in each case will be the

relative urgency of international and domestic problems, the ambition and self-restraint of the political actors, and the nature of the President's inability. In a word, the Amendment is only technically self-executing. Nonetheless, it contains all that a constitutional device should: a set of presumptions about the process of exercising power and an implicit expectation that it will be applied in a mood of restraint. Once the Amendment is ratified a Vice President will know that he has a constitutional obligation to seek support if deterioration of the President's health threatens the political order. Moreover, a President will know that a temporary declaration of inability is an accepted condition under the Constitution and that if he so declares, a Vice President will be available during this period to exercise the executive prerogatives without drawing into question his constitutional authority. However difficult the Amendment may be to apply, its greatest service is in making at least this much certain.[32]

Many of Longaker's predictions have become a reality in the last six years. There will be a division of opinion about the failure of the Reagan administration to use the Twenty-fifth Amendment. At least the concept was used, and there was an awareness of some of the problems in applying it if our top officials choose their own version of maintaining or transferring the duties of the president.

It is assumed that "inability to serve" will be primarily a political issue based on accurate and adequate medical input. One way to insure the latter is to have a well-trained senior White House physician with a full knowledge of both the medical and political problems of the Twenty-fifth Amendment. He or she must realize that the responsibilities include not only the care of the president but at times the care of the nation. The White House physician must have a well-defined and acceptable political route, such as the proposed protocol, to make his or her concern about the president's inability to serve" known to the vice president.

In view of the importance of the president's physician in evaluating presidential disability, we recommend that the following guidelines be adopted in defining the role of the presidential physician.

1. He or she is now selected and should continue to be selected by the president.

2. To be an effective personal physician, the time-honored concept of patient-doctor confidentiality must be in broad terms maintained.

3. A possible code of conduct for the president's physician would include:

a. From the beginning of his appointment the physician must have a knowledge of the history, medical implications, and use of the Twenty-fifth Amendment.

b. He or she should be familiar with the views of the American Medical Association Council on Medical Ethics regarding patient-doctor confidentiality and those instances when it can be departed from in the national interest.

c. He or she should have an early meeting with the president regarding the use of the Twenty-fifth Amendment due to illness. The physician should also seek a meeting with the president, the vice president, the chief of staff, and the legal counsel to the president to establish if possible a written protocol regarding the use of Section 3.

d. He or she should possess the knowledge, humility, and expertise to obtain consultation to insure the best medical care for the president. As previously noted, Dr. Daniel Ruge, who met with the physicians' committee, pointed out that the president's physician, because of his office, had easy access to any consultant or group of consultants that he wished to see the president.

In 1964, during the drafting of the Twenty-fifth Amendment, former President Truman made the following statement: "I don't think, in the enormous emergency that we would be faced with under the circumstances if the President did become disabled, that we can wait much longer in meeting the problem. We must face it and solve it, or else we could find ourselves in an extremely grave situation if we continue to leave it to chance." The Twenty-fifth Amendment has been in force for twenty years. Section 2 has been used on two occasions. Section 3 was the basis of President Reagan's letter that made Vice President Bush the acting president for eight hours. To date we fortunately have not been faced with implementing Section 4. To quote President Truman's statement, "we face an extremely grave situation if we continue to leave to chance" the institution of workable medical and political guidelines to define presidential disability. We would stress that these guidelines or a suitable protocol be instituted *before* the president takes office to avoid the confusion that occurred in President Reagan's administration.

Though it is difficult to prove that illness has been a major factor in the decisions of world leaders that subsequently affected world history, there is considerable evidence that this might be the case. This thesis is aptly expressed by Dr. Milton Greenblatt, professor of psychiatry at UCLA School of Medicine: "There is a body of evidence that shows that illness and exhaustion affected global world decisions made by Presidents Woodrow Wilson and Franklin Delano Roosevelt, and that ulcers, hypertension, coronary disease, stroke, and many other ailments beset world leaders perhaps more than ordinary citizens."[33]

Professor Louis Halle, a distinguished political science scholar who was in the State Department for several years, writes as follows:

> I have talked with doctors in Washington, and they say that if the American public knew what the strain does to even the toughest, they would be horrified. Washington wives know this, but of course it's confidential. They know the number of men who appear calm, all day—presiding or participating at meetings in

Washington—but when they go home in the evening they sometimes lock the door behind them, and smash the furniture, and chew up the rugs. This is almost literally so. Doctors have told me of some of the physical symptoms, like breaking out in rashes, diarrhea, and so on—just these ordinary symptoms of the strain. But of course it goes to the point where men break down, where perhaps they are no longer wholly responsible.

One of the things that is a bit frightening is that President Franklin D. Roosevelt was totally incompetent to be President of the United States in his last year. He'd had twelve years of this kind of thing, and if anyone put a paper in front of him that last year it transpired he couldn't read it. And he was negotiating with Russia at Yalta, and things like that, under circumstances where he was no longer altogether present mentally, so to speak.[34]

The issue was perhaps best summarized by former Secretary of State Dean Rusk: "The international list of those who have carried great responsibility while ill is long and there are fleeting glimpses of decisions which good health might have turned another way."[35]

Notes

Preface

1 The original article on the man "37 years of age" was by James A. Nicholas, Charles L. Burstein, Charles J. Umberger, and Philip Wilson, "Management of Adrenocortical Insufficiency during Surgery," *AMA Archives of Surgery* 71 (1955): 737–42.

2 Howard Bruenn, "Clinical Notes on the Illness and Death of President Franklin D. Roosevelt," *Annals of Internal Medicine* 72 (1970):579–91.

3 See, for example, Bert Park, *The Impact of Illness on World Leaders* (University of Pennsylvania Press: Philadelphia, 1986). Park, who is a neurosurgeon and student of American history, does a masterly job of documenting the maladies of important historical figures in the twentieth century. Our work, though similar in intent, focuses more closely on the American presidents and on the policy impact of their illnesses.

---

1. Illness and History

1 Dean Rusk, "Summitry," *Foreign Affairs*, April 1960. See also Hugh L'Etang, *The Pathology of Leadership* (New York: Prentice-Hall, 1970), p. 9.

2 Rusk, "Summitry," p. 2.

3 See *New York Times*, July 26, 1972, or *Washington Post*, July 27, 1972, for details of Eagleton's debacle.

4 "Eagleton Tells of Shock Therapy on Two Occasions," *New York Times*, July 26,

1972, p. 1. See also "Eagleton Reveals Illness," *Washington Post*, July 26, 1972, p. 1.

5 "Eagleton Says Allegation of Drunken Driving Is Lie," *New York Times*, July 28, 1972, p. 1; "Eagleton says Story 'Damnable'," *Washington Post*, July 28, 1972, p. 12.

6 See *New York Times* or *Washington Post* July 28, 1972, for editorials calling on Eagleton to resign.

7 Ibid.

8 "How the Eagleton Story Finally Got to the Public Domain," *Washington Post*, July 26, 1972, p. 2.

9 Ibid.

10 "The Public's Right to Health Data: We Must Know More about Our Leaders' Health," *Washington Post*, March 26, 1978.

11 Quoted in *New York Times*, July 31, 1972.

12 James Reston, *Washington Post*, July 20, 1972.

13 Ibid.

14 James David Barber, *The Presidential Character: Predicting Performance in the White House* (Englewood Cliffs, N.J.: Prentice-Hall, 1972), p. 6.

---

2. Woodrow Wilson

1 Charles Mee, *The End of the Order: Versailles, 1919* (New York: Elsevier Press, 1980), pp. xvl, 259. Mee's excellent study of World War I and its aftermath gives a strong sense of the unbelievable carnage and destruction wrought by the war.

2 Ibid. See also Joseph P. Tumulty, *Woodrow Wilson As I Knew Him* (New York: Garden City Publishing, 1927).

3 Edwin Weinstein, *Woodrow Wilson: A Medical and Psychological Biography* (Princeton: Princeton University Press, 1981), pp. 333–47. For primary sources on Wilson's entry into Paris, see Ray Stannard Baker, *Woodrow Wilson and World Settlement* (New York: Garden City Publishing, 1923), 1:12–18. For an assessment of the effect of Wilson's illness on the presidency from another physician's perspective, see Bert Park, *The Impact of Illness on World Leaders* (Philadelphia: University of Pennsylvania Press, 1986).

4 Mee, *End of the Order*, p . 12.

5 Ibid.

6 S. W. Livermore, "The Sectional Issue in the 1918 Congressional Elections," *Mississippi Valley Historical Review* 25 (1948):29–60.

7 Mee, *End of the Order*, p. 14, and Weinstein, *Woodrow Wilson*, p. 330. Although

most historians agree with the interpretation laid out by Livermore (see above) that parochial and domestic issues would probably have returned a Republican majority to Congress, Wilson's politicking did nothing to help the situation.

8   William Bullitt and Sigmund Freud, *Thomas Woodrow Wilson: A Psychological Study* (Boston: Houghton-Mifflin, 1967). Much of what Freud and Bullitt say about Wilson's neurotic and self-defeating behavior may or may not be true, but the tone of the study suggests that the authors were patently unsympathetic —and often unfair—to their subject.

9   Weinstein, "Woodrow Wilson's Neurological Illness," *Journal of American History* 57 (1970):324–51. In this article, and in his subsequent book on Wilson, Weinstein is considerably more fair and evenhanded in his appraisal of Wilson's illnesses than were Freud and Bullitt. In making our own assessment, we follow Dr. Weinstein's lead and are heavily indebted to his work in this area.

10   Weinstein, "Wilson's Neurological Illness," p. 324.

11   Ibid.

12   We note here that there are alternative interpretations to Wilson's illness and that the diagnosis of the president's maladies is still the subject of a heated dispute. See, for example, Michael F. Marmor, "Wilson, Strokes, and Zebras," *New England Journal of Medicine* 307 (1982):528–35; see also Juliette L. George, Michael F. Marmor, and Alexander L. George, "Issues in Wilson Scholarship: References to Early 'Strokes' in the *Papers of Woodrow Wilson*," *Journal of American History* 70 (1984): 845–53. See also Park, *Impact*, for further discussion. These alternative diagnoses are a subject to which we return in the last section of this chapter; we simply make note here that, although we agree with Dr. Weinstein's interpretation, the matter is by no means closed.

13   See, for example, John D. Moses and Wilbur Cross, *Presidential Courage* (New York: W. W. Norton, 1980), p. 134, for a recent example of medical biographers who refer to young Wilson as a "pathetic figure." See also Baker, *Woodrow Wilson and World Settlement*, 1:77, for a source more contemporaneous to Wilson which makes the same assumption.

14   Weinstein, *Woodrow Wilson*, p. 20.

15   Moses and Cross, *Courage*, p. 134, and Baker, *Woodrow Wilson*, 1:37.

16   Weinstein, *Woodrow Wilson*, pp. 17–18, suggests dyslexia as the cause of Wilson's early difficulties reading; see also Freud and Bullitt, *Thomas Woodrow Wilson*, p. 5, for a psychoanalytic interpretation.

17   Baker, *Woodrow Wilson and World Settlement*, 1:74.

18   Ibid., p. 77.

19   Weinstein, *Woodrow Wilson*, p. 20; quoted from Cary T. Grayson, *Woodrow Wilson:*

An Intimate Memoir (New York: Garden City Publishing, 1960), p. 80.

20   Weinstein, *Woodrow Wilson*, pp. 20–21.

21   From *The Collected Papers of Woodrow Wilson*, quoted in Weinstein, *Woodrow Wilson*, p. 21.

22   See, for example, Baker, *Woodrow Wilson and World Settlement*, 1:77.

23   William B. Hale, *Woodrow Wilson* (New York: Garden City Publishing, 1912), p. 51.

24   Weinstein, *Woodrow Wilson*, p. 24.

25   Ibid., p. 49.

26   Ibid.

27   Ibid.

28   Ibid., p. 50.

29   Both studies by Freud and Bullitt and by Weinstein suggest that it was Wilson's unhappiness over his love affair with Hattie and his own ambivalence over the study of the law that were at the root of Wilson's "very severe cold." His abrupt departure without taking leave of any of his friends suggests as much. See Bullitt and Freud, *Thomas Woodrow Wilson*, 36–38.

30   Weinstein, *Woodrow Wilson*, p. 55.

31   For Wilson's scholarly development, see, for example, James Kerney, *The Political Education of Woodrow Wilson* (New York: Century, 1926), and Henry W. Bragdon, *Woodrow Wilson: The Academic Years* (Cambridge, Mass.: Harvard University Press, 1967).

32   Wilson's behavior in 1895 is best described by Weinstein, *Woodrow Wilson*, pp. 117–27; most biographers have overlooked Wilson's health during the 1890s, and one who has not (Marmor) disputes Weinstein's interpretation. For an alternative set of impressions, see Marmor, "Wilson," pp. 528–35.

33   Weinstein, *Woodrow Wilson*, pp. 133, 135.

34   Ibid., p. 127.

35   Weinstein, "Wilson's Neurological Illness," p. 325.

36   For example, Marmor, "Wilson," pp. 528–35, and George, Marmor, and George, "Issues," p. 848.

37   Weinstein, *Woodrow Wilson*, p. 141.

38   Ibid.

39   Ibid.

40   Ibid., p. 147.

41   Ibid.

42   Ibid., p. 148. Arthur S. Link, who is Wilson's foremost biographer and editor of Wilson's papers, had suggested prior to Weinstein's study that Wilson's sudden

personality changes between 1895 and 1896 were indicative of some severe, probably physiological, pathology. In this regard, see Arthur S. Link, *Woodrow Wilson: Revolution, War, and Peace* (Arlington Heights, Ill.: University of Illinois Press, 1979).

43   Ibid.

44   The term "anosognosic," used by Weinstein to describe Wilson's personality, means literally "ignorant of disease." Weinstein comes back to this term when describing Wilson's denial of serious illness; it is a character trait that would figure importantly in Wilson's later, more serious illnesses. See Bullitt and Freud, *Thomas Woodrow Wilson*, pp. 80, 188, for a psychoanalytic discussion of this pathology.

45   Weinstein, *Woodrow Wilson*, p. 153.

46   Bragdon, *The Academic Years*, p. 275.

47   Ibid.; see also Weinstein, *Woodrow Wilson*, p. 153.

48   Weinstein, *Woodrow Wilson*, p. 168.

49   See Bullitt and Freud, *Thomas Woodrow Wilson*, p. 188.

50   Ibid.

51   Weinstein, *Woodrow Wilson*, p. 159.

52   Bragdon, *The Academic Years*, p. 303.

53   Ibid.

54   Weinstein, *Woodrow Wilson*, p. 160.

55   Ibid.

56   Ibid., p. 161; see also Bragdon, *The Academic Years*, p. 303.

57   See Marmor, "Wilson," and George, Marmor, and George, "Issues," for the opposing view.

58   See, for example, Link, *Revolution, War, and Peace*.

59   Most biographers have made note of Wilson's medical breakdown in 1906: Baker, *Woodrow Wilson and World Settlement*, 1:201; Moses and Cross, *Courage*, p. 149; Link, *Revolution, War and Peace*, p. 33.

60   Weinstein, *Woodrow Wilson*, p. 165; in our opinion, Dr. Weinstein does a masterly job in this particular section of his study gathering the data and drawing a convincing medical portrait of a man suffering a succession of cerebrovascular accidents. Where Weinstein differs from previous biographers, especially those cited above, is in his assertion that the malady was not simply a "retinal hemorrhage," but an indication of severe neurovascular disease. Moreover, Weinstein further believes that Wilson's "transient weakness" in 1907 is further proof of vascular pathology (p. 188). In all, Weinstein counts four major and minor strokes between 1900 and 1907.

61 Ibid.

62 Ibid.

63 Ibid., p. 166.

64 Ibid.

65 Ibid.

66 See Ray Stannard Baker, *Woodrow Wilson: Life and Letters (1890–1910)* (New York: Doubleday, Page, 1927), pp. 226–27.

67 See Weinstein, *Woodrow Wilson*, pp. 171–73; and Baker, *Woodrow Wilson*, p. 230, for fuller details of Wilson's increasing unhappiness at Princeton.

68 Ibid., p. 173.

69 Weinstein, *Woodrow Wilson*, p. 176.

70 Ibid., p. 178

71 Ibid, p. 222.

72 See Link, *Revolution, War and Peace*, p. 145.

73 Weinstein, *Woodrow Wilson*, p. 226.

74 Excellent and in-depth treatments of the story of Wilson's entry into politics are given in Arthur Link, *Wilson: The Road to the White House* (Princeton: Princeton University Press, 1947), and Baker, *Woodrow Wilson: Life and Letters: Governor 1910–1913* (Garden City, N.Y.: Doubleday, Doran, 1931).

75 Weinstein, *Woodrow Wilson*, pp. 226–27; see also Link, *Road to the White House*, pp. 131–37, for a fuller treatment of Wilson's campaign tactics and speeches.

76 Weinstein, *Woodrow Wilson*, pp. 226–27.

77 Wilson's speech is quoted in Weinstein, *Woodrow Wilson*, p. 236, who makes note of Wilson's curious use of self-referential and anatomical language; Link, *Road to the White House*, p. 352, also makes note of Wilson's erratic behavior during this time.

78 Weinstein, *Woodrow Wilson*, p. 236.

79 Link, *Road to the White House*, pp. 147–55.

80 Weinstein, *Woodrow Wilson*, p. 249.

81 Link, *Wilson: The New Freedom* (Princeton: Princeton University Press, 1956); for a fuller description of Wilson's early days in the White House, see Gene Smith, *When the Cheering Stopped* (New York: William Morrow, 1964), pp. 7–15. Almost all of Wilson's biographers seem to agree that Wilson's first two years in the White House were his finest and most effective.

82 Weinstein, *Woodrow Wilson*, p. 251.

83 Ibid.

84 Ibid., p. 252.

85 Link, *The New Freedom*, p. 47.

86 For a fairly distorted account of Wilson's medical problems, see Cary T. Grayson, *Woodrow Wilson: An Intimate Memoir* (New York: Holt, Rinehart, and Winston, 1960). If one is to believe Grayson's account in his book, Wilson's physician was remarkably uninformed about his patient's previous illnesses.

87 Weinstein, *Woodrow Wilson*, p. 254.

88 Ibid., p. 255.

89 Ibid., p. 256.

90 Ibid., p. 255.

91 See Smith, *When the Cheering Stopped*, pp. 46–48, and Weinstein, *Woodrow Wilson*, pp. 254–57, for Wilson's reactions to his wife's illness and death.

92 Baker, *Woodrow Wilson and World Settlement*, 4:330.

93 The interpretation here of Wilson's bizarre behavior is Weinstein's (*Woodrow Wilson*, p. 259), but others, including Link, have made note of the president's rash actions.

94 Weinstein, *Woodrow Wilson*, p. 259.

95 Ibid.

96 Ibid.

97 Wilson's "surprise" meeting and quick marriage to Mrs. Galt are described in a number of places: see, for example, Smith, *When the Cheering Stopped*, p. 14, and Weinstein, *Woodrow Wilson*, pp. 279–83.

98 Weinstein, *Woodrow Wilson*, pp. 279–83.

99 Weinstein, *Woodrow Wilson*, p. 295; Marmor disputes Weinstein's interpretation here; see, for example, Marmor, "Wilson," p. 530, and George, Marmor, and George, "Issues," p. 435.

100 Weinstein, *Woodrow Wilson*, p. 295.

101 Ibid.

102 Weinstein, *Woodrow Wilson*, p. 297. Colonel House was a close friend of Wilson's, who enjoyed the president's confidences. Many of Weinstein's diagnoses are drawn from House's "clinical" impressions.

103 Ibid.

104 Ibid.

105 Ibid., p. 305.

106 Quoted in Weinstein, *Woodrow Wilson*, p. 313.

107 Ibid., p. 298.

108 Freud and Bullitt, *Thomas Woodrow Wilson*, pp. 200–201.

109 Wilson's abhorrence for the war into which the United States had been drawn is amply documented in Link's biography, as well as in the psychological portrait

drawn by Freud and Bullitt, *Thomas Woodrow Wilson*, p. 200.

110   See Weinstein, *Woodrow Wilson*, p. 321.

111   The accounts of both Weinstein and Freud and Bullitt—as well as the impressions recorded in the diaries by Wilson's contemporaries—attest to Wilson's increasing emotionalism and erratic behavior; see, for example, Edmund W. Starling, *Starling of the White House* (New York: Simon and Schuster, 1946), pp. 97–98. Starling, who was a Secret Service agent, noted that as early as December 1917, Wilson's outbursts and directives became unpredictable and erratic.

112   Weinstein, *Woodrow Wilson*, p. 323; see also Freud and Bullitt, *Thomas Woodrow Wilson*, p. 205, on Wilson's forgetfulness and "leaky mind."

113   Weinstein, *Woodrow Wilson*, p. 323.

114   Weinstein, *Woodrow Wilson*, p. 324.

115   Weinstein, *Woodrow Wilson*, p. 329, quoted from the *Public Papers of Woodrow Wilson*.

116   Mee, *End of the Order*, p. 146; see also p. 14 for a description of the problems facing Wilson and his European allies.

117   Ibid.

118   Wilson's working habits: Mee, *End of the Order*, pp. 62–64; Smith, *When the Cheering Stopped*, pp. 43–46.

119   Mee, *End of the Order*, p. 65.

120   Ibid.

121   Ibid.

122   Quoted in Weinstein, *Woodrow Wilson*, p. 335.

123   Grayson, *An Intimate Memoir*, p. 85.

124   Weinstein, *Woodrow Wilson*, p. 337.

125   *End of the Order*, p. 167.

126   On Wilson's illness on April 3: Grayson, *An Intimate Memoir*, p. 85; Weinstein, *Woodrow Wilson*, pp. 337–38; Mee, *End of the Order*, pp. 167–72; Marmor, "Wilson," pp. 530–31; Smith, *When the Cheering Stopped*, pp. 48–50.

127   Weinstein, *Woodrow Wilson*, p. 339.

128   Ibid.

129   Ibid., p. 340.

130   Observations of Wilson's strange behavior, and the quotation from Grayson's diary, are cited in Weinstein, *Woodrow Wilson*, p. 342.

131   Weinstein, *Woodrow Wilson*, p. 342.

132   Ibid.

133   Ibid., p. 343.

134 Ibid., p. 344.
135 Ibid.
136 Quoted in Mee, *End of the Order*, p. 316.
137 Weinstein, *Woodrow Wilson*, p. 345.
138 Ibid.
139 Link, *Revolution, War, and Peace*, p. 77.
140 Ibid.
141 Weinstein, *Woodrow Wilson*, p. 353.
142 Ibid., p. 354.
143 Tumulty, *As I Knew Him*, p. 447.
144 Weinstein, *Woodrow Wilson*, p. 355.
145 Ibid.
146 Ibid., p. 356.
147 Ibid., p. 357.
148 Ibid., p. 359.
149 Ibid., p. 360.
150 Ibid., pp. 364–65.
151 Ibid., p. 359.
152 Grayson, *Memoir*, p. 114.
153 Weinstein, *Woodrow Wilson*, p. 363.
154 Ibid., p. 364.
155 Ibid.
156 Ibid., p. 370.

---

3. *Franklin D. Roosevelt*

1 Howard G. Bruenn, "Clinical Notes on the Illness and Death of President Franklin D. Roosevelt," *Annals of Internal Medicine* 72 (1970):579–91. See also John
Gunther, *Roosevelt in Retrospect* (New York: Harper and Bros., 1950); Elliott
Roosevelt, ed., *FDR: His Personal Letters* (New York: Duell, Sloan, and Pearce,
1950); William Hassett, *Off the Record with FDR* (New York: Allen and Unwin,
1949); and James Bishop, *FDR's Last Year* (New York: Morrow, 1974).
2 "Roosevelt Health Long In Doubt," *New York Times*, April 12, 1945. Admiral
McIntire's comments are also contained in this article.
3 James A. Farley, *Jim Farley's Story: The Roosevelt Years* (New York: Whittlesey
House, 1948), p. 95.
4 John B. Moses and Wilbur Cross, *Presidential Courage* (New York: W. W. Norton,
1980), p. 203.

5   Ibid.

6   Hassett, *Off the Record*, p. 239.

7   Ibid.

8   Bruenn, "Clinical Notes," p. 585. See also Ross McIntire, *White House Physician* (New York: G. P. Putnam's Sons, 1946), for an alternative diagnosis.

9   Bruenn, "Clinical Notes," p. 591.

10   Ibid.

11   Ibid.

12   Ibid.

13   Papers of Edwin A. Watson, Watson Collection, Manuscripts Room, Alderman Library, University of Virginia, Charlottesville, Virginia.

14   William M. Moore, "FDR's Image: A Study in Pictorial Symbols" (Ph.D. diss., University of Wisconsin, 1946).

15   Bruenn, "Clinical Notes," p. 584.

16   Papers of Edwin A. Watson.

17   Betty H. Winfield, "FDR's Pictorial Image, Rules, and Boundaries," *Journalism History* 5 (Winter 1978–1979):4.

18   Ibid.

19   Moore, *FDR's Image*.

20   See, for example, Hassett, *Off the Record*, for details of Roosevelt's last days.

21   James MacGregor Burns, *Roosevelt: The Lion and the Fox* (New York: Harper and Row, 1964).

22   L'Etang, *Pathology of Leadership*, p. 88.

23   Michael Beschloss, *Kennedy and Roosevelt: The Uneasy Alliance* (New York: W. W. Norton, 1980), and Alfred B. Rollins, *Roosevelt and Howe* (New York: Alfred A. Knopf, 1962). Details of Roosevelt's recovery and reentry into public life after his initial bout with polio are taken from Beschloss, *Kennedy and Roosevelt*.

24   Beschloss, *Kennedy and Roosevelt*, p. 58.

25   Ibid.

26   Ibid.

27   Karl Wold, "Roosevelt's Health," *Look Magazine*, Feburary 15, 1949.

28   Beschloss, *Kennedy and Roosevelt*, p. 63.

29   L'Etang, *Pathology of Leadership*, p. 90.

30   Ibid., p. 89.

31   Winfield, "FDR's Pictorial Image," p. 34.

32   L'Etang, *Pathology of Leadership*, p. 90.

33   McIntire, *White House Physician*, p. 75.

34   Harold Ickes, *The Secret Diary of Harold Ickes* (New York: Simon and Schuster,

1954), 2:184.

35   Farley, *Farley's Story*, p. 187.

36   Ickes, *Secret Diary*, p. 185.

37   Ibid.

38   Farley, *Farley's Story*, p. 192.

39   Ibid.

40   Beschloss, *Kennedy and Roosevelt*, p. 189.

41   Ibid.

42   L'Etang, *Pathology of Leadership*, pp. 91–92.

43   Bruenn, "Clinical Notes," p. 581.

44   Gunther, *Roosevelt in Retrospect*, p. 355.

45   Ibid.

46   Farley, *Farley's Story*, p. 365.

47   Ibid.

48   Beschloss, *Kennedy and Roosevelt*, p. 256.

49   Ibid.

50   Ibid.

51   Ibid.

52   Ibid.

53   See Harry S. Goldsmith, "Unanswered Mysteries in the Death of Franklin Roosevelt," *Surgery, Gynecology, and Obstetrics* 149 (1979):905.

54   Bruenn, "Clinical Notes," p. 581.

55   Ibid. p. 583.

56   Ibid., p. 586.

57   See, for example, Moses and Cross, *Presidential Courage*, pp. 206–7.

58   Bruenn, "Clinical Notes," p. 586.

59   Ibid.

60   Moses and Cross, *Presidential Courage*, p. 207.

61   Ibid.

62   Ibid.

63   Federal Bureau of Investigation, FOIA file 219,162, letter dated December 26, 1944.

64   Details of this investigation are in the FOIA file cited above, document 62-76894-8, p. 2 (FBI FOIPA files), hereinafter referred to as the Tamm Memorandum.

65   The words are special agent Tamm's, taken from his memo to J. Edgar Hoover, Tamm Memorandum, p. 2.

66   Ibid.

67   Ibid.

68   Ibid.

69   Ibid.

70   Moses and Cross, *Presidential Courage*, p. 206.

71   See L'Etang, *Pathology of Leadership*, p. 90; and Moses and Cross, *Presidential Courage*, p. 191.

72   L'Etang, *Pathology of Leadership*, p. 90.

73   Ibid.

74   Gunther, *Roosevelt in Retrospect*, p. 365.

75   Bruenn, "Clinical Notes," p. 589.

76   Ibid.

77   Ibid.

78   Tamm Memorandum, p. 6.

79   On Roosevelt's use of aliases: FOIA file 81-DFI-1259, obtained through the National Naval Medical Center, Bethesda, Maryland. The summary of this research appears in a private letter written by the chief legal officer at the command to the authors, dated November 17, 1981. The complete list of names that FDR used follows: George Adams, John Cash, Mr. Delano, Roy F. David, Mr. Elliott, James D. Elliott, Mr. Fox, Mr. Ford, G. A. Forkes, Ralph Frank, Rolph Frank, Frank A. McCormack, D. Rhodes, Dan R. Rhodes, D. Rhoades, Dan R. Rhoades, Dan F. Rhodes, Daniel F. Rhodes, Mr. Rhodes, Mr. Rolphe, Fred Rosen, Fred D. Rosen, F. David Roy.

80   Goldsmith, "Unanswered Mysteries," p. 919.

81   Ibid.

82   See, for example, Burns, *Roosevelt*, for an excellent summary on World War II's effect on domestic politics.

4. Diplomacy and Failing Health

1   L'Etang, *Pathology of Leadership*, pp. 97–98.

2   Ibid.

3   Ibid.

4   Frances Perkins, *The Roosevelt I Knew* (New York: Viking Press, 1946), p. 312.

5   L'Etang, *Pathology of Leadership*, p. 96.

6   Ibid.

7   Ibid.

8   Charles L. Mee, *Meeting at Potsdam* (New York: M. Evans, 1975), p. 37.

9   Bruenn, "Clinical Notes," p. 588.

10   Alvin A. Barach, "Franklin Roosevelt's Illness: Effect on Course of History," *New*

York State Journal of Medicine, November 1977, p. 2154.

11   See also L'Etang, *Pathology of Leadership*, p. 99.

12   Ibid.

13   Bruenn, "Clinical Notes," p. 589.

14   See also L'Etang, *Pathology of Leadership*, pp. 105–8, for a description of Roosevelt's entourage.

15   Burns, *Roosevelt*, p. 66.

16   Barach, "Roosevelt's Illness," pp. 2154–55.

17   Ibid.

18   Bruenn, "Clinical Notes," pp. 589–90.

19   Ibid., p. 155.

20   Ibid., p. 589.

21   Burns, *Roosevelt*, p. 199; see also William Bullitt, "How We Won the War and Lost the Peace," *Life Magazine*, August 30, 1948.

22   Ibid.

23   Ibid.

24   Bruenn, "Clinical Notes," p. 588.

25   L'Etang, *Pathology of Leadership*, pp. 119–21.

26   Mee, *Potsdam*, p. 37.

27   Bullitt, "How We Won." Bullitt's comments, which are poorly substantiated, were written just as the cold war was beginning.

28   L'Etang, *Pathology of Leadership*, p. 99.

29   Francis L. Biddle, *In Brief Authority* (Garden City, New York: Doubleday, 1962), p. 376.

30   Barach, "Roosevelt's Illness," p. 2154.

31   McIntire, *White House Physician*, p. 211.

32   Oral History Project, Harry S. Vaughn, Truman Library, Independence, Missouri.

33   Hassett, *Off the Record*, pp. 327–28.

34   Ibid., p. 329.

35   Ibid.

36   Bruenn, "Clinical Notes," p. 590.

37   Ibid.

38   Ibid.

39   Gunther, *Roosevelt in Retrospect*, p. 369.

40   Ibid.

41   Bruenn, "Clinical Notes," p. 590.

42   Ibid.

43   Ibid.

44   Gunther, *Roosevelt in Retrospect*, p. 369.

45   See the *New York Times*, April 13 and 14, 1945, for reactions to the president's death.

46   Ibid.

47   McIntire's public comments are recorded in the *New York Times* article, "Roosevelt Health Long in Doubt" (unattributed), April 13, 1945, p. 1.

48   Bruenn, "Clinical Notes," p. 590.

49   Ibid.

50   Personal correspondence with the authors, courtesy of Mrs. McGown, Richmond, Virginia.

---

5. John F. Kennedy

1   Joan Blair and Clay Blair, *The Search for JFK* (New York: Beckley Publishing, 1976). This excellent and evenhanded study by the Blairs provided an immense amount of material for our analysis of Mr. Kennedy's health problems. To our knowledge the Blairs' work is the first—and the best documented—to point out the great lengths to which Mr. Kennedy and his family went to hide his illness.

2   Kenneth P. O'Donnell and David F. Powers, *Johnny, We Hardly Knew Ye* (Boston: Little, Brown, 1972), pp. 7–9.

3   Pierre Salinger, *With Kennedy* (Garden City, New York: Doubleday, 1966), pp. 40–41. For another analysis of Kennedy's politics, from a slightly different perspective, see also Garry Wills, *The Kennedy Imprisonment* (Boston: Little, Brown, 1981), pp. 127–28.

4   The politics behind the health issue during the 1960 campaign for the Democratic nomination are described in Wills, *Kennedy Imprisonment*, p. 128; Salinger, *With Kennedy*, pp. 40–41; Blair and Blair, *Search*, pp. 575–76.

5   See also Jack Anderson, "The Candidates—How Healthy Are They?" *Parade*, April 10, 1960, pp. 4–5, for media attention to this problem prior to the Democratic Convention.

6   The importance of the "vigor" theme in Kennedy's 1960 campaign—and his subsequent administration—is amply explored in Wills, *Kennedy Imprisonment*, pp. 143–45. In one illustrative passage, Wills points out how zealously Kennedy protected this image:

> Sorensen's book tells us how carefully Kennedy crafted his symbols. When his back troubles forced him to use crutches, these signs of weakness were abandoned whenever he moved into an area of the White House where he could be

seen. On the other hand, his rocking chair was an acceptable sign of relaxation. . . . The chair stood for relaxation, not weakness. The President declared the need for "vigah," and sent his "frontiersmen" off on fifty-mile hikes.

7   See Salinger, *With Kennedy*, p. 40.
8   O'Donnell and Powers, *Johnny*, p. 103.
9   Salinger, *With Kennedy*, pp. 40–41.
10   The details behind the medical opinion proffered in this case are from Kennedy's personal physician, Janet Travell, and appear in her book *Office Hours: Night and Day* (Mount View, Calif.: World Publications, 1968), pp. 332–34.
11   Blair and Blair, *Search*, pp. 575–76.
12   Press response to this event was remarkably muted; see, for example, the July 18, 1960 issue of *U.S. News and World Report*, and David Wise, "Now It Seems Democrat's Race Is to the Healthiest," *New York Herald Tribune*, July 6, 1960, pp. 1–6.
13   By way of explaining the media's sympathetic treatment, Salinger issued the "fairness" statement the day after his press release; Salinger, *With Kennedy*, p. 42.
14   "I'm the healthiest candidate" line is from O'Donnell and Powers, *Johnny*, p. 7.
15   From the preface to Robert F. Kennedy's *John F. Kennedy: As We Remember Him*, edited by Goddard Lieberson (1965); also cited in Blair and Blair, *Search*, p. 22.
16   Blair and Blair, *Search*, p. 582.
17   Ibid.
18   Wills, *Kennedy Imprisonment*, p. 32; see also Blair and Blair, *Search*, p. 26.
19   Blair and Blair, *Search*, p. 26.
20   Ibid., p. 21.
21   Ibid., p. 42.
22   Kennedy's travel history during this time was pieced together through personal interviews with his friends by the Blairs, *Search*, pp. 56–106.
23   Ibid.
24   Ibid.
25   Ibid.
26   Wills offers a more negative interpretation of the events surrounding the PT 109 incident in Wills, *Kennedy Imprisonment*, pp. 131–34; see also Blair and Blair, *Search*, pp. 177–86.
27   Ibid.
28   Ibid., p. 177; the Blairs were the first to document Kennedy's having an illness as early as 1943.

29   Ibid.

30   A possible explanation for Kennedy's "jaundiced" color may have been that he was taking Atabrine, an antimalarial drug which American soliders stationed in the South Pacific regularly took as a prophylactic; his possible taking of Atabrine would not necessarily mean that he had contracted malaria.

31   Blair and Blair, *Search*, p. 387.

32   See, for example, James MacGregor Burns, *John Kennedy: A Political Profile* (New York: Harcourt, Brace, 1960).

33   For a thorough clinical description of Addison's disease, see Robert H. Williams, *Textbook of Endocrinology*, 5th ed. (Philadelphia: W. B. Saunders, 1974), pp. 270–74.

34   Thomas Addison's original description of the disease that bears his name is from Williams, *Textbook*, pp. 271–72.

35   Ibid.

36   Kennedy's first campaign is well described in O'Donnell and Powers, *Johnny*; see Blair and Blair, *Search*, pp. 432–44.

37   Blair and Blair, *Search*, p. 432.

38   Lee's description is in Blair and Blair, *Search*, p. 476.

39   Ibid., p. 212.

40   Ibid., p. 560. The real curiosity in this message is that the first documented evidence we have of an Addisonian crisis in JFK points to 1948—a year after these cables were sent; the nature of the "hair" prescriptions remains a mystery.

41   Ibid.

42   Ibid., p. 576.

43   Ibid.

44   Ibid.

45   Ibid.

46   Ibid.

47   Ibid.

48   Ibid., pp. 578–79.

49   Ibid.

50   Ibid.

51   Ibid. The medical evidence of Kennedy's Addison's disease is thoroughly and carefully researched in Blair and Blair, "The Health Question: An Answer," *Search*, pp. 556–79. Further evidence of Kennedy's medical problems—and confirmation of the veracity of the Blairs' research—has been given to us by a confidential source.

52   Ibid.

53   Ibid. We cannot explain the confusion over whether or not Kennedy was confirmed as an Addisonian in 1954, unless the physicians in question did not have full access to JFK's previous medical records.

54   Ibid.

55   At least three newspaper articles were published that mentioned Senator Kennedy's operation: (a) *New York Times*, October 11, 1954, p. 39; (b) *New York Times*, October 21, 1954, p. 17; and (c) *New York Times*, February 26, 1955, p. 28.

56   The original article on the man "37 years of age" was by James A. Nicholas, Charles L. Burstein, Charles J. Umberger, and Philip Wilson, "Management of adrenocortical insufficiency during surgery," *AMA Archives of Surgery* 71 (1955): 737–42.

57   This "simple" medical puzzle, however, was not fully and openly solved until 1967, when Dr. John Nichols pieced together the 1955 medical article on Kennedy and the *New York Times* articles; see Nichols, "President Kennedy's Adrenals," *Journal of the American Medical Association* 201 (1967):115–16.

58   Burns, *John Kennedy*, pp. 156–60.

59   Ibid.

60   Travell, *Office Hours*, pp. 327–28.

61   Burns, *John Kennedy*, p. 160.

62   The fact that Mr. Kennedy's adrenal malfunction was not due to tuberculosis is supported by Dr. John K. Lattimer, who obtained copies of x rays from the autopsy performed on President Kennedy. Dr. Lattimer writes:

> These [the adrenals] were well visualized on the x-rays of the mid-portion of the body, and no abnormal calcification could be seen to suggest tuberculosis or earlier hemorrhage of the adrenals. It is my firm belief that the President suffered from spontaneous bilateral adrenal atrophy.

From John K. Lattimer, *Kennedy and Lincoln: Medical and Ballistic Comparisons of Their Assassinations* (New York: Harcourt Brace Jovanovich, 1980), p. 220.

63   Travell, *Office Hours*, pp. 327–28.

64   Wills, *Kennedy Imprisonment*, p. 127.

----

6. *The Twenty-fifth Amendment and the Decisions of History*

1   Rudolph Marx, *The Health of Presidents* (New York: Putnam Books, 1969); Milton Plesur, "The Health of Presidents," in *The Presidency Reappraised*, ed. Rexford

G. Tugwell and Thomas E. Cronin (New York: Praeger Publishers, 1974); Charles A. Roos, *Bulletin of Medical Library Association*, 1960, p. 49.

2   Hugh L'Etang, *Pathology of Leadership*.

3   Michael P. Riccards, "The Presidency in Sickness and in Health," *Presidential Studies Quarterly*, summer 1977, Center for the Study of the Presidency.

4   Ibid., pp. 227–29.

5   Richard H. Hansen, *The Year We Had No President* (Lincoln: University of Nebraska Press, 1962), pp. 75–78.

6   John D. Feerick, *The Twenty-fifth Amendment* (New York: Fordham University Press, 1976).

7   Robert S. Robins and Henry Rothschild, "Hidden Health Disabilities and the Presidency: Medical Management and Political Considerations," *Perspectives in Medicine and Biology*, winter 1981, pp. 240–53.

8   Laurence Barrett, *Gambling With History* (Garden City, N.Y.: Doubleday, 1982), pp. 115–17.

9   Personal interview with the authors at the Miller Center of the University of Virginia, Commission for the Study of the 25th Amendment, 1987.

10   Ibid.

11   Ibid.

12   William Safire, "The President Takes the 25th," *New York Times*, July 19, 1985.

13   Personal interview with the authors at the Miller Center of the University of Virginia, Commission for the Study of the Twenty-fifth Amendment, 1987.

14   William Safire, "The Operating Room," *New York Times*, January 5, 1987.

15   Personal communication to the Miller Center of the University of Virginia, Commission for the Study of the Twenty-fifth Amendment, 1987.

16   Ibid.

17   Personal interview with the authors at the Miller Center of the University of Virginia, Commission for the Study of the Twenty-fifth Amendment, 1987.

18   Ibid.

19   Herbert Brownell, "Presidential Inability: The Need for Constitutional Amendment," *Yale Law Review* 68 (1958):189.

20   Personal interview with the authors.

21   William J. Curran, "Presidential Inability to Function," *New England Journal of Medicine*, 1986, pp. 301–2.

22   Robert S. Robins and Henry Rothschild, "Hidden Health Disabilities and the Presidency."

23   Milton Greenblatt, "Power and Impairment of Great Leaders," Distinguished Psychiatrist Lecture, American Psychiatric Association Annual Meeting, May

2, 1983.

24 William Safire, "The Operating Room."

25 American Medical Association, "Current Opinions of the Council on Ethical and Judicial Affairs of the AMA," 1986.

26 Personal correspondence with authors.

27 Personal interview with authors. The period during and following the president's surgery was further complicated by another problem, reported by Jack Anderson and Dale van Atta. "Highly placed" White House sources claimed that while Mr. Reagan was undergoing surgery, Vice President Bush was knocked unconscious for a time during a game of tennis. Though there apparently were no sequelae to the incident, the White House seemed to feel uneasy enough about the fact that both the president *and* vice president were out of commission —if only for a short time—that they never reported the incident. (See Anderson and van Atta, *Washington Post*, January 27, 1988.)

28 Francis D. Moore, *Metabolic Care of the Surgical Patient* (Philadelphia: Saunders Publishing, 1959), pp. 28–29, 111–12.

29 Personal communication with authors.

30 John D. Feerick, *The Twenty-fifth Amendment* (New York: Fordham University Press, 1976).

31 Oral History Project, Harry S. Vaughn, Truman Memorial Library, Independence, Missouri.

32 Richard Longaker, "Presidential Continuity: The Twenty-fifth Amendment," *UCLA Law Review*, April 1966, p. 560.

33 Greenblatt, "Power and Impairment."

34 Personal communication with the authors.

35 Rusk, "Summitry," p. 1.

Index

Addison's disease, 181, 196; and Kennedy, x, 162, 163, 180, 181, 182, 183–84, 186, 188, 191; use of cortisone in, x, 182, 189

Agnew, Spiro, 209

Anderson, Jack: on Eagleton's illness, 5

Andropov, Yuri: and illness, 3

Axson, Stockton: on Wilson's personality, 29

Barber, James David: on personalities of U.S. presidents, 10

Barrett, Laurence: on the shooting of Ronald Reagan, 213–15

Bartels, Dr. Elmer: on Kennedy's illness, 187–88, 189, 190, 191

Bayh, Birch: on Twenty-fifth Amendment, 228, 233

Begin, Menachem: and illness, 2

Blair, Joan and Clay: biography of John F. Kennedy, 161, 166–67, 172, 189, 198; on Kennedy's illnesses, 170, 181, 187, 188

Billings, Lem: on Kennedy's illness, 171

Brezhnev, Leonid: and illness, 3

Brownell, Herbert, 227

Bruenn, Dr. Howard J.: clinical notes on Roosevelt's death, 152–54, 155, 157; description of Roosevelt's illnesses, viii, 79, 101, 103, 105, 106–7, 108, 131, 150, 151; on medical management of Roosevelt's illnesses, 78, 79, 80–81, 82, 105, 108, 114, 115, 117, 124, 125, 147–48, 152

Buchen, Philip: on implementation of Twenty-fifth Amendment, 220–21, 222

Bullitt, William: on Roosevelt at Yalta, 131–32, 133, 146; on Wilson's health problems, 15

Burns, James MacGregor: on Kennedy's illness, 195, 196, 197

Bush, George P.: and presidential succession, 216–17

Chernenko, Constantin: and illness, 3

Cleveland, Grover: and illness, 204–5

Connally, John: on Kennedy's illness, 162, 196

Curran, William: on presidential disability, 229–30

Daniels, Margaret Truman: on Roosevelt's health, 107–8, 147; Secret Ser-

vice protection of father, 149
Duvalier, Jean Claude: and illness, x

Eagleton, Thomas: and candidacy for
vice president, 3, 5; description of
medical problems, 3, 4; Dr. Karl Menninger's assessment of, 7; *New York
Times* calls for resignation, 5; press
reaction to resignation, 6, 8–9; resignation from presidential race, 6
Early, Steven, 154; and press reports on
Roosevelt, 84, 108, 109, 110, 119; and
use of FBI, 111, 112, 113, 115–17
Eden, Anthony: observations of Roosevelt, 132
Eisenhower, Dwight D., 162, 227;
described by Rusk, 1; health problems,
205–6; succession agreement with
Richard Nixon, 205, 207
En-lai, Chou: and illness, 2

Farley, James: observations of Roosevelt's
illnesses, 77, 97, 98, 99, 102
Federal Bureau of Investigation: investi-
gation of press leaks, 111–12, 115–17
Feerick, John D.: on Twenty-fifth Amend-
ment, 208, 233
Fielding, Fredrick: on use of the Twenty-
fifth Amendment, 213, 214, 216, 217,
218, 235
Ford, Gerald R.: use of Twenty-fifth
Amendment, 209
Franco, Francisco: and illness, 2
Freedom of Information Act: use of, x,
10
Freud, Sigmund: psychoanalytic inter-
pretation of Wilson's illness, 15

Gunther, John: on Roosevelt, 101–2, 121
Garner, John Nance: on Roosevelt, 99
Grayson, Dr. Cary, 18, 222; as Wilson's

physician, 11, 48–49, 51–52, 54, 55,
61, 62, 65, 67, 69–71, 72–73, 96
Greenblatt, Milton: on presidential disability, 231, 240

Halle, Louis: on presidential illness,
240–41
Harriman, Averell: on Roosevelt, 125
Hart, Gary: on Eagleton's illness, 4
Hassett, William: observations of Roose-
velt's illnesses, 77, 150
Hopkins, Harry, 128, 132, 133; illnesses
of, 127
Howe, Louis: political advice to Roose-
velt, 87, 88, 89, 90

Ickes, Harold: observations of Roosevelt's
illnesses, 97, 98

Kastenheimer, Robert W.: on Twenty-fifth
Amendment, 237
Kennedy, John F., ix, 162, 165, 170, 199,
200
—illnesses of, 167–68, 169, 170,
176–78, 180, 184–86; Addison's disease 162, 163, 180, 181, 182, 183–84,
186, 188, 191; chronic back problems,
177, 178, 179, 190–91; press accounts
of, 162, 163–64, 187, 190, 193–94,
202; surgery, 191, 192
—and Lyndon Johnson, 161, 164, 165
—military career, 173, 174–76, 179
—political career, 188; congressional
campaign (1946), 182, 183, 184; presidential campaign, 161, 163, 165
—summary of health problems, 11,
199–201
Kennedy, Joseph P., 173–74; and John F.
Kennedy's medical problems, 168,
169, 184, 192; on Roosevelt, 99, 103–4
Kennedy, Robert F., 164; on brother's

health, 166, 189

Khrushchev, Nikita: described by Rusk, 1

King, MacKenzie: on Roosevelt, 146

Knorr, Norman: on presidential disability, 236

Krock, Arthur: on Kennedy's illness, 172, 192

Lahey, Dr. Frank, 119; medical consultation on Roosevelt, 80, 105, 116–17

L'Etang, Hugh: on medical historiography, 203; on Roosevelt, 114, 115

Link, Arthur S.: on Wilson's politics, 47

Lodge, Henry Cabot: opposition to Treaty of Versailles, 15, 67

Long, Breckenridge: on press accounts of Roosevelt's illness, 111, 112

Longaker, Richard: on presidential disability, 237–38

Lukash, Dr. William, 226, 227

McGovern, George: consultation with Dr. Karl Menninger, 7; on Eagleton's illness, 4, 5; knowledge of Eagleton's illness, 7

McIntire, Dr. Ross T., ix, 96, 102, 117, 154, 157–58, 222; management of Roosevelt's illnesses, 76, 78, 96, 100; press statements, 84–85, 148, 156

Madison, James, 204

Menninger, Dr. Karl: on Eagleton's illness, 7

Mondale, Walter, 236

Moran, Lord Charles: on Roosevelt, 121

Murphy, Robert: on Roosevelt, 147

Nixon, Richard M.: use of Twenty-fifth Amendment, 209

Paullin, Dr. James A.: medical consultation on Roosevelt, 80, 153–54, 158–59

Perkins, Frances: on Roosevelt, 121–22

Pompidou, Georges: and illness, 2

Presidential succession: Eisenhower and Nixon, 207; general problems, 204, 206; history of, 207, 208; and Presidential Succession Act, 207; President Johnson, 207; President Kennedy, 207. See also Twenty-fifth Amendment

Reagan, Ronald W.
—health problems, 203, 213, 220, 233, 234–35
—use of Twenty-fifth Amendment, xii, 216, 239–40; interpretation of, 213, 214–16, 216–17, 218, 219, 220

Reston, James: reaction to Eagleton's illness, 8

Riccards, Michael: on illness of Eisenhower, 205–6; on illness of presidents, 204

Robins, Robert S.: on presidential disability, 212, 230

Rockefeller, Nelson, 209

Roosevelt, Franklin D., ix, 160, 240, 241
—and Churchill, 76, 100, 123, 124, 125, 127, 130, 132, 151
—death of, 85, 152–54; press reports of, 155–56
—illnesses of, 75, 76, 78, 82, 100, 106, 126, 148; at Bethesda Naval Medical Center, 78, 112, 118–19; cardiovascular, 75, 78–79, 80–81, 82–83, 93–94, 100, 108, 115, 126, 131; gastrointestinal, 77, 78, 104, 105–6, 107, 115; Mrs. Roosevelt's observations, 77, 95, 122, 125; onset of polio, 86–87; and press reports, 83–84, 92, 95, 107, 108, 109, 112, 119, 155–56; during World War II, 100, 103, 105, 114, 119; at Yalta, 123–24, 125, 126, 127–30, 131, 146

—marriage to Eleanor Roosevelt, 86
—political career of: New York governorship, 89, 90–91; 1920 vice presidential campaign, 86; 1924 Democratic
   convention, 89–90; 1932 presidential
   campaign, 95; 1944 presidential campaign, 101, 102, 103, 110; secretary of
   the navy, 86
—and Stalin, 123, 128, 129, 131, 132
—summary of health problems, 10,
   92–93
Roosevelt, James, 122; observations of
   father's illness, 104
Rostow, Mortimer: reaction to Eagleton's
   illness, 8
Rothschild, Henry: on presidential disability, 212, 230
Ruge, Dr. Daniel, 226, 227, 232; during
   Reagan's surgery, 215, 216
Rusk, Dean: on illness and world leaders, 1, 2, 241

Safire, William: on presidential disabil-
   ity, 231; on Twenty-fifth Amendment,
   218–19
Salinger, Pierre, 163, 164, 197
Smuts, Jan, 13
Stephan, Paul: on Twenty-fifth Amend-
   ment, 223–26
Stettinius, Edward: at Yalta, 127, 132

Thurmond, Strom, 217
Tito, Marshal: and illness, 2
Travell, Dr. Janet: on Kennedy's illness,
   195–96, 197
Troy, Matthew J.: political reaction to
   Eagleton's illness, 8
Truman, Harry S., 151, 162, 237; on
   presidential succession, 228–29, 239;
   on Roosevelt's health, 107, 108, 147;
   selection as vice president, 103; Secret

Service protection, 148–49
Tse-tung, Mao: and illness, 2
Twenty-fifth Amendment, 216, 217, 219;
   description of, xi, xii, 208–10, 211;
   legal aspects of, 208, 211, 223–26; legislative history of, 208, 209–10, 239;
   and presidential disability, 208,
   210–11, 212, 221, 222, 227, 229–30,
   232, 235–36; presidential succession,
   ix, 208–10; and president's physician,
   220, 222, 223, 227–28, 231, 232, 235;
   problems with, 212, 213, 218, 223,
   227, 230–32, 234–35; recommendation for reform of, 238–39; and vice
   president, 216, 217, 220, 237, 238. See
   also Presidential succession

Watson, Edwin, 147; notes on Roosevelt,
   81, 103
Weinstein, Dr. Edwin: on medical historiography, 15; on Wilson's denial of
   illness, 28, 29; on Wilson's early childhood, 15; on Wilson's neurologic
   diseases, 15, 26–27, 37, 46, 47–48,
   49–50, 52, 53, 56, 57, 63–64, 65,
   67, 69
Wills, Garry: on Kennedy, 198–99
Wilson, T. Woodrow, ix, 160, 240
—illnesses of: as a child, 17–18; at
   Davidson College, 19; at Johns Hopkins University, 23; as Princeton University professor, 25; as Princeton University student, 19–20; at University
   of Virginia Law School, 20–22
—and League of Nations 65, 66, 69, 72
—neurologic illnesses of, 26, 33–34,
   36–37, 41, 42–43, 47, 52, 67, 68, 73;
   and denial of, 28–29, 30, 46, 62, 65,
   69–70, 73; and Mrs. Wilson's management of, 69–71, 73; physicians' interpretations of, 37, 38, 68, 73

—political career: New Jersey governorship, 44–45; presidential campaign, 45–46; as president of United States, 46–47, 54, 55, 57, 58, 66, 69–71
—at Princeton University: problems as president of, 32–33, 34–35, 35–36, 39–41, 43
—summary of health problems, 10–11

—at Versailles conference, 14–15; illnesses at, 60–61, 62; observations of Wilson's behavior, 64, 65; unexplained behavior, 59, 60, 61, 62, 63, 64; Wilson's peace plan, 59
Wilson, Dr. Philip: description of Kennedy's operation, 192–93

About the Authors

Kenneth R. Crispell, M.D., is University Professor of Medicine and Law Emeritus at the University of Virginia. Dr. Crispell has served as medical school dean and vice president for the health center at the University of Virginia. An internist and endocrinologist by training, Dr. Crispell has published widely within his own subspecialty as well as in the fields of bioethics and medicolegal affairs.

Carlos F. Gomez is a medical student at the University of Virginia School of Medicine. He is currently a fellow in the Pew Program at the University of Chicago, where he is pursuing a doctorate in public policy studies.

Library of Congress Cataloging-in-Publication Data
Crispell, Kenneth R., 1916–
Hidden illness in the White House / by Kenneth R. Crispell and
Carlos F. Gomez.
p.   cm.
Bibliography: p.
Includes index.
ISBN 0-8223-0839-8
1. Presidents—United States—Diseases—History—20th century.
I. Gomez, Carlos F, 1958–   . III. Title.
E176.1.C915   1988
973'.09'92—dc19
[B]   88-7158